YELLOWSTONE TRAILS
A HIKING GUIDE

Mark C. Marschall
Joy Sellers Marschall

Yellowstone National Park • Wyoming 82190
www.YellowstoneAssociation.org

Published by: The Yellowstone Association
             Box 117
             Yellowstone National Park, WY 82190

Illustrations by: Dan Biechler on pages 18, 22, 23, 31, 32, 46, 55, 63, 115, 120
Photographs and other illustrations by authors, unless noted
Library of Congress Number: 90-070639
ISBN 0-89288-197-6 (SC)
0-934948-12-7 (Spiral)

Cover Design: Adrienne Pollard
Back Cover Photos: ©Yellowstone Association, Tom Murphy, Mark Marschall

PREFACE

I started writing *Yellowstone Trails* in 1978 after spending a grand total of six summers in the park. During my summer breaks from college, I pumped gas for the Yellowstone Park Service Stations. I hiked the trails on all my days off and went on a long multi-day hike each fall before school started up again. After graduation, I took a seasonal job with the National Park Service, giving guided walks and issuing backcountry permits. At the time, I thought my six summers of hiking experience made me an expert.

Yellowstone Trails is now 35 years old and, sitting here with my wife and coauthor, Joy, putting the finishing touches on the tenth edition, we realize that the book, the park, and the author have all changed considerably. *Yellowstone Trails* has 120 more pages than that first edition—with what we hope are improved maps and graphics, better trail descriptions, and updated information on the park's dynamic ecosystem. Since 1978, Yellowstone National Park has experienced the sweeping fires of 1988, the reintroduction of the wolf, the displacement of cutthroat trout in Yellowstone Lake by lake trout, and the visible effects of a changing climate. These events, either directly or indirectly, have altered the park and the hiking experience from what it was 35 years ago. As for the author, I've added 20 years of Yellowstone hiking experience to complement my original, self-proclaimed expert status. Both by hiking on my own and by patrolling as a National Park Service backcountry ranger, I've learned a great deal about Yellowstone's trails since that first edition.

Each time we revise the book we're surprised by the amount of new information that turns up for the latest edition. Yet, even if you read this entire book and digest all the details contained in these pages, you will find something new— something not in the book—on your next hike in the park. Whether it's your first or fiftieth Yellowstone hike, approach it with your eyes, ears, and nose open and your mind ready to process what you are sensing. Undoubtedly, you will experience something you haven't before: a different mixture of scents in a field of wildflowers, a nuance in a raven's call, or the pattern of grizzly tracks on a wet path. It's like watching a great movie, one that you've seen before, and discovering something you hadn't noticed or understood the first time around.

Yellowstone Trails was originally envisioned as an inexpensive, accurate, and comprehensive guidebook, one that would be kept up to date with frequent revisions and minimal price increases. We hope that this edition lives up to that goal. We want you to have a great experience when you hike in Yellowstone. This park is a reservoir of physical and spiritual beauty. It represents so much more than just a place to go hiking. Enjoy it without harming it. Push yourself, but remember there are people waiting for your safe return. &

Mark C. Marschall
with Joy Sellers Marschall

YELLOWSTONE NATIONAL PARK BACKCOUNTRY REGULATIONS

The following are paraphrased from their legal origin in the Code of Federal Regulations. For a complete list of the regulations, contact the National Park Service. All overnight trips into the backcountry require a Backcountry Use Permit.

- Weapons other than legally permitted firearms are not allowed.
- No pets are allowed in the backcountry. Horses, mules and llamas are the only domestic animals allowed.
- It is illegal to leave garbage or litter in the backcountry.
- Fires are allowed only in established fire rings.
- Only dead and downed timber may be used for firewood.
- Do not feed or harass wildlife.
- Collecting any souvenir specimens of any kind—rocks, antlers, bones of animals, or otherwise—is not allowed.
- Do not disturb any cultural or prehistoric artifacts.
- All food, when not in use or being transported, must be stored out of reach of bears.
- Dumping or depositing any waste within 100 feet of any stream or other body of water is not allowed. Dish washing is not allowed in any body of water.
- A Yellowstone National Park fishing permit and knowledge of the regulations are required for fishing.
- Bathing, dishwashing, or cooking in thermal features is not allowed.
- Gathering nuts, berries, mushrooms, etc., for personal consumption in the park is allowed.
- Backcountry patrol cabins are strictly for official use. Breaking into one, other than in a life-threatening emergency, is prohibited. ❧

Throughout this guide you will notice that certain trails have this warning:

BEAR MANAGEMENT AREA

These trails travel throughout areas that have scheduled closures or restrictions on their use during certain times of the year. This is an attempt by the National Park Service to allow bears undisturbed use of prime habitat. A list and a map of the scheduled closures are posted at every ranger station or can be viewed in the *Backcountry Trip Planner*, available from Yellowstone National Park, (307) 344-2160, or www.nps.gov/yell/planyourvisit/backcountrytripplanner.htm. ❧

CONTENTS

Preface...3
Yellowstone National Park Backcountry Regulations 4
Acknowledgements 6

PRE-HIKE INFORMATION 8
How to Use This Guide..8
Suggested Short Hikes 9
Suggested Medium-Distance Hikes 11
Suggested Long Hikes..13
A Guide to Maps 14
The Maps in This Book..15 & 190
Backcountry Permits & Continental Divide Trail............................16
Day Hiking and Backpacking Equipment..19
Backcountry Camping..21
Coexisting with Bears..24
Water Treatment 32
River and Stream Crossings 35
Weather...36
Points of Interest in the Backcountry 38
Wildlife 42

TRAIL DESCRIPTIONS..49
Northwest Corner 51
Gallatin Mountains and Mammoth Area 60
Lower Yellowstone River Area...76
Tower Area 85
Northeast Corner 91
Lamar River Area..95
Pelican Valley Area 102
Canyon Area 113
Norris Area..124
Central Plateau Area...127
Madison Valley Area 131
Firehole Valley Area..133
Shoshone Lake Area 143
Bechler River and Falls River Area..148
Snake River Area 161
Thorofare Area 170

BACKCOUNTRY CAMPSITES..180

APPENDIX 188

MAPS...190-236

INDEX..237

ACKNOWLEDGEMENTS

This book has always been a group effort. Even when we were living in Yellowstone we couldn't cover every trail every year. Now that we're in Yosemite National Park, we depend even more on others for Yellowstone updates. This edition was especially helped by Ivan Kowski and Dagan Klein of the NPS's Central Backcountry Office, Chris Glen of the Trails Office, and international grizzly bear expert Kerry Gunther of the Bear Management Office (who we're lucky to have known since before he was famous). Backcountry rangers Kevin Dooley, Brian Helms, George Kittrell, Sarah McCormack, Michael Curtis, and Liz Voigt also provided detailed notes and updates on their areas. These and other backcountry rangers are the ones who are out on the trails day in and day out, axing and sawing fallen logs, checking for bear activity, ensuring trails are marked and signed, cleaning campsites, hanging food poles, watching out for the well-being of the hikers, and protecting the park's wilderness resources. Thanks to them and to the NPS trail crews for making Yellowstone's system of trails what it is today.

Luckily we didn't have to completely depend on others for updates on the trails for this revision. This time we were able to make three extended trips to Yellowstone and travel a variety of trails, reconfirming the significant contrast with hiking in California's Sierra Nevada, where it's always sunny, most rivers and creeks have bridges, and grizzly bear have been absent for a hundred years. These Yellowstone trips were greatly aided by friends' generous lodging and logistical support: Bill and Colette Daigle-Berg, Ann Marie Chytra and Pat Navaille, Ray and Daryl Fenio, Margie and Rick Fey, Bruce and Melinda Sefton, Bill and Jean Guza, Tara and Dave Ross, and Karen and Matt Vandzura. Reconnecting with these friends was as important to us as reconnecting with the park and its trails.

Since the last revision two longtime friends and Yellowstone backcountry rangers, Dave Phillips and Jerry Mernin, passed away unexpectedly. They both were mentors to a long string of newbies, showing us by their actions and words how to be a backcountry ranger. They demonstrated that despite the myth of the "lone ranger", it is collaboration with others and perseverance in effort that gets things done. We are grateful to have shared time on the trail and food around the campfire with them.

In the 35 year history of *Yellowstone Trails*, the book has received assistance from a wide range of characters. Many of the people on this list should be in a *Who's Who* of Yellowstone's backcountry, and we're honored to have been associated with them. They reviewed trail descriptions, edited text, or supplied information on some aspect of Yellowstone's backcountry or backcountry travel. They are: Steve Anderson, Rick Bennett, Laura Bittner, Ann Marie Chytra, Colette Daigle-Berg, Terry Danforth, Rick DeLappe, Bob Flather, Joe Fowler, Luann Freer, Bonnie Gafney, Jean Guza, Michael Keator, Randy King, Jessica Knoshaug, Harlan Kredit, John Litherland, Dennis Lojko, Rick McAdam, Mark McCutcheon, Gerald Mernin, Marv Miller, Andrew Mitchell, Pat Navaille, Bundy Phillips, Tiffany Potter, Scott Powers, Doug Ridley, Ann Rodman, Brad Ross, Dave Ross, Mike Ross, George Sechrist, Doug Smith, Dunbar Susong, Cat Syrbe, Tim Townsend, Boone Vandzura and Anita Varley. Thanks to GIS specialists Chris Overbaugh and Luca Guglielmetti for creating the base layers for all 34 of the maps.

If there are errors or confusing sections in this book, or if you have suggestions, please contact us c/o Yellowstone Association, P.O. Box 117, Yellowstone NP, WY 82190, or e-mail us at: mcmarschall@hotmail.com. ❧

HOW TO USE THIS GUIDE

Yellowstone National Park's backcountry covers over 2 million acres and contains over 1,000 miles of trails. It is hard for most of us to comprehend such a large, wild area. Not surprisingly, it is also hard to choose which trail to hike—unless, of course, you use this book.

Start with the Pre-Hike section. First is a list of suggested hikes, ingeniously divided into short, medium, and long categories. This list will give you trail names, distances, and page numbers so that you can look up and read the specific trail descriptions. Next, there is map information, including a map of Yellowstone that shows you how the park is divided up into areas. If you want to hike in a specific area, look at the park map and the table below it to find the page number for the specific map for that area. Use the index at the back of the book if you only know the name of the place where you want to hike.

The Pre-Hike section has a variety of general information that may help you choose a trail and make your hiking more enjoyable. Because traveling in grizzly bear country is a major concern for backcountry users, there is a segment devoted to the subject. The following topics are also covered in the Pre-Hike section: backcountry permits, hiking equipment, backcountry camping techniques, water treatment, weather, stream crossings, fire ecology, petrified forests, thermal features, and wildlife.

The Pre-Hike section is followed by specific trail descriptions for 120 different trails. The trail descriptions are grouped by geographical regions of Yellowstone. Near the back of the book, there is a complete listing of Yellowstone's Backcountry campsites, including any restrictions that may apply to individual sites. You will find 34 topographic maps at the end of the book; all backcountry campsites are marked by a symbol (▲) on these maps. ♠

SUGGESTED SHORT HIKES

	Distances (roundtrip)		Page #
Starting from Mammoth Area:	Miles	Km	
Grizzly Lake	4	6.5	61
Bunsen Peak	4	6.5	72
Osprey Falls	9	15	72
Beaver Ponds Loop	5	8	73
Rescue Creek	8*	13*	80
Starting from Tower Area:			
Yellowstone River P.A.	4	6.5	86
Lost Lake Loop	4	6.5	87
Mt. Washburn	6	9.6	113
Starting from Northeast Entrance Road:			
Slough Creek (T.H. to first meadow)	4	6.5	91
Pebble Creek (Warm Creek T.H. to upper meadows)	4	6.5	92
Lamar River (T.H. to Cache Creek)	6.2	10	95
Starting from Lake/Bridge Bay/Fishing Bridge Area:			
Pelican Valley (to bridge)	6.8	10.8	102
Storm Point	2	3	110
Elephant Back	3.6	5.8	130
Avalanche Peak	4	6.5	179
Starting from Canyon Area:			
Mt. Washburn	6	9.6	113
Grebe Lake	6	9.6	120
Cascade Lake	4.4	7	121
Starting from Norris Area:			
Solfatara Creek (first 3 miles)	6	9.6	124
Artist Paint Pot	0.6	1	126

*Denotes one-way distance trailhead to trailhead.
Abbreviations used:
C.G. – Campground
P.A. – Picnic Area
R.S. – Ranger Station
T.H. – Trailhead

SUGGESTED SHORT HIKES

	Distances (roundtrip)		Page #
Starting from Madison Area:	Miles	Km	
Purple Mountain	6	10	131
Starting from Old Faithful Area:			
Lone Star Geyser	5	8	133
Observation Point Loop	2	3	135
Mystic Falls	3	5	137
Fairy Falls	5	8	139
Shoshone Lake (via DeLacy Creek)	6	10	146
Starting from Grant Village/Lewis Lake/South Entrance Area:			
Shoshone Lake (via Dogshead)	8	13	147
Riddle Lake	5	8	169
Yellowstone Lake Overlook	2	3	169
Starting from Bechler Area:			
Cave Falls T.H. to Bechler Falls	2.6	4.2	154
Cave Falls/Bechler Falls Loop	7	11	154
Starting from Grassy Lake Road:			
Terraced Falls	3.2	5	158

*Denotes one-way distance trailhead to trailhead.
Abbreviations used:
C.G. – Campground
P.A. – Picnic Area
R.S. – Ranger Station
T.H. – Trailhead

SUGGESTED
MEDIUM-DISTANCE HIKES

	Distances (roundtrip)		Page #
Starting from West Entrance/U.S. 191 (Gallatin Highway) Area:	**Miles**	**Km**	
Sky Rim Trail Loop	18	29	52
Crescent Lake/High Lake Loop	23	37	57
Sportsman Lake	22	35	58
Gneiss Creek	14*	22.5*	132
Starting from Mammoth Area:			
Mt. Holmes	20	32	62
Bighorn Pass	16	26	64
Fawn Pass	24	38.5	66
Electric Peak	18	29	69
Sepulcher Mountain Loop	12	19	70
Blacktail Creek T.H. to Hellroaring T.H.	14*	22.5*	77
Blacktail Creek T.H. to Knowles Falls	11	18	81
Starting from Tower Area:			
Yellowstone River (Tower R.S. to Gardiner)	20.5*	33*	88, 77
Garnet Hill Loop	7.5	12	88
Specimen Ridge (Yell. Riv. P.A. to Lamar Riv. T.H.)	18.5*	29*	89
Starting from Northeast Entrance Road:			
Pebble Creek (Pebble Creek T.H. to Warm Creek T.H.)	12*	19*	92
Bliss Pass (Pebble Creek T.H. to Slough Creek T.H.)	21*	34.6*	94
Republic Pass (Thunderer T.H. to Cooke City)	17*	27*	98, 97
Starting from Lake/Bridge Bay/Fishing Bridge Area:			
Pelican Valley Loop	16	26	102
Park Point	13	21	172

*Denotes one-way distance trailhead to trailhead.
Abbreviations used:
C.G. – Campground
P.A. – Picnic Area
R.S. – Ranger Station
T.H. – Trailhead

SUGGESTED
MEDIUM-DISTANCE HIKES

	Distances (roundtrip)		Page #
Starting from Canyon Area:	Miles	Km	
Mt. Washburn (Dun. Pass T.H. to Glacial Boulder T.H.)	11*	18.5*	113, 115
Seven Mile Hole	11	17.5	116
Observation Peak	11	17.5	122
Howard Eaton (Ice Lake T.H. to Cascade Creek T.H.)	10.5*	17*	122

Starting from Old Faithful Area:

Mallard Lake Loop	11.8	19	135
Fairy Creek	13.5	21.6	138
Shoshone Lake via Lone Star Geyser	17	27	144

Starting from Grant Village/Lewis Lake/South Entrance Area:

Shoshone Lake Loop	11	17.5	147
(Lewis River Channel Trail to Dogshead Trail)			
Heart Lake	15	24	162
Heart Lake T.H. to South Entrance T.H.	23.5*	38*	162
Mt. Sheridan Lookout	22	35	164

Starting from Bechler Area:

Bechler R.S. to Colonnade Falls	17	27.5	150
Dunanda Falls	16	26	153
Robinson Creek (West Boundary Trail)	18	30	154

Starting from Grassy Lake Road:

*Denotes one-way distance trailhead to trailhead.
Abbreviations used:
C.G. – Campground
P.A. – Picnic Area
R.S. – Ranger Station
T.H. – Trailhead

SUGGESTED LONG HIKES

Grassy Lake to Union Falls .... 15 .... 24.5 155

	Distances (roundtrip)		Page #
	Miles	Km	

Fawn Pass–Fan Creek–
Sportsman Lake Loop:
Starting from Glen Creek T.H. .... 43 .... 69 ...... 68, 58,
74, 66

Starting from Fawn Pass T.H.
(Milepost 22 on U.S. 191 [Gallatin Highway]) .... 42 .... 67 ..... 66, 68,
58, 74

Pelican Valley–Lamar Valley
Pelican Valley T.H. to Lamar River T. H. .... 33* .... 53* .. 109, 95

Hoodoo Basin
Lamar River T.H. to Hoodoo Basin and
park boundary back to Lamar River T.H. .... 57 .... 91 ..... 95, 100
Pelican Valley T.H.–Frost Lake–Pahaska Teepee .... 35.5* .... 57* .. 109, 101

Heart Lake–Snake River–South Boundary Loop
Heart Lake T.H. to Heart River Trail to Snake River Trail to South
Boundary Trail to Harebell Jct. to Heart Lake
to Heart Lake T.H.. .... 56.5 .... 90.5 .. 162, 164
166, 168

Thorofare Trail–Two Ocean Plateau–Heart Lake
Nine Mile T.H. to Thorofare R.S. to
Two Ocean Plateau Trail to Trail Creek
Trail to Heart Lake T.H. .... 76* 122* 172,
167, 178,
176, 162

Bechler River–Shoshone Lake–Old Faithful
Cave Falls to Bechler River Trail to Shoshone Lake
to Lone Star Geyser T.H. at Old Faithful .... 34* 54.5* 150,
144

*Denotes one-way distance trailhead to trailhead.
Abbreviations used:
C.G. – Campground
P.A. – Picnic Area
R.S. – Ranger Station
T.H. – Trailhead

A GUIDE TO MAPS

The 34 topographic maps included in this book should be sufficient for planning hikes and navigating on most maintained trails in Yellowstone National Park. Nearly all the maps come in one of two scales: either approximately 1 inch: 2.5 miles or 1 inch: 1.3 miles. The maps show trails, topographic lines, forest cover, roads, creeks, rivers, lakes, ranger stations, and designated backcountry campsites. Remember, if trail signs and markers are down and a trail is hard to follow, these maps might not be detailed enough to find your way.

Stand-alone topographic maps are better than the maps in this book for finding your exact location along a trail, especially when hiking off-trail, and for identifying landmarks and mountain peaks. The maps with the greatest detail are the U.S. Geologic Survey (USGS) 7.5-minute maps. However, you may need to hire a llama just to carry all the 7.5-minute maps required for a 3- or 4-day hike. If you are planning an off-trail hike, use these maps, but otherwise, the level of detail will be overkill.

Probably the best combination of scale, accuracy, size, price, and durability is the "Yellowstone Series" of maps put out by National Geographic. This is a series of four maps covering all of Yellowstone National Park and the Forest Service areas adjacent to the park boundary. Each National Geographic map covers about nine USGS 7.5-minute maps, has a scale of 1:63,360, and is printed on durable, waterproof paper. These maps are excellent for navigating trails and are sufficient for some off-trail travel as well. See the appendix for ordering information for USGS and National Geographic maps. ❧

THE MAPS IN THIS BOOK

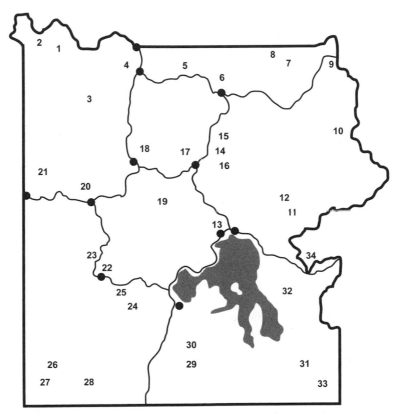

Map#	Area	Page #
1	Northwest Corner	191
2	Northwest Corner (enlarged)	192, 193
3	Gallatin Mountains	194, 195
4	Mammoth	196, 197
5	Lower Yellowstone	198
6	Tower	199
7	Slough/Pebble Creeks	200
8	Slough Creek	201
9	Northeast Corner	202, 203
10	Lamar	204, 205
11	Pelican Valley	206
12	Pelican Valley (enlarged)	207
13	Lake/Fishing Bridge	208
14	Canyon	209
15	Mt. Washburn	210
16	Canyon (enlarged)	211
17	Grebe/Cascade Lakes	212
18	Norris	213
19	Central Plateau	214
20	Madison	215
21	Gneiss Creek	216
22	Firehole Valley	217
23	Old Faithful	218
24	Shoshone Lake	219
25	Shoshone Lake (enlarged)	220, 221
26	Bechler	222, 223
27	Bechler (enlarged)	224, 225
28	Grassy Lake	227
29	Snake River	228, 229
30	Heart Lake	231
31	Thorofare	232, 233
32	Yellowstone Lake (east)	234
33	Thorofare (enlarged)	235
34	Avalanche Peak	236

BACKCOUNTRY PERMITS

A backcountry use permit is required for all parties staying overnight in the backcountry. If you are day hiking, you don't generally need a permit, but you are still responsible for observing all backcountry regulations. (Off-trail day hiking in some areas, such as Two Ocean Plateau, may require a special permit. Check at a permit-issuing station, listed on following page, for details.) Yellowstone uses a designated backcountry campsite system for overnight trips. A backcountry use permit does two things: it reserves a backcountry campsite for each night of your trip and it lets the rangers know your trip itinerary. Permits cost $3 per person per night (as of 2015) and are available at the permit-issuing stations listed on the following page. Backcountry use permits must be obtained in person and are issued only 48 hours or less before the first day of your trip. When you go in to get your permit, you'll choose backcountry campsites for each night of your trip. If you select a campsite that has already been reserved by another party, you'll be asked to choose a different site. Because most backcountry campsites are one-party sites, you and your group most likely will have your reserved campsites to yourselves.

It is possible to make an advance reservation for backcountry campsites. For an advance reservation, fill out a trip-planning worksheet (available online, through the mail, or at permit-issuing stations). Then submit the worksheet either through the mail, by fax, or in person at a permit-issuing station (see next page for contact details). There is a $25 fee for this service. You will receive a confirmation of your reservation. Keep in mind that, within 48 hours of the day you plan to start your trip, you will need to go in person to a permit-issuing station to exchange the reservation confirmation for a backcountry use permit. Only a portion of backcountry campsites in each section of Yellowstone is allowed to be reserved in advance.

If all the campsites in an area are taken, you may want to simply day hike into the area, you may delay your hike until a campsite becomes available, or you may choose to go hiking in a less popular area—that's why you bought the trail guide, right? If it sounds like the Park Service is running the backcountry like a motel, remember that there are many people wanting to use the campsites. By keeping areas from becoming overcrowded and overused, the Park Service is ensuring the preservation of the backcountry and a quality experience for those who venture into it.

The *Backcountry Trip Planner,* **published by the National Park Service,** has a rough map of backcountry campsites and a listing of their restrictions. This planner is free and is available at any ranger station, by writing or calling Yellowstone's Central Backcountry Office, or by downloading it from the office's website (see below for contact details). Also, a comprehensive list of Yellowstone backcountry campsites and their restrictions is located near the back of this book (pages 180–187). The topographic maps, which begin on page 180, show backcountry campsite locations. Because locations of backcountry campsites may change from year to year, the best way to determine the exact location of your campsite is by looking at the official campsite map posted in all permit-issuing stations. Once on the trail, there will be signs pointing out the location of the campsites.

Sign in and out at the trailhead register. If you are overdue and rangers see that you have actually signed in at the register, they can then narrow their search to that backcountry area. This advice is especially important for day hikers.

Contact Details:
Central Backcountry Office
P.O. Box 168
Yellowstone N.P., WY 82190
(307) 344-2160
www.nps.gov/yell/planyourvisit/backcountrytripplanner.htm

Permit-Issuing Stations:

Bechler Ranger Station	Old Faithful Ranger Station
Bridge Bay Ranger Station	South Entrance Ranger Station
Canyon Visitor Center	Tower Ranger Station
Grant Village Backcountry Office	West Yellowstone Visitor
Mammoth Backcountry Office	Information Center

CONTINENTAL DIVIDE TRAIL (CDT)

The Continental Divide National Scenic Trail is a proposed hiking route that runs from Mexico to Canada and follows, within 25 miles, the continental divide for its entire length. It is a younger version of this country's great trails such as the Pacific Crest and Appalachian trails. The CDT was designated by Congress in 1978 and is still being developed. When completed, it will total 3,100 miles and travel through the states of Montana, Idaho, Wyoming, Colorado, and New Mexico, as well as 25 national forests, 4 Bureau of Land Management districts, private lands, and 3 national parks—including Yellowstone.

The route through Yellowstone uses a number of existing trails that travel near the continental divide. At the time of this writing, none of these trails were marked as being part of the CDT, although all were marked and maintained as a regular part of Yellowstone's trail system. In the future the CDT may be signed at trail junctions, and there may be a special marking on the existing orange trail markers that will designate the CDT. In this trail guide, those trails that are part of the CDT route will be designated by the CDT logo in the trail description and on the maps.

Remember that the CDT route through Yellowstone was not designated for any special qualities, but solely for the fact that it travels near the continental divide. Sections of the trail are quite interesting, but don't let the name give you the impression that it is a high alpine route. Unless you are doing the entire trail from Mexico to Canada and want to stay true to the route, I would recommend a number of other multi-day trails through Yellowstone rather than the CDT (see Suggested Long Hikes on page 13).

If you are planning to follow the CDT through Yellowstone, be certain to contact the Central Backcountry Office for their information sheet. ❧

Great Gray Owl

DAY HIKING AND BACKPACKING EQUIPMENT

The two most popular methods of exploring Yellowstone's backcountry are day hiking and backpacking. Day hiking simply means starting a hike and returning on the same day. Backpacking refers to hiking into the backcountry and camping for one or more nights.

By day hiking, you can avoid buying and carrying a lot of expensive equipment. In fact, you probably already own the essential items needed for summer day hiking in Yellowstone. The basic hiking wardrobe starts with a pair of comfortable walking shoes. When I started hiking here, heavy, leather mountaineering boots were the only acceptable footwear for the serious Yellowstone hiker. They took a couple years to break in, caused blisters, and doubled in weight when they got wet. What more could you want in footwear? Now, thankfully, trail running shoes and lightweight nylon and leather hiking boots are the footwear of choice for day hikers. These shoes don't offer much protection from moisture (unless they have a Gore-Tex or other waterproof feature), but they are so comfortable and lightweight that the trade-off is worth it. Probably the most popular all-around day-hiking/backpacking shoe among experienced Yellowstone hikers is a lightweight, all-leather Gore-Tex boot (weighing around 3 lbs. or less). To the shoes, add a pair of loose, comfortable pants, preferably made of a material that isn't very water absorbent and that dries quickly. Supplex nylon pants, cotton/nylon blend pants, or lightweight wool pants (early or late in the season) are much better than jeans. Many people hike in shorts and only put the pants on if they get cool. If you don't like slathering massive amounts of toxic insect repellent onto your bare legs during mosquito season, you might consider wearing the light nylon pants. A t-shirt supplemented by either a long-sleeved fleece made of polypropylene-type fabric or a wool sweater gives you a flexible outfit. (Obviously, during cooler weather you'll need some extra clothing.) You'll also need a small daypack to carry:

THE DAY HIKING ESSENTIALS

Raingear. Remember, it can rain anytime no matter what the forecast said.

A warm hat. It'll keep your head dry and prevent heat loss through your head, should you get cold.

A container for drinking water. Any canteen or plastic container that doesn't leak will do.

Insect repellent. Often necessary between mid-June and late August.

Sunscreen. Wrinkles and weather-beaten skin are no longer trendy; skin cancer never was.

A first-aid kit suited to your needs.

For longer day hikes, consider taking: a map, compass (or GPS unit), small flashlight or headlamp, Swiss army knife, water filter, and food and matches. An overnight hike obviously requires all of the above equipment and then some. Before taking your first overnight backcountry trip, it will be well worth your while to look through one of the many books dealing with backpacking equipment, techniques, and food.

For an overnight hike in Yellowstone you'll need to bring some extra warm clothing and a sleeping bag suitable for the expected nighttime temperatures (see Weather section, page 36). A shelter of some sort is a must. A tarp is nice and light, but in a blowing rain or during insect-biting season, a tent can be worth every ounce of extra weight. One hundred feet of cord or rope, a stuff sack for hanging food and garbage, and a couple of plastic trash bags will also be needed (see Backcountry Camping section, page 21). For cooking, a backpacking stove is required at some of Yellowstone's campsites and is generally a good idea anywhere because it will still work even when it's raining or snowing and dry firewood is scarce. Fires are allowed in the fire rings at many backcountry campsites, but usable firewood is becoming scarce near some of these sites. In collecting wood for a fire, remember that regulations allow only downed timber to be used. Chopping down live or standing dead trees, or breaking off branches of either, is not allowed. A small backpack saw can come in handy for cutting up large logs at sites where small firewood is scarce. And finally, **always bring first aid material for preventing and treating blisters.** I have seen blisters take the fun out of numerous multi-day backpacking trips, even among otherwise well-equipped, in-shape hikers. ❧

Spring Beauty
- white or pink flowers
- blooms June–July
- moist soils
- lance-shaped leaves
- a favorite food of grizzlies

BACKCOUNTRY CAMPING

C amping in Yellowstone's backcountry allows you to experience the park on a much more intimate level than day hiking does. And the more days you're out, the deeper your appreciation will be for the wilderness. The feeling that comes from sitting at camp and watching the landscape around you change from evening to night, and from dawn to day, transcends my limited descriptive vocabulary. To fully appreciate Yellowstone's backcountry, you must go out overnight.

Of course, bears will be on your mind—and rightfully so. But you can reduce your worrying by using good camping technique. Look the area over for any sign of bear activity (see Coexisting with Bears section, page 24) and check for any animal trails (call them "game trails" and you'll sound more knowledgeable) passing through the camping area. If you see evidence of recent bear activity in the campsite, do not camp there. You do not want to risk having the bear revisit the campsite while you are there. Move to another campsite, even if you're tired. Rangers check backcountry campsites periodically and close them if there is bear activity, or if other hikers have reported bears in that camp. This keeps your chance of being given a permit for a campsite with recent bear activity to a minimum.

Set up your tent as far away as possible from the cooking area, food storage tree, main trail, or any game trails. One hundred yards is not too far, but local topography may limit the distance to less than that (see diagram on page 22). Bears routinely use trails at night, and in the unlikely event that a bear investigates your camp, it will probably be drawn to the areas with the strongest food odors. If you keep your sleeping area food-odor free and, if possible, upwind from your cooking and food storage areas, you will greatly reduce the chance of having a bear visit your tent.

Do all your cooking and food preparation at the fire ring/cooking area. Keep food odors to a minimum. Avoid frying foods. Freeze-dried foods or meals cooked in plastic bags are especially handy and allow for easier cleanup. Wash dishes immediately after eating. If fires are allowed at your campsite, burn any garbage from the meal, but make sure the fire is hot enough to burn it completely. Pick any unburned garbage or food out of the fire and put it in your trash bag before you go to sleep. If you cooked a particularly odorous meal, you should consider changing clothes. Washing after your meal is also a good idea. And most important, before you go to sleep, you must store your food, garbage and anything that may carry food odors out of reach of bears.

In most campsites in Yellowstone, the National Park Service has put up either a pole or cable between trees to be used for food storage. These poles or cables are usually located near the fire ring/cooking area so the food odors can be concentrated in one spot at the campsite. Store your food in one sealed plastic

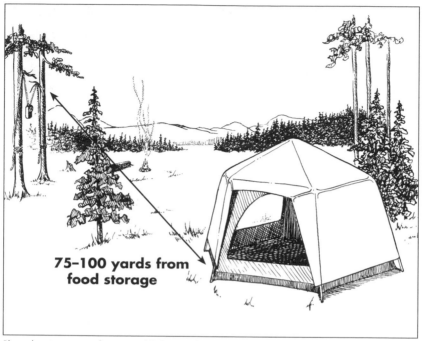

75–100 yards from food storage

Place sleeping area as far as possible from trails, streams, and cooking/food storage area.

Hanging Food

1. Pick two trees about 20–25 feet apart.
2. Go to one tree and throw the end of a 50-foot piece of rope over a branch that is at least 17 feet off the ground.
3. Go to the other tree and do the same with another 50-foot piece of rope.
4. Attach food bag to the ends of both ropes.
5. Pull ropes tight so that the food bag is equidistant between the two trees. Take as much of the sag out of the ropes as possible and make sure the food bag is at least 12 feet off the ground and 4 feet from the tree branches.
6. Tie ropes off at the base of the trees.

bag, your garbage in another sealed plastic bag, and then put both plastic bags into a nylon stuff sack, which should be used only as a food storage sack and not for your sleeping bag afterward. Take a 50-foot length of cord or rope and tie some weight (a piece of wood or rock) to one end. Throw that end of the rope over the pole or cable. Lower the weighted end back down to the ground. Position the rope in the middle of the pole or cable, then attach the stuff sack and hoist it up. Make sure it is at least 12 feet off the ground. Tie the other end of the rope off around one of the trees. If there is no pole or cable at your campsite, you will need an extra 50 feet of cord or rope to hang your food (see Hanging Food diagram, facing page at bottom left). In 2012, the National Park Service changed the regulations for use of bear-resistant food containers (BRFCs) in Yellowstone. The new policy states: "BRFCs can be stored on the ground at the base of the food pole or, if a food pole is not present, in the cooking area, a minimum of 100 feet from any sleeping area (300 feet recommended)."

For disposing of human waste, choose a spot at least 100 feet away from any water source, and away from your sleeping area. Dig a small hole 4–8" deep, place the waste in the hole, and cover it back over with the extra dirt. A small backpacker's trowel is a useful tool for this task. Burning toilet paper at the waste site may start a forest fire. Instead, burn it at the campfire ring. Do not attempt to bury any extra food or garbage, as bears will just dig it up. Burn it or pack it out. When you leave your campsite, make sure the fire is out. Pick out any foil from the ashes and any litter left behind in the area. 🐾

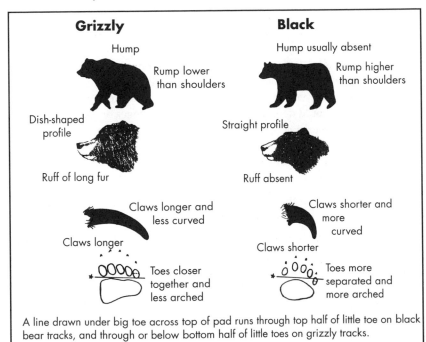

Grizzly

Hump

Rump lower than shoulders

Dish-shaped profile

Ruff of long fur

Claws longer and less curved

Claws longer

Toes closer together and less arched

Black

Hump usually absent

Rump higher than shoulders

Straight profile

Ruff absent

Claws shorter and more curved

Claws shorter

Toes more separated and more arched

A line drawn under big toe across top of pad runs through top half of little toe on black bear tracks, and through or below bottom half of little toes on grizzly tracks.

COEXISTING WITH BEARS

The Greater Yellowstone Ecosystem is home to over 500 grizzly bears and an unknown number of black bears (bears are hard to spot and even harder to count). Many hikers have heard about the incredible strength, stealth, and cleverness of grizzly bears, and have read about grizzlies killing people in Yellowstone and Glacier national parks. Thus, even though the statistical chance of being injured by a bear is very small, it is at the front of most people's minds as they are traveling in the backcountry. And that is good, to an extent. The danger from bears is real. You cannot eliminate the danger, but you can considerably reduce it by your actions.

Bears are unpredictable. Although seeing a bear in the backcountry is a great thrill, you can never be sure how the bear will react if it sees you. For this reason, most hikers prefer to avoid meeting bears in the first place. The following list of suggestions should help you prevent such an encounter.

- **Ask at a visitor center or ranger station** if there have been bears spotted recently along the trail you wish to hike. Also check for posted warning signs at the trailhead register.

- **Check for recent bear tracks and scat.** If you see recent bear sign, it obviously tells you that a bear is using the trail. The bear may just be using the trail at night, when it knows there are no people present, or it may be using the trail during the day. If there are many tracks going both ways, then your chances are probably greater of encountering the bear than if there is just a single set of tracks (especially if it is going opposite of your travel direction). If you see small cub tracks with the adult tracks, then your danger meter should definitely be in the red. Also check at your backcountry campsite for recent sign of bears—scat, tracks, or any indication that the fire pit has been scattered about or dug up by a bear. Consider moving to another campsite in this situation, even if it's not the one assigned to you. Report all bear sign to a ranger station when you return.

- **Hike in a group of three or more people.** This seems to greatly reduce the chance of a bear encounter or attack.

- **Make noise to keep from surprising a bear.** Bears will usually leave an area if they know you're coming. Although the constant ringing of a bell, rattling of a rock in a can, or off-key singing of your companion will warn a bear of your presence, it may also take a good deal of the enjoyment out of hiking. Thus, it will usually suffice to only make the noises intermittently, being sure to ring, rattle, or sing well in advance of any blind spots on the trail.

- **Don't hike at night**. Bears often use the trails after dark.

- **Use proper camping techniques** (see Backcountry Camping section, page 21).

Bear Encounters

In spite of taking the above precautions, you may still encounter a bear on your backcountry trip. These people–bear encounters usually fit into one of three broad categories:

1) Encountering a bear from a distance; bear may or may not see you.
2) Close range encounter, often involving a charge, possibly an attack.
3) An encounter in your campsite.

I'll discuss these situations one at a time, knowing that in an actual encounter they may overlap. You should also realize that there are no absolutes when dealing with bears. Each bear has a different personality, and the same situation may cause one bear to attack while another flees. (Grizzlies do seem to be more aggressive than black bears.) Even though there have been many bear encounters and attacks in North America from which to make inferences on bear behavior, it is difficult to draw conclusions due to the incredible number of variables that are part of each incident. I have drawn on numerous sources (see appendix), including my own experience in investigating bear incidents and observing bears in Yellowstone, for the following information and suggestions. No course of action is guaranteed to work every time. This is just part of the inherent risk of traveling in grizzly country.

Encountering a bear from a distance might occur while you are hiking in or near a large open area and see a bear feeding or walking about 100–200 yards away, and the bear apparently hasn't yet sensed your presence. This is the most common type of bear encounter in Yellowstone's backcountry.

- If the bear hasn't seen you, turn around and slowly go back the way you came. Leave this trail to be hiked another day. If you choose to detour around the bear, give it as wide a berth as possible. Watch the bear to determine its direction of travel and choose your detour accordingly. If it is a grizzly sow with cubs, I would not try a detour, and if possible, just go back the way I came.

- There is probably no reason to draw attention to yourself in such an encounter. If you can leave the area without the bear knowing you were there, all the better. Running or quick motions are probably a bad idea. Bears have a tendency, as do other predators, to chase things that run from them.

- If the bear senses (smells, hears, or sees) you from a distance, it often will leave the area. Some bears—those that have become habituated to human presence—may know you are nearby but will exhibit no outward reaction.

BEAR-INFLICTED HUMAN INJURIES IN YELLOWSTONE NATIONAL PARK, 1969–2011

In 2012, the National Park Service's Bear Management Office in Yellowstone compiled data from the last 43 years of bear attacks within park boundaries, and put out an information sheet summarizing their findings (see appendix for more information). Some interesting statistics came from their report:

Of the 43 people injured by grizzly bears in the backcountry in 43 years:

5 (12%) died from their injuries

40 (93%) were in groups of fewer than 3 people

18 (42%) were in groups of 2 people

22 (51%) were traveling solo

Hiking groups of 3 or more people are just as common as solo hikers, yet hikers in parties of 3 or more account for only 7% of all injuries. This suggests that hiking with at least 2 other people is less likely to result in being injured by a bear.

22 (51%) were attacked while traveling off-trail

19 (44%) were attacked while traveling on designated trails

Because substantially more people hike on trail than off, this data suggests that hiking off trail is proportionately more likely to result in being injured by a bear.

2 (5%) were attacked in backcountry campsites

41 (95%) were attacked while hiking

26 (60%) involved females with young (as reported—may be higher)

37 (86%) reported their attacks as surprise encounters

From 1980 through 2011, 43 people were injured by bears (35 by grizzly bears, 5 by black bears, and 3 by bears where the species was not identified) within the park. Of these 43 injuries only 9 (21%) were women. Of the 9 incidents involving women there was no evidence linking menstruation to any of these attacks. See the table on page 142 for more information on grizzly bear caused human fatalities in Yellowstone's backcountry.

• If the bear senses you from a distance and starts advancing slowly or stands up, it is probably trying to determine what manner of creature it has sensed. The correct response to this situation is not clear. It may be beneficial to help the bear identify you by waving your arms, talking in an even voice, and moving upwind of the bear. With any luck, once the bear has identified you as a human, it will leave the area.

• Climbing a tree or running over to a tree to climb it can both be interpreted by a bear as fleeing. And one of our strong assumptions is that bears chase people that attempt to flee or run. Grizzly bears have gone high up into trees after people by climbing limb over limb as we do. (Black bears can climb just about any tree.) If you choose to climb a tree, do it when the bear is still far in the distance and not actively charging, and get at least 15–20 feet off the ground, higher if possible. Remember that injuring yourself by falling out of a tree, or by being pulled out, may be just as dangerous a course of action as choosing not to climb.

The close range encounter usually occurs when a hiker is coming around the bend of a trail or over the rise of a hill and surprises a bear at close range. It probably happens when something prevents the bear from seeing, smelling, or hearing you in time to flee. Some habituated bears may just go back to what they were doing before you surprised them, but most bears will eventually either flee, bluff charge, or attack. If your presence is making the bear nervous she may huff, woof, clack her teeth, or slap the ground with her paws. If you see this behavior consider backing away slowly, while continuing to watch the bear for a reaction.

• In a close range encounter the NPS advises hikers not to run from the bear and I believe this is the single most important thing you should remember. DO NOT RUN. A person cannot outrun a bear and running likely incites the bear to chase and attack—even a quick one or two steps towards a tree or cover may do it.

• If the bear does charge, and you have ready access to pepper spray, now is the time to use it. (See the section on pepper spray, page 30, for more detailed information.)

• We have had instances in Yellowstone where a bear has stopped its charge right in front of a person, "a bluff charge". In these cases defending yourself by pushing, hitting, or kicking the bear seems to be the wrong move as the bears responded by biting or clawing the person. If I had a bear stop a charge right in front of me (and was unable to deploy pepper spray), I would stay still or back away slowly, talk softly to it, and hope that it would turn away. I would try to not look it in the eye. If I made a movement or action that seemed to provoke the bear, I would not do it again. If the bear moved away, I would stay still until it was out of sight or at least 100 yards away. At least that is what I would try to do.

• If the bear continues the charge into an attack and you either don't have pepper spray, or have chosen not to use it, the NPS recommends that you "play dead" either just before or just after the bear hits. This drastic action has almost always resulted in hikers escaping an attack with only minor injuries. In past attacks in Yellowstone, it appears as if fighting back or movement may prolong the attack, and only after resistance has stopped does the attack cease. A reasonable theory is that the bear charges and attacks during a surprise encounter because it perceives a person as a threat. The bear attacks out of defense. As long as a person fights or shows signs of life, the person remains a perceived threat to the bear.

A bear encounter in your campsite occurs when you are in your campsite and a bear enters, or prowls around, the perimeter of the camping area. This usually happens at night and is, potentially, a very dangerous situation. A bear that willingly comes this close to people has probably had a past association with people and our food. This is a much different situation than surprising a bear at close range and having the bear react defensively. This type of bear is probably after food and may even, in rare circumstances, view you as prey. This is a situation where having bear spray is a real advantage.

• If the bear enters the camping area while you are up and about, you should retreat slowly from the bear, possibly throwing down things (not food) to distract the bear. Watch the bear as you retreat to see if you can determine its intentions. If the bear comes close enough to spray with pepper spray, use it. If you do not have pepper spray, and the bear continues to approach or follow you as you try to leave, make noise, throw things at the bear, and be as aggressive as seems prudent. If and when the bear leaves the area, do not go to sleep, nor move camp a short distance and try to sleep there. Stay awake all night, and when there is enough light in the morning, pack up your camp and hike out of the area. When you get back to the trailhead, report this type of incident to rangers immediately so they may close the campsite and prevent others from having the same experience.

• If the bear enters the camping area while you are asleep and pulls you or one of your party out of the tent, this is the time to fight back. Do not play dead in this situation. This is one of those extremely rare situations that have occurred periodically in Yellowstone and other areas in bear country. The person being attacked usually isn't capable of resisting the bear, so it is up to the rest of the group to distract or deter the bear. Definitely use your pepper spray. This is a volatile situation and everyone is in danger of being injured, but without help, the person being dragged off will almost certainly be killed.

• I sleep with my bear spray in my tent, next to my sleeping bag. I want my spray readily available if a bear comes into my tent. If you are camping with another person and only have one canister, make certain that both of you can reach it during the night and make certain your partner is ready to take the necessary actions in the event of a nighttime attack.

PLAYING DEAD

Leave your pack on. Lie on your stomach. Interlock your fingers over the back of your neck and bring your elbows up to cover your face. Your pack offers protection for your back, leaving only your buttocks and legs exposed. The bear may bite and scratch you, but you must remain still and silent. This sounds incredibly difficult, but many "ordinary" people have done it. People who have played dead and been bitten and scratched by grizzlies have told me that they weren't aware of any pain during the attack. Once the bear leaves you, don't move, as the bear may be watching you from a short way off, looking for signs of life. Continue listening, and only move when you are sure the bear has left the area.

WHEN NOT TO PLAY DEAD: The NPS offers the following advice: "If the bear has not reacted aggressively, and has not initiated a charge or otherwise acted defensively, you should back away. Never drop to the ground and 'play dead' with a bear that has not been aggressive or defensive. Being submissive or 'playing dead' with a curious bear could cause the bear to become predatory. A defensive bear will charge almost immediately during a surprise encounter, and will charge with its head low and ears laid back. A curious or predatory bear will persistently approach with its head up and ears erect. When approached by a curious or predatory bear you should be aggressive and fight back."

Now that you're feeling very unsure of entering the backcountry, remember again that the chance of encountering a bear is small, especially after taking the proper precautions. Also, the National Park Service helps to prevent hikers from encountering bears by closing off certain areas of the backcountry when these areas have more than the usual amount of bear activity. But a certain amount of fear, or at least consciously thinking about grizzlies, as you hike or camp is part of the Yellowstone experience. Even with all the rangers, regulations, and permits, this is still a wild place, and your safety may hinge simply on a matter of chance. To some people, all the precautions and assurances aren't enough. The presence of bears and the real or perceived danger may make hiking in Yellowstone so nerve-wracking that the trip becomes unpleasant. Evaluate your fears before you start your trip. Being afraid of bears is not foolish. Don't go if the thought of bears is going to make you miserable. Hiking in the backcountry should be an enjoyable experience, not a terrifying one.

On the other end of the spectrum, there are those people who seek out bears instead of trying to avoid them. Although observing a bear in the backcountry can be the thrill of a lifetime, encountering a bear risks not only your life but also the future of that bear. Grizzly bears, in particular, cannot cope with human disturbance. In the wild they are unsure of hikers and usually avoid them whenever possible. If a grizzly is disturbed often enough by hikers and would-be observers, it may leave a prime feeding area to escape this disturbance. Or, rather than trying to escape the cause of the disturbance, the bear may attack it. With the shortage of remaining grizzly habitat in the lower 48 states, we can't afford to let Yellowstone's grizzlies lose precious feeding areas due to disturbances we can easily prevent. Limit your disturbance of the bears and heed closures for the bear's safety and yours. ♣

PEPPER SPRAY–CAPSICUM REPELLENT FOR BEARS

The National Park Service recommends that Yellowstone hikers carry capsicum pepper spray and use it to deter attacking bears. Many recreational and professional backcountry travelers have been carrying it for years and studies have found it to be an effective, non-lethal tool in stopping aggressive behavior in bears. Carrying pepper spray does not guarantee your safety in the backcountry. The best preventive measure you can take is to practice the safe hiking and camping strategies outlined in this book and recommended by the NPS.

Capsicum (or the derivative capsaicin) is a powerful local irritant of soft tissue, causing inflammation and constriction of the respiratory tract and inflammation of the eyes. The most effective spray dispersal canister appears to be the cloud-pattern spray type (similar to a mini fire extinguisher), which gives a wider pattern of coverage than a narrow-stream type spray. The cloud pattern makes it easier to hit the bear's eyes, nose and mouth—the target areas. There is evidence that even the sound made by the cloud-type canister may have a deterrent effect. Manufacturers claim ranges of up to 25–40 feet for their products. This is obviously very dependent on wind conditions.

A 2008 study of bear encounters in Alaska, as well as recent incidents of successful pepper spray use in Yellowstone, show pepper spray to be effective deterrent in both predatory and surprise encounters with bears. The Alaska study found that in 92% of close range encounters with grizzly bears, and in 90% with black bears, spray stopped the undesirable behavior. In aggressive encounters, pepper spray stopped the aggressive behavior in 85% of the grizzly incidents and 100% of the black bear incidents.

If you choose to carry bear spray, make certain you are prepared to use it. The canister should be readily accessible, preferably in a holster and not inside your pack. Practice drawing the spray canister until you can do it smoothly without looking. Under stress you are much more likely to deploy the spray quickly and efficiently if you have done a number of repetitions beforehand. Lastly, at the trailhead, loosen the tension

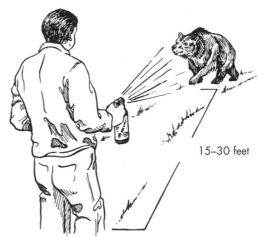

Pepper Spray
has a limited range.
Always be aware of
wind direction.

15–30 feet

setting on the plastic thumb safety so that you can easily access the spray button if needed.

The NPS recommends that when being charged by a bear hikers should start to spray the charging bear when it is about 30-60 feet away. The spray will not hit the bear at that distance but the bear will be moving so fast that you should start spraying before the bear is actually in range. Use a slight side to side motion and spray a 2-3 second blast so that the bear must pass through the cloud of bear spray before it gets to you. Aim lower rather than higher so that the bear can't run under the spray cloud. Keep spraying until the bear breaks off the charge. Remove yourself from the area of the bear without delay as the effect of the spray may soon wear off.

One reason to always carry a full canister is that you may need to spray the bear more than once. In the Alaska study, for 18% of the incidents (involving both grizzly and black bears) one dose of bear spray was not enough. After initially being sprayed these bears resumed their threatening behavior and required repeated spraying until the users could remove themselves from the situation.

Don't use pepper spray like mosquito repellent. Don't spray it on your tent, or clothes, or around your campsite in the hope of repelling bears. It only works when it is sprayed in a bear's face.

Pepper spray is not a substitute for caution in bear country. Your best defense against an attack is to stay alert while hiking and do what you can do avoid surprise encounters. There is still a lot to be learned about pepper spray and bears. Stay informed. The sources I used are listed in the appendix. 🐾

Water Filter

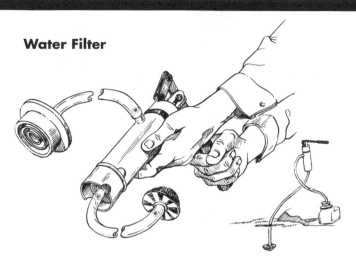

WATER TREATMENT

That cold, clear, fast-moving stream certainly looks refreshing on a hot day. The water has a crispness to it that you just don't get from the kitchen tap back home. Of course, this stream may also contain some microscopic critters your digestive system won't like. *Giardia* protozoa and *Campylobactor* bacteria are the two organisms most frequently accused of causing trouble. Both can cause mild-to-extreme intestinal distress. Other, less common surface water contaminants found in North America include viruses such as *Hepatitis*, the protozoan *Cryptosporidia*, and the bacteria *E. coli*. Unfortunately, there has not been enough sampling done to know if, in any given body of water in Yellowstone, any of these organisms are actually present. You definitely can't tell by looking or tasting. So whether or not it's needed, treating your water is the only way to be certain the water you're drinking isn't harmful.

Giardia lamblia, the most common human intestinal parasite in the U.S., is a pear-shaped protozoan that, when ingested in food or drink, may attach itself to the intestinal lining. This changes the absorptive capacity of the intestine and causes the symptoms of giardiasis. These symptoms appear one to three weeks after exposure and may include an explosive onset of watery diarrhea, cramps, gas, abdominal distention, nausea, loss of appetite, vomiting, fever, and chills (whew!). Acute symptoms usually last five to seven days. If not treated by medication, giardiasis may go into a chronic stage that is characterized by periodic bouts of less severe symptoms. Check with a physician to see if your case is worth treating with drug therapy. Scientists know that many of the types of animals found in Yellowstone carry a species of *Giardia* and that these *Giardia* may be deposited into water sources through animal feces. Beavers, for instance, are often blamed for passing on *Giardia*, but whether these species of *Giardia* affect humans has not been proven conclusively.

Campylobactor jejuni, a bacterium, is second only to *Giardia* as a cause of acute waterborne diarrheal disease. It can be carried in the intestinal tracts of humans and many domestic animals, and can be transmitted to humans through water polluted by such carriers. Once in our intestines, the bacterium causes patchy destruction of the mucus lining which, in turn, may cause bloody diarrhea, abdominal pain, cramps, and fever. These symptoms appear three to five days after ingestion and cease within 48–72 hours. The illness is self-limiting, and drug therapy is not essential in most cases. If you're out of the backcountry and back in civilization when the illness strikes, it's still worth visiting a physician to play it safe.

After hearing the unattractive details of these illnesses, you're probably more interested in learning how to treat your water. Disinfecting water for drinking can be done a number of ways: filtration, boiling, purifying with an ultraviolet (UV) light device, and treating with halogens (chlorine or iodine). Treating with halogens, while effective, involves many variables and won't be discussed here. (See appendix for references on water treatment.) Purifiers that use UV light are increasingly popular. Filter systems are easily obtained and available in a variety of sizes and prices, but manufacturer's directions must be followed. The maximum effective filter pore size for *Giardia* is 5 microns; for enteric bacteria, such as *Campylobactor*, it is 0.2 microns. Only a filter that uses chemicals will neutralize viruses, but viruses should be rare in Yellowstone backcountry water found at altitudes above areas of human use. Pre-filtering may be necessary for cloudy water, and the filter elements have to be replaced or cleaned periodically according to the manufacturer's recommendations.

WASH YOUR HANDS

Recent research, including a study done on high-altitude lakes and streams in the Sierra Nevada mountains (see appendix), found that you are actually more likely to be infected by *Giardia* and other microbes through poor sanitary practices among you and your hiking companions than from untreated water. To avoid any hostile finger-pointing, make sure everyone on your trip practices what we all learned in kindergarten: always wash your hands after going to the bathroom (or, as the case may be, ducking behind the nearest lodgepole pine) and definitely before cooking and eating. Vigorous cleaning and rinsing will rid your hands of most miniscule culprits. If you really want to be careful, antibacterial quick-drying gels or hand wipes are widely available and might prove to be more valuable than your water filter. ❧

Another effective way to treat water in Yellowstone is to bring it to a boil. In the past, numerous publications have recommended treating water by boiling it anywhere from 1 to 30 minutes, depending on the altitude. It appears now that this was overkill. All diarrheal pathogens and viruses are very heat-sensitive, killed within 5 minutes at 131°F, and more rapidly at higher temperatures. Bacteria are slightly more heat resistant but will be killed, along with the *Giardia*, by any water brought to a boil, as disinfection is occurring during the time required to heat water from 140°F to boiling. Physicians of the Wilderness Medical Society have stated that any water brought to a boil, even at high altitude, should be safe to drink. For added safety, let the boiled water stand covered for a few minutes. A convenient way to handle water for long trips is to boil enough drinking water each night for use on the trail the next day. That way, the water has a chance to chill down overnight so that it's cool by morning. ❧

AVOID BECOMING DEHYDRATED

Yellowstone has very low humidity. Perspiration evaporates rapidly, which means you may not need as much deodorant as usual, but you will need more water. For a full-day hike, most people need four or more quarts of water. Unfortunately, even when it's available to them, few people will actually drink that much water on a hike. As a result, dehydration may limit their performance and energy level. Force yourself to drink, even when you're not thirsty. On hot days, don't drink too much at once; instead, drink a little and drink often. Luckily, almost every trail in Yellowstone has an abundance of water nearby, and those that don't are mentioned in the trail descriptions. Should you or someone in your hiking party develop symptoms such as significant fatigue, vomiting, diarrhea, or even an odd loss of appetite, serious dehydration may be to blame. Eating or drinking may seem unthinkable to the victim; however, it is crucial that the dehydrated hiker ingest liquids and food in small quantities. Once severe dehydration has set in, drinking water alone may actually aggravate the condition. The quickest and least painful way to recover is to drink an Oral Rehydration Solution (ORS), which will replenish both water and electrolytes in the body. The recipe for an ORS is simple: ½ teaspoon salt, 6 teaspoons sugar, and 1 quart (or liter) of water (see appendix for references). Consider preparing the salt and sugar, in correct quantities, ahead of time and packing the extra ounce of weight with you. Extreme dehydration occurring far in the backcountry is an emergency; even if you have to use untreated or obviously dirty water to mix the ORS, the benefits will far outweigh the health risks of the potentially contaminated water. ❧

RIVER AND
STREAM CROSSINGS

The trails of Yellowstone cross many rivers and streams, most of which are purposely not bridged. To perpetuate a wild feel to the area, the National Park Service has made backcountry bridges an exception rather than the rule. This not only maintains the wilderness appearance of a river, but also forces hikers to regard Yellowstone's backcountry differently than a more "developed" backcountry area, both in their trip planning and in what is demanded of them physically. So in Yellowstone, unless you're able to find a fallen log on which to cross a stream, you'll have to wade to get to the other side. Here are some suggestions that should help you in your stumblings through Yellowstone's ice-cold waters.

Fording Tips

• If many crossings, or one especially wide crossing, are to be included on your hike, wear wading shoes. Many people use old running shoes or river runner sandals. Rocky streambeds can wreak havoc on bare feet and the pain can make it hard to keep your mind on your balance.

• Don't wade a stream with your hiking boots on. Wet shoes not only cause blisters; they also cause cold feet. Also, if the crossing is higher than where you can roll up your pants, take them off or wear shorts. I believe it was Plato who once said, "Wet pants are cold pants."

• You don't have to cross a stream exactly at the trail. Many times there is a shallower or easier crossing a short way up or downstream.

• If a ford is fast and over thigh deep, forget it. Try another spot or look for a logjam. One slip in that depth of fast water with a backpack, and you could easily drown. Crossing a creek on fallen logs can be a convenient alternative to wading, but wet logs, especially without bark, can be incredibly slippery. Be aware that the consequences of a fall from a log into a fast, deep creek are even worse than a slip while wading.

• If you do cross a deep, fast stream, be certain to unbuckle your pack's waist strap.

• Avoid hazardous stream crossings altogether by picking another trail or waiting for the streams to go down. The trail descriptions in this guide provide information on each major stream crossing. ❧

WEATHER

The weather and your ability to deal with it are important factors in the success of your hike. As mothers have been telling us all along, getting too cold and wet, or too hot, is not good for us. You might notice that when you ask a Yellowstone ranger what the day's weather will be, the ranger will hesitate and then, while looking very uncomfortable, mutter something about "partly cloudy, chance of rain." It's close to impossible to make an accurate forecast. On any given day in Yellowstone, the weather can be hot and sunny one minute, sprinkling rain with flashes of lightning the next, and turning to windy hail and even snow the next.

Sudden afternoon storms are not uncommon during the summer season, usually blowing in from the south or southwest. Lightning often travels with these storms. If you are on an exposed ridge or peak and hear thunder, don't wait to see how far away the lightning is—descend to lower ground as quickly as possible. Research suggests, however, that you should stop moving and assume the lightning position if you actually become exposed to lightning, even if you are still in open terrain. While people have died trying to make it to a distant sheltered area (the theory is that, in an open area, if you are the tallest point while upright and moving, you become a lightning rod), no one has died in the lightning position (Gookin 2). In brief, the lightning position is a low squat, with your feet together, your arms wrapped around your legs, and your eyes closed. (For more details, go to the website for the National Outdoor Leadership School: www.nols.edu.)

Most of Yellowstone's trails are at an elevation of 7,000–9,000 feet above sea level, so that when it gets cloudy, it gets cool. When it rains, it's a cold rain. Getting cold and wet can easily lead to hypothermia, a lowering of the body's core temperature, which can sometimes lead to death. For the majority of hikers in Yellowstone, hypothermia is one of the biggest dangers they'll face. It's well worth your time to know how to prevent and treat it. Put on extra layers of clothing <u>before</u> you get wet or cold. Warning signs of hypothermia include uncontrollable or violent shivering; slow, slurred speech; stumbling; and memory lapses and drowsiness. If someone in your hiking group is showing signs of hypothermia, immediately find shelter from any wind and rain, remove the hiker's wet clothes, put the hiker in a dry sleeping bag, and help restore the hiker's body heat by administering warm drinks. Never offer the hypothermic hiker alcohol—while it may make the hiker feel warm, it will actually lower the hiker's core body temperature.

It's not always cold and wet in Yellowstone. In fact, most summer days are sunny and dry. As nice as this weather feels, there are still some weather issues to take into consideration. At Yellowstone's high elevation, the effects of the sun are magnified. It's quite easy to get a first rate sunburn in no time at all. Protect your eyes with sunglasses and your skin with sunscreen, especially if traveling over snow.

What to expect from the weather on the Yellowstone Plateau:
Mid-May to mid-June: 20–40°F on clear nights, 45–70°F on sunny days. Rain is common, but it can snow heavily at any time. Snow may still be on the ground in the forests and at high elevations. Trails may be wet and mucky. Streams are rising. Flowers are blooming at lower elevations. Insects are not yet a problem. Migratory birds arrive. Migratory mammals are at low elevations but are beginning to move to summer range.

Mid-June to mid-July: 25–40°F on clear nights, 65–85°F on sunny days. Weather improves in July. Meadows may still be wet and mucky; trails are wet but may dry by the end of this period. Streams are at their highest. Mosquitoes are reaching their peak. Flowers are blooming over most of the park. Migratory mammals have moved to their summer range.

Late July to mid-August: 25–40°F on clear nights, 65–90°F on sunny days. Most days are sunny with an occasional afternoon rain. Mosquitoes are declining. Trails are dry. Streams are receding. Flowers are blooming at higher elevations. Migratory mammals are on high ridges and meadows. Berries are ripe on bushes.

Late August to late September: 15–35°F on clear nights, 55–70°F on sunny days. When the weather is fair and sunny, the hiking at this time of year is very enjoyable. Heavy snowfalls are possible during this time, so be certain to carry the proper cold weather gear. The large animals are congregating at the lower elevations and this is an excellent time to view them. Stream levels are down. Hunting season opens outside the park in some areas—wear bright clothing if hiking near the boundary.

October: 5–35°F on clear nights, 40–55°F on sunny days. When the weather is fair and sunny, the hiking at this time of year is very enjoyable, especially at lower elevations. Heavy snowfalls are common during this month, so be certain to carry the proper cold weather gear. The animals are congregating at the lower elevations, and this is an excellent time to view them. Streams levels are down. ❧

Spotted Sandpiper
• head held low
• body tilted forward
• tail bobs up and down constantly

POINTS OF INTEREST IN THE BACKCOUNTRY

Hiking is usually more enjoyable when you understand or know something about the things you're seeing along the trail. Guidebooks on flowers, trees, mammals, and birds are helpful in this respect, and are available from Yellowstone's visitor centers. National Park Service ranger-naturalist walks into the backcountry are another aid. Knowledge gained on one of these walks can often be applied on your own hikes along other trails in the park. The following section of this guide presents information on some of the interesting features found in the backcountry and provides just a hint of the huge body of knowledge that awaits those hikers eager to discover more. Be careful, though; a little knowledge can be a dangerous thing. Learning about Yellowstone can turn into a lifelong addiction.

Hydrothermal Areas (Hot Springs and Geysers)

A hydrothermal area is a place where water that has been heated by a deep chamber of molten rock comes to the surface in the form of geysers, hot springs, mud pots or fumaroles. There are other hydrothermal areas in the world, but Yellowstone contains more geysers than the rest of these areas combined. The most impressive examples of Yellowstone's hydrothermal features are found in the Upper, Midway, and Lower geyser basins along the Firehole River, and also at Norris Geyser Basin. These areas are all accessible by boardwalks and short, paved paths. Inexpensive trail leaflets and ranger-naturalist guided walks provide detailed information on these features. If you're interested in hydrothermal features, you may want to visit these frontcountry sites first so that you'll understand more about what you're seeing when you do visit the backcountry hot springs. Two of the larger backcountry hydrothermal areas are the Shoshone Geyser Basin and the Heart Lake Geyser Basin, both of which contain active geysers. Some other interesting backcountry sites include Ponuntpa Springs and the Mushpots in the Pelican Valley area, Imperial and Lone Star geysers in the Firehole Valley area, Highland Hot Springs on the Mary Mountain Trail, and Washburn Hot Springs on the Washburn Spur Trail. There are many other smaller thermal areas scattered throughout the backcountry that may or may not be found on maps. Part of the intrigue of hiking in Yellowstone is unexpectedly finding one of these areas on your own. Remember that bathing, washing dishes, and cooking are not allowed in thermal features or their runoff channels. The preservation of the delicate mineral formations and the fragile ecosystems living here is a greater priority than a hot bath.

Fires burning in Pelican Valley in 1994.

Forest Fire Areas

Each summer and fall, forest fires burn in different areas of Yellowstone. Most of these are relatively small. The forest fires of 1988, however, had a major impact on Yellowstone's backcountry. Approximately 800,000 acres in the park burned. The fires of 1988 touched almost every area of the park.

Fires continue to occur each year in Yellowstone, but nowhere close to the size and intensity of the 1988 fires. The year 2003 was considered a big fire year, but the total area burned was still "only" around 29,000 acres. There are many sections of trails in the park that have not experienced recent fires, and even those areas that have burned did so to varying degrees. In some places, entire trees burned completely, while in other spots only the understory burned and the forest canopy was untouched. This fire diversity has left us with patterns of different intensities of burn throughout the forest. These patterns are called fire mosaics, and are especially visible from overlooks and high peaks (such as Mt. Washburn and Mt. Sheridan). Many books have been written about wildfires—about the chronology of events, the management policies, the firefighting effort, and the effects of these incredible fires. I will only touch on the subject briefly here.

When a fire strikes a forest, it may burn away the forest canopy. This allows more sunlight to reach the forest floor, and soon grasses, flowers, bushes, and new trees spring up (some 1988-burned areas in Yellowstone contained over 100 seedlings per square meter by summer 1993). Studies have shown that the number of plant species increases after a fire and reaches a peak after about 25 years. Then, as the trees grow back up and the forest canopy again forms, the plant diversity decreases drastically. As you'll notice, there isn't much variety to the plant life in a typical lodgepole pine forest.

The number of mammals and birds also increases after a fire. Grazing animals and root-eating rodents are attracted by the sudden abundance of ground-level plants. Some birds nest in the trees killed by the fires while others come to feed on the insects these trees attract. As the forest grows back and its diversity decreases, the diversity and number of birds, rodents, and grazing animals also decreases.

It's been nearly 25 years since the fires of 1988, but in most subsequent years there have been major, albeit much smaller, wildfires. In traveling through recently burned areas, I've noticed some positives and some negatives from a hiker's point of view. The primary detractor is the increased soot and heat while hiking. The lack of forest canopy lets the sun glare down without any shade, the blackened trees seem to absorb and then radiate a portion of the sun's heat, and some of the burned areas go on for miles. It all makes for hot hiking. Even sitting down for a rest can leave your clothes and pack streaked in soot. Also, beware of taking shelter among burned standing trees during windstorms; some trees have been burned almost completely through at their bases and may need only a small amount of wind to be blown down.

On the plus side, there is new undergrowth with large patches of purple fireweed, yellow arnica, and green grass that seems so much brighter when contrasted with the black background. And, of course, deer, elk, and moose are more noticeable, either because they move to the burned areas to feed or because they are simply easier to see due to the lack of foliage. With the forest canopy gone, there are now new views of surrounding peaks where before all you could see were the trees a few yards in front of you. Even the burned trees themselves present images of interesting patterns and forms, which might take your mind off the soot and the heat. Will the scorched earth ruin your hike? All I can say for sure is that the burned areas are worth taking a look at. You may hate them or you may find them fascinating, but you shouldn't miss the opportunity to see them for yourself.

Backcountry Waterfalls

Trying to describe the individual beauties of Yellowstone's different backcountry waterfalls would be hard for most writers, and a definite mistake for this one. Let me just present you with a list of some of the park's highest backcountry falls and leave the rest to your imagination. None of them are ugly, and they are all worthwhile destinations.

- Union Falls, Ouzel Falls, Silver Scarf Falls, Dunanda Falls, Colonnade Falls, and Terraced Falls, along with many others in the Bechler area.

- Fairy Falls and Mystic Falls in the Firehole River area.

- Osprey Falls, Wraith Falls, and Knowles Falls in the Mammoth area.

Petrified trees near Crystal Creek.

Fossil Forests

Yellowstone has the most extensive fossil forests of any known area in the world. Some of these petrified tree stumps are standing upright. This may be the position in which they originally grew millions of years ago, or they may have been moved by geologic forces after becoming fossilized and are only now upright by coincidence. I know which theory I like best. These trees became petrified when they were saturated with volcanic outpourings from Yellowstone's numerous past volcanic eruptions. This silica-rich volcanic material filled the cell cavities of the trees, thus preserving their structure for us to view and study today. The species of fossilized trees—sycamores, walnuts, magnolias, chestnuts, oaks, redwoods, maples, and dogwoods—indicate that Yellowstone must have had a much warmer climate in the distant past. The best place to view the standing petrified trees is near the Specimen Ridge Trail. Pieces of petrified wood may also be found along many of the trails in the eastern section of the park, near the volcanic Absaroka Range, or in the northwest corner along the Sky Rim Trail. Just remember that collecting specimens is a violation of park regulations. Leave them for others to discover as you did. ❧

WILDLIFE

The opportunity to view wildlife is one of the main reasons people venture into Yellowstone's backcountry. Watching an animal act and react in its natural surroundings, away from the crowds, can be a very satisfying experience. Perhaps the most interesting aspect to Yellowstone's wildlife is their self-sufficiency. Finding all their own food, protecting themselves from predators, raising their young, and surviving long, cold winters are all part of an animal's life here. As happens in any natural area, some die each year due to winter, predators, old age, disease, or a combination of these factors. But their death makes room for other animals, and their bodies return to the soil or provide food for scavengers. This is how the animals have lived for centuries in Yellowstone, and we as hikers are privileged to be able to watch as this cycle continues. The following segment contains general information on some of Yellowstone's more famous animals.

Grizzly Bears

Grizzly bears represent different things to different people. To some, the grizzly is an indicator of the wildness of a place; if a piece of land has grizzlies, then it still must be somewhat untamed and uncivilized. To others, the bear is an intelligent animal, with human-like attributes, that just wants to live out its life and be left alone. And to many, the grizzly bear is a powerful predator to be respected and feared. What is particularly fascinating about grizzlies is how hard their behavior is to predict. The bear's behavior and habits always seem to be one step ahead of the people who think they know the bear the best. Just when researchers, rangers, park management, local residents, photographers, or hikers think they know what a grizzly will do or how it will react in a certain situation, it does something different. It may be that we are poor observers and have a hard time "thinking like a bear," or it may be that the bear's behavior is constantly evolving in response to a changing environment. Whichever it may be, the grizzly is truly an unknown quantity—a wild card. In our orderly society, we seem to find this particularly intriguing.

When the grizzlies emerge from their dens between March and April, Yellowstone is still covered with deep snow. The bears feed on the carcasses of winter-killed animals during this period and can be very protective of the carrion, often burying it and chasing off other hungry scavengers, such as ravens and coyotes. More recently, since the reintroduction of wolves, grizzlies have been observed chasing wolves off of wolf-killed bison carcasses and feasting on the "free" bison steaks. When the elk begin calving in May, grizzlies start preying on elk calves, searching them out where they hide or chasing them down. During late May and June, the cutthroat trout begin moving out of Yellowstone Lake and up into tributary streams to spawn, though in drastically reduced numbers due to predation from introduced lake trout. With fewer trout, there is more competition for prime fishing spots. Where once there was enough for many bears to share the trout wealth, now it is just the dominant adult male bears who end up scooping out the cutthroat gathered in these streams. As the season progresses and new vegetation begins to emerge and mature, grizzlies also turn to plants, such as grasses and clover, for a part of their diet.

In mid-summer, the bears graze on clover, dandelion, elk thistle, and the roots of yampa and biscuitroot. A bear's dexterity in digging out the yampa roots is impressive, as the roots are small and the plants very delicate. Throughout the summer, grizzlies may prey on an occasional elk as well as dig up pocket gophers. If you see a grizzly intensely digging in a meadow with periodic lunges and flurries of activity, the quarry is probably a pocket gopher. These tiny animals must be quite a delicacy to the grizzly, as a bear seems to move a lot of earth just to get a gopher in its mouth. Later on, in August and early September, the bears also feed on grouse whortleberry and huckleberries.

At higher elevations, grizzlies can forage for two energy-rich food sources: army cutworm moths and whitebark pine nuts. The army cutworm moths live in talus slopes from July through September, finding shelter underneath the scree. Grizzly bears feed on the moths by the thousands, scrounging through loose rocks with their paws and licking the undersides clean. During a 30-day period, a grizzly can consume enough army cutworm moths to fulfill nearly 50% of its energy requirements for an entire year (see appendix). In years past, whitebark pine nuts were an important autumn food source for grizzlies. As winter temperatures in the Northern Rockies have become more moderate, pine beetles have been able to get a foothold in higher elevations where the whitebark grow and are killing an increasing number of these pines. A 2009 aerial survey found 95% of forest stands containing whitebark pine had measurable mountain pine beetle activity. Where whitebark pine remain and are still producing cones the bears search out caches of pine nuts that red squirrels have gathered for the winter. The bears come in and ransack the caches while the squirrels are left to chatter in frustration from a nearby tree. In years of poor pine nut production, bears must find another fall food source. This may result in them hunting for food in developed areas or backcountry campsites. There are other natural food sources available to bears in the fall, and some bears do prey on elk, but I'm sure it's a lot easier raiding a squirrel's nut cache than it is chasing down an elk.

When winter arrives, the grizzlies den up in a natural shelter of some sort, a log pile or a cave, for instance. A bear may also dig its own den under the roots of a tree. It's been theorized that grizzlies may wait until a heavy falling snow before they move into their dens. This snow covers their tracks and covers the den, insulating the bear and helping to assure it of an undisturbed winter slumber.

Elk

Of Yellowstone's large mammals, elk are both the most abundant and most often spotted in the backcountry. Most elk summer near high meadows where they feed on grasses, sedges, and forbs. Big Game Ridge, Two Ocean Plateau, the Gallatin Range, and the upper Miller Creek and upper Lamar River areas are all excellent spots to view elk during the summer. In the fall, the elk move to lower elevations for the mating season. The bulls perform their famous antler-to-antler battles and sound their challenging bugles as they strive to acquire, and hoard, a harem of females. Some of the best fall viewing spots for elk are Swan Lake Flats, Gallatin River Valley, Slough Creek, Big Game Ridge, and Two Ocean Plateau.

Bison

Yellowstone's bison are actually hybrid descendants of the plains bison and the mountain bison. Mountain bison originally inhabited Yellowstone but were hunted to near extinction by the late 1800s. Plains bison were then brought into the park to supplement the population, and the two species interbred. The present bison population, though, has taken after the mountain bison in their migrating habits and behavior. Unlike the huge herds that roamed the plains, Yellowstone's bison generally travel in small bands of 10–40 animals, consisting of cows, young bulls, calves, and occasional mature bulls. The bison may gather in larger herds during the mating season, from mid-July to mid-August, and on wintering grounds. These herds may contain as many as 450 animals. Many of the bull bison travel in their own small groups of 3–8, and often, when a bull gets on in age, it no longer travels with the herd and may be seen feeding by itself miles from any other bison. Like the elk, the bison spend the winters at lower elevations such as the lower Yellowstone River area, Firehole Valley, and Lamar Valley. Many bison winter in Pelican Valley and Hayden Valley which, at almost 8,000 feet, aren't low, but are filled with lush vegetation for grazing. To reach this vegetation, a bison must push aside a lot of snow with its head and hooves. In early summer, the bison move surprisingly quickly to high meadows where they graze until September. During this period, their mountain bison blood is readily apparent; they will wander above the tree line and scamper along rocky ledges that seem more appropriate for bighorn sheep. Places where you might spot bison during the summer include Little Firehole Meadows, upper Lamar Valley drainages, Specimen Ridge, Hayden Valley, and Pelican Valley.

Bison have butted or gored dozens of people in Yellowstone, often resulting in injury and, in a couple cases, even death. While most bison in the backcountry will run from you, some old bulls will seem to be oblivious to your presence. They aren't. And they can move very fast when they want to. Always keep at least 100 yards between you and any bison; while hiking, detour around them, going off the trail if you must. Being gored by a bison usually leaves you with a deep, gaping, puncture wound in the thigh or buttocks; a lasting, ugly scar; and short-term embarrassment when you explain to the rangers how it happened.

Wolves

Wolves roamed Yellowstone from at least 1,000 years ago until the 1930s, when government hunters eliminated them as a viable population. Experts believe that wolves were part of the original post ice age ecosystem of Yellowstone. Wolves were reintroduced to Yellowstone in 1995 and 1996. As of December 2014, there were apporximatley 106 wolves in 11 packs in the park. The wolves have reoccupied Yellowstone's entire wolf habitat. Wolves need a place with a year-round elk (or other ungulate) population. In Yellowstone, the wolves have preyed on deer, bison, moose, and pronghorn; even though elk have been their main source of prey, for some packs a healthy percentage of their winter calories come from bison.

The most likely places to spot wolves from the highway are Hayden Valley, along the Canyon-Fishing Bridge Road, and Lamar Valley, along the park's Northeast Entrance Road. During the summer in the backcountry, wolves may be seen in the Lamar and Northeast Entrance area, the Thorofare area, Pelican Valley, Heart Lake and Two Ocean Plateau, Nez Perce Creek, and Hayden Valley. While hiking, the best way to see wolves is to stay on the trail. Hiking off-trail usually makes so much noise that the wolves will hear your approach and vanish before you can see them. Surprisingly, there have been numerous sightings made from backcountry campsites. People sitting in their sites, usually around dusk and while not making much noise, have had wolves walk through nearby meadows.

Other Animals

Coyotes are often spotted in large open meadows such as Hayden Valley, Pelican Valley, and Gardners Hole. They spend the summers in these meadows searching for mice and pocket gophers. These rodents are their main food during summer, but in winter coyotes feed heavily on the carcasses of elk and bison.

Black bears may turn up just about anywhere in Yellowstone, although you probably won't see them begging for food along the roadside as in years past. Black bears seem to prefer forested areas to large open valleys and are fairly secretive creatures in the wild. While black bears have been responsible for very few backcountry injuries to hikers, they should still be treated as potentially dangerous and avoided, especially sows with cubs.

Coyote *[Canis latrans]*

Appearance delicate

Height	16–20 in (0.4–0.5 m)
Length	3.5–4.25 ft (1.1–1.3 m)
Weight	20–35 lbs (9–16 kg)
Color	varies from gray to tan to rust
Ears	long and pointed
Muzzle	long and narrow
Legs	thin and delicate
Feet	small 2 in (5 cm) wide 2.5 in (6 cm) long
Tail	hangs straight down or out

Wolf *[Canis lupis]*

Appearance massive

Height	26–36 in (0.6–1.0 m)
Length	4–6 ft (1.2–1.8 m)
Weight	70–80 lbs (32–36 kg)
Color	varies from white to black to silver-gray
Ears	rounded and relatively short
Muzzle	large, broad and blocky
Legs	thick and long
Feet	very large 3.5–4 in (9–10 cm) wide 4–5 in (10–13 cm) long
Tail	hangs straight down or out

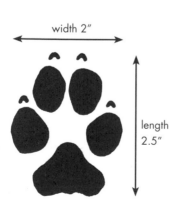

width 2"

length 2.5"

width 3.75"

length 4.75"

With one exception, bighorn sheep are not regularly seen along the park's trails. The sheep spend the warm months on high, inaccessible ridges grazing on the alpine plants and getting their water from the snow. Mt. Washburn is the one trail where the chance of spotting bighorn is fairly good.

Moose are occasionally seen along the park's trails, especially near lakes, ponds, and willow-lined streams, where they feed on aquatic vegetation. The upper Yellowstone River, lower Pelican Valley, Bechler Meadows, Gallatin River, Gardners Hole, and Madison Valley are some of the better places to look for moose.

Mountain lions, also known as cougars, are much more abundant in Yellowstone than one might think. They range over the entire park but are seldom seen. Probably the most efficient killer among the world's big cats, mountain lions routinely kill deer and elk by stalking them at close range, leaping onto the back, and delivering a powerful bite into the neck at the base of the skull. The good news is that there is no record of a mountain lion attacking a human in Yellowstone. Reports of mountain lion attacks elsewhere are rare but get a lot of media attention.

The park also appears to be home to lynx. In the year 2000, lynx were listed as a threatened species in the lower 48 states under the federal Endangered Species Act. A comprehensive study on lynx within Yellowstone's park boundaries was conducted from 2001 to 2004. Evidence such as DNA hair snares, tracks, and reported sightings confirmed that lynx inhabit the central and eastern portions of Yellowstone. Lynx can be extremely difficult to tell apart from their much more common relative, the bobcat. They both weigh about 30 pounds and have tufted ears. The distinctive feature of lynx is their much larger paw size (bigger than a mountain lion's) and their long hind legs. Should you observe a lynx in the backcountry, take note of your location, any distinguishing features of the lynx, such as color and approximate size, and if possible, measure its tracks. Be sure to report your sighting of this rare species at any ranger station or visitor center.

Yellowstone has over 220 species of birds that live within, or migrate through, its boundaries. Trumpeter swans, osprey, American white pelicans, bald eagles, golden eagles, and sandhill cranes are a few of the more spectacular. All bird species need to nest away from disturbances; if, while hiking, you should spot a bird nesting, observe it from a distance and leave if it appears distressed by your presence.

There are 11 native and 5 non-native species of fish residing in the waterways and lakes of Yellowstone. Yellowstone's aquatic ecosystem is probably best known for its cutthroat trout; Yellowstone Lake and Yellowstone River contain the largest inland cutthroat trout population in the world. There are actually three subspecies of cutthroat trout that occur in Yellowstone: Yellowstone cutthroat, Snake River cutthroat, and westslope cutthroat. Illegally introduced, non-native lake trout now pose a severe threat to the survival of the Yellowstone cutthroat trout in Yellowstone Lake and its tributaries. Discovered in the lake in 1994, lake trout are voracious predators—one adult lake trout can consume about 41 cutthroat trout each year. The introduction to the Thorofare area, page 170, further describes the lake trout issue. Details about recent efforts to reestablish a westslope cutthroat trout population in the northwest corner of Yellowstone can be found in the description for the Crescent Lake/High Lake Trail on page 57. ♣

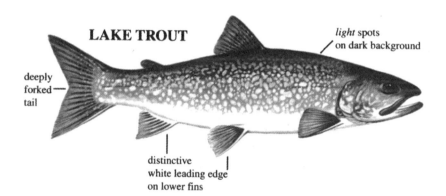

LAKE TROUT

light spots on dark background

deeply forked tail

distinctive white leading edge on lower fins

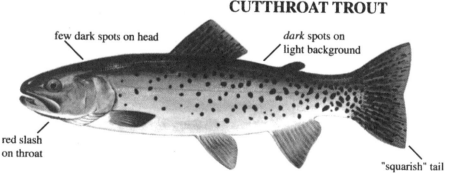

CUTTHROAT TROUT

few dark spots on head

dark spots on light background

red slash on throat

"squarish" tail

TRAIL DESCRIPTIONS

This book's trail descriptions can be used to help you decide which trail to take, when to take that trail, and how difficult the hiking will be. The trail descriptions are divided into 16 different geographical areas of Yellowstone; each area has an introduction that gives general information about that area and its trails. Following the introduction are individual trail descriptions for the area, beginning with a listing of distances, in miles and kilometers, from the trailhead to points along the trail. Hiking distances in the guide are not always exact but are accurate to within a half mile. (One mile equals 1.6 kilometers.) Following this information is the trail description. For longer trails, the description begins with general information about the trail conditions, scenery along the way, opportunities to see wildlife, and anything else that may help you decide if that's the trail for you. Next comes the more detailed information that, when used in conjunction with the maps included in this book, will help you in the actual navigation along the trail. One note of caution: this guide will not be enough for you to navigate a trail if the NPS doesn't regularly maintain the trail markers and trail signs on a trail. If you find yourself on a poorly marked section of trail, look for blazes on trees and for trail clearing cuts on logs along the trail. This should be a relatively unusual occurrence, because all the trails described in this book are listed in the NPS's Backcountry Management Plan as consistently maintained trails.

The descriptions in the guide do cover a variety of trail conditions, and for each of these conditions certain variables should be taken into consideration. For instance, the depths of most stream crossings are given, but these, of course, will vary with how well you choose a spot to cross, if there has been much recent rainfall, and the schedule of the snowpack melt and runoff. Mosquito concentrations and the degree to which they annoy hikers is a rather subjective matter and can be altered by such variables as cold weather, welcome breezes, and the hiker's own mental state. Because of the numerous mountain streams in Yellowstone's backcountry, the availability of drinking water is not usually a problem and will only be mentioned if there is a shortage and a need to bring extra water with you. It is up to you to decide whether or not you need to purify your water from these streams. (See Water Treatment section, page 32.)

Throughout this guide you will notice that certain trails have this warning:

BEAR MANAGEMENT AREA

These trails travel throughout areas that have scheduled closures or restrictions on their use during certain times of the year. This is an attempt by the National Park Service to allow bears undisturbed use of prime habitat. A list and a map of the scheduled closures are posted at every ranger station or can be viewed in the *Backcountry Trip Planner*, available from Yellowstone National Park, (307) 344-2160, or www.nps.gov/yell/planyourvisit/backcountrytripplanner.htm.

NORTHWEST CORNER

The northwest corner of Yellowstone is a place of ups and downs. High, steep ridges and low valleys mean long climbs and descents for hikers. Not much level walking is done here. Once atop the rugged heights, the view of the forested hills, mountain peaks, streams, and lakes below is simply inspiring. Chances of seeing wildlife are good any time of the year in this area. Elk and deer live on the high ridges in the summer and along the river valleys in the spring and fall. Moose feed along the willow-lined streams, and bighorn sheep inhabit the steep slopes and mountain ridges near Sheep Mountain and Bighorn Peak. Grizzly bears use this area all season long, but it is particularly attractive to them in August and September when they feed on the whitebark pine nuts at the higher elevations. All trails in this area start from trailheads on U.S. 191 (Gallatin Highway), which runs between Bozeman and West Yellowstone, Montana. ♣

DAILEY CREEK TRAIL   Map #1, 2

Dailey Creek Trailhead (milepost 31, U.S. 191) to:

Dailey Creek Cutoff Trail Jct.	2 miles	3 km
Tepee Creek Cutoff Trail Jct.	2.4	3.8
Dailey Pass	5.3	9
Sky Rim Trail Jct.	6	9.6

The Dailey Creek Trail provides the easiest access from U.S. 191 to the Sky Rim Trail. There are good opportunities to spot elk during spring and fall. Grizzly bears and wolves also frequent this area, as the tracks and scat will indicate.

From the trailhead, the trail climbs gradually through meadows and open hillsides and soon reaches the Dailey Creek Cutoff Trail junction. The cutoff trail turns east. Look for the first trail marker in a clump of trees up the drainage to the east. The cutoff travels approximately 2 miles over a ridge to meet the Black Butte Trail. To stay on the Dailey Creek Trail, continue hiking north. In less than a mile, the trail arrives at another trail junction. Stay right (north) to remain on the main trail. The Tepee Creek Cutoff Trail heads off to the left (west) and travels approximately 1 mile up through meadows to the park boundary and the Tepee Creek Trail in the Gallatin National Forest. About 4 miles from the trailhead, the Dailey Creek Trail becomes steeper as you approach Dailey Pass. The pass is about 1,600 vertical feet above the trailhead. To reach the Sky Rim Trail, you now follow the trail up the ridge to the northeast, climbing about 400 more vertical feet. ♠

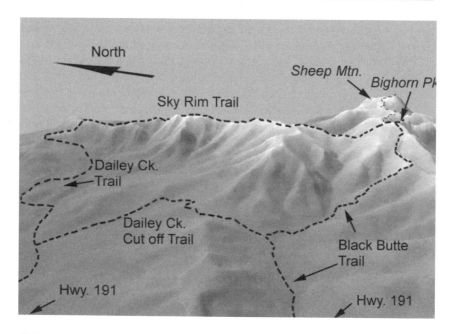

SKY RIM TRAIL

Map #1, 2

From Dailey Creek Trail Junction (6 miles from Dailey Creek Trailhead) to:

Bighorn Peak.. 4 miles.........6.5 km
Specimen Creek Trail Jct. .... 6.5.............. 10.5
Shelf Lake .... 7................. 11
Sheep Mountain .... 8................. 13

The Sky Rim Trail provides the best prolonged dose of mountain scenery in Yellowstone. As it follows the boundary ridge of the park, the trail travels across the summits of two peaks and offers sweeping vistas of mountain ranges in all directions. Chances of viewing wildlife along this route are very good. Elk and bighorn sheep feed in high meadows visible from the trail. Ravens, hawks, and eagles may be spotted soaring above or even below you. Marmots and pikas scurry among the rocks. Mountain goats frequently are seen roaming alone or in groups of two or three. Also look for outcrops of petrified wood among the volcanic rock along the boundary ridge.

Several sections of this trail are steep, rocky, and exposed. Watch your footing. The trail may be hard to follow in places, and will be marked with NPS boundary markers and rock cairns. To reach the Sky Rim Trail, you have three choices: start at the Dailey Creek Trailhead and hike 6 miles, start at the Black Butte Trailhead and hike 7 miles, or start at the Specimen Creek Trailhead and hike 8.5 miles. I've listed mileages and described the trail as if one was starting the Sky Rim Trail from its junction with the Dailey Creek Trail. Be certain to bring plenty of water on this hike, because the only source of water is melting snow, which may be gone by mid-August. One warning: The Montana State Sheep Hunt occurs in this area for ten days during the beginning of September. Because this trail is right on the boundary, you may find yourself in the middle of a flurry of sheep hunting activity—legal and otherwise. This would be a good week to hike somewhere else.

You can make a very enjoyable 18-mile loop hike by traveling up the Dailey Creek Trail, then following the Sky Rim Trail to the Black Butte Trail, and finally hiking down the Black Butte Trail to the cutoff trail back to the Dailey Creek Trail and out to the trailhead.

Starting at the junction with the Dailey Creek Trail, the Sky Rim Trail follows the boundary ridge of the park. The ridge consists of a series of small summits that must be ascended, then descended. Because of all the up and down, these are hard miles, and the trail definitely seems longer than the miles listed above.

There are two areas along this initial section of trail where hikers have had trouble finding the route. The first occurs after about 2.7 miles at a big, broad, open ridge marked by 2-foot tall white park boundary posts with red tops. Here the trail tread disappears. Stay on the crest of this ridge and continue hiking in a southerly direction until you regain the trail. About a mile farther, you'll come to the second potentially confusing area. Here, the trail descends into a saddle in the ridge, and the tread again disappears. From the saddle you simply must make your own route up the steep, rocky ridge to the southeast until you gain the top of that ridge. From the top, the trail will then again become evident. The junction with Black Butte Trail is marked with a metal trail sign, orange markers, and rock cairns in a small clump of trees in this area. If you want to take the Black Butte Trail, go straight down (south) from these trees (there will probably not be any trail tread) until you locate the trail and additional orange markers.

To continue on the Sky Rim Trail from the trail junction area, stay on the ridge top and head east. You must immediately descend to another saddle, which is in the middle of some precipitous terrain, then scramble up to the summit of Bighorn Peak. From here, the trail is easy to follow as it descends and traverses three more small summits to the junction with the Specimen Creek Trail. The Specimen Creek Trail travels ½ mile down to Shelf Lake and then 8 more miles out to U.S. 191. After the junction, the Sky Rim Trail continues steeply up Sheep Mountain, climbing about 1,000 feet in 1 mile to the summit. When you first see the summit of Sheep Mountain you may wonder why a drive-in movie screen is sitting on top. Don't wait around for the show, because that large object is actually a piece of radio-relaying equipment. Look instead for the bighorn sheep that are occasionally spotted in this area. &

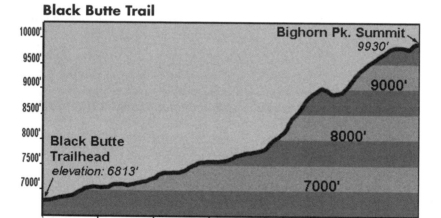

BLACK BUTTE TRAIL   Map #1, 2

Black Butte Trailhead (milepost 38, U.S. 191) to:

Dailey Creek Cutoff Trail Jct... 2 miles.........3 km
Sky Rim Trail Jct. .... 6.7 .... 10.7
Summit of Bighorn Peak 7 11

The Black Butte Trail travels from U.S. 191 to the Sky Rim Trail and provides the shortest, as well as the steepest, route to the summit of Bighorn Peak. There is a spectacular view in all directions from the top of the trail. The trail climbs

3,100 feet in 7 miles as it follows the forested valley of Black Butte Creek and winds past the Gallatin Petrified Forest. Exposed pieces of petrified wood are common throughout this area. Also watch for moose and mule deer low on the trail and bighorn sheep and bears higher up. In recent years, the extensive stands of whitebark pine on the upper sections of this trail have suffered a high mortality rate caused by the mountain pine beetle. This increased mortality is being repeated throughout the Greater Yellowstone Ecosystem and appears to be caused by the beetles' ability to move into high altitude areas, and into the resident stands of whitebark pine, that were previously out of reach of the pine beetle before the recent warming trend. Scientists believe that the milder winters, with earlier snowmelt, are decreasing the over-winter mortality of the beetles (Gibson 3). While it lasts, the remaining population of whitebark pine provides an ideal late summer and fall habitat for grizzlies that feast on pine nuts cached away in middens by squirrels. Take precautions for encountering grizzly bears and avoid solo hiking. From the summit of Bighorn Peak, it is about 3 miles to Shelf Lake following the Sky Rim Trail east. 🐾

MISTAKEN IDENTITIES

Gray Jay
- short beak
- fluffier appearance than nutcracker

Clark's Nutcracker
- wicked-looking beak
- strong contrast between black and white on wings and tail

SPECIMEN CREEK TRAIL   Map #1, 2

Specimen Creek Trailhead (milepost 26, U.S. 191) to:
Sportsman Lake Trail Jct. .... 2 miles......... 3 km
Crescent Lake/High Lake Trail Jct. .... 6 .... 9.5
Shelf Lake 8 13
Sky Rim Trail Jct. 8.5 14

The Specimen Creek Trail travels from U.S. 191 to Shelf Lake and the junction with the Sky Rim Trail on the park's north boundary. The Specimen Creek Trail offers good opportunities to see wildlife. Bighorn sheep frequent the slopes of Meldrum Mountain and from October to June elk gather in the valley.

For the first 6 miles, the Specimen Creek Trail climbs slowly through the forest and meadows along Specimen Creek and its north fork. In August 2007, the lightening-caused Owl Fire burned a total of 2,800 acres in this part of the park, including sections of the Specimen Creek Trail. Starting about 1.5 miles from the trailhead, there are now spotty burns and partially burned trees. Watch for falling snags along the trail. In the section of the trail just before the Sportsman Lake Trail junction, the intense heat of the fire left behind heavily burned sections of forest. (The fire burned right through backcountry campsite WE1, which is located at the Sportsman Lake Trail junction. A few trees were left alive, including those holding a food storage pole, so the campsite was not moved. The area is blackened from the fire, but the meadow on the east edge of the campsite and along the creek itself was not burned, leaving a nice viewing area for wildlife. If you camp at this site pitch your tent in the meadow area due to the potential for falling snags near stands of trees.) Four miles from the trailhead, the trail crosses the North Fork of Specimen Creek and leaves the burned area completely. The trail above and below this crossing has become very rocky and rutted from recent heavy spring stream flows; trail work, including a ½-mile reroute, was started in 2012 and when done, the new trail will travel on the east side of the valley at the base of the hill.

At the junction with the Crescent Lake/High Lake Trail the grade increases, and by the time you reach Shelf Lake two miles away, you will have climbed 1,100 feet. With Sheep Mountain looming above, Shelf Lake is a pleasant spot to rest, enjoy the scenery, and refill your water bottles. It's now about a ½-mile hike up to the boundary ridge and the Sky Rim Trail. ✿

CRESCENT LAKE/HIGH LAKE TRAIL   Map #1, 2

From Specimen Creek Trail Junction (6 miles from Specimen Creek Trailhead) to:

Crescent Lake .... 1.5 miles...... 2.2 km

High Lake .... 6 .... 9.5

Sportsman Lake Trail Jct. 10 16

Specimen Creek Trailhead via Sportsman Lake Trail .... 17 .... 26.5

This trail travels from the Specimen Creek Trail to the Sportsman Lake Trail. It offers the opportunity for a superb 23-mile loop hike that takes you past two lovely alpine lakes and over an abundance of wild mountain country. Although the area feels rugged, the environment of the alpine lakes is fragile. The thin soil layer is a long time in forming and plant life grows slowly. Treat these places gently. Bring campstoves, since wood fires are prohibited at High Lake, and be certain to pack out all trash—even if it isn't yours.

In recent summers, campers at High Lake have come away with captivating wildlife anecdotes. In one case, an overnight group watched—and, after sunset, listened to—grizzly bears devouring a wolf-killed elk carcass along the lakeshore. On another occasion, two backpackers spent most of the night awake, listening to the screams of a pair of dueling mountain lions. High Lake and the East Fork of Specimen Creek have also been making headlines in the world of Yellowstone fisheries. In 2006, aquatic biologists began a four-year project to restore genetically pure westslope cutthroat trout to this watershed. During the first year, scientists used a fish toxin called rotenone to eliminate the existing, non-native population of Yellowstone cutthroat trout—a species park managers had introduced to the watershed in 1937. In the summer of 2007, High Lake was stocked with westslope cutthroat trout adults and fry. In subsequent years, the restoration team repeated this process down the rest of the drainage to U.S. 191. Catch-and-release fishing is now permitted in High Lake and in the streams below it, down to the man-made fish barrier (a little less than 3 miles in from the trailhead). Below the barrier, standard park fishing rules apply.

At the time of publication, this trail continues to be very difficult to follow in places. There are sections with no tread, and there is minimal trail marking. It's a primitive trail. Even rangers have become "temporarily misplaced" here. There is a maze of game trails in this area, so always make certain you are on the main trail (and haven't strayed onto a game trail by mistake) by continually looking for trail markers. This trail can be even more difficult to follow if there is snow on the ground, so think twice about early or late season trips. Check at the West Entrance Ranger Station for current information on this trail. A map and compass or GPS are a must.

The Crescent Lake/High Lake Trail starts from the Specimen Creek Trail, 6 miles in from the trailhead on U.S. 191. The first 1.5 miles to Crescent Lake climb 900 feet up the side of a forested valley. The lake sits in a cirque with an 800-foot cliff rising above it. The trail from Crescent Lake to High Lake is relatively new and might not be on topographic maps put out before 1985 (and is incorrectly marked on some newer maps). From Crescent Lake, the trail travels northeast, climbing up the side of a forested valley. The trail climbs out of that valley and follows below the north boundary ridge of the park for about 2 miles. Along this section you will be able to look down to the south into a beautiful valley below you. Don't drop down into that valley, as the trail stays high in this section. The trail eventually crests the boundary ridge and descends into the basin containing High Lake.

High Lake is a beautiful, secluded spot, and the feeling of serenity and accomplishment that comes from sitting along its shore is well worth the toil of the hike. From the lake, the Crescent Lake/High Lake Trail continues down the East Fork of Specimen Creek, dropping about 700 feet in the 4 miles before it joins the Sportsman Lake Trail. From this junction, it's 7 miles back to the Specimen Creek Trailhead on U.S. 191. &

SPORTSMAN LAKE TRAIL–WEST Map #1, 2, 3

Specimen Creek Trailhead (milepost 26, U.S. 191) to:

Sportsman Lake Trail Jct.	2 miles	3 km
Crescent Lake/High Lake Trail Jct.	6.8	10.9
Sportsman Lake	11	17.5
Electric Divide	14	22.4
Glen Creek Trailhead, Mammoth–Norris Road	24	38.5

The Sportsman Lake Trail travels 24 miles from U.S. 191 (Gallatin Highway) to the Mammoth–Norris Road. It follows the East Fork of Specimen Creek, passes by Sportsman Lake, crosses the Gallatin Range, and ends in Gardners Hole. This segment of the guide describes the trail from its starting point on U.S. 191 to Sportsman Lake. The trail east of that is covered in the Gallatin/ Mammoth Area section under Sportsman Lake Trail–East, page 68. Due to the concentrations of grizzly bears, off-trail travel is prohibited in the Sportsman Lake area.

Starting from the Specimen Creek Trailhead, you actually follow the Specimen Creek Trail for the first 2 miles of this hike. The meadows in this area are home for moose all year round, and elk gather here from late September through May. About ¹/₂ mile before reaching Sportsman Lake Trail itself, effects of the August 2007 Owl Fire begin. First, burned patches of forest and meadow appear, and then, after turning onto Sportsman Lake Trail and crossing the footbridge over Specimen Creek, heavily burned areas are apparent for the first two miles of the trail. The Sportsman Lake Trail follows the East Fork through areas of forest and meadow with very few living trees left. The Owl Fire moved from the ridge top on the south (uphill) side of the trail and continued across the creek on the north (downhill) side, exposing previously hidden rocky slopes. During the month following the fire, trail crew and rehabilitation workers established drainage bars along this section of trail. The many charred trees left standing are potential falling hazards. On a positive note, a recently burned wilderness area quite often makes for better wildlife watching—that pesky, thick vegetation is finally out of the way.

There are two more bridged crossings of the East Fork in this section of the trail, one at 3 miles and the other at 4 miles. Evidence of the Owl Fire is almost completely gone at the four-mile footbridge. The trail then veers away from the East Fork and meets the Crescent Lake/High Lake Trail. It's 3.4 miles to High Lake from this junction. The Sportsman Lake Trail continues east, climbing gradually up to a low pass and then dropping down (500 feet in a mile) through burned forest to Sportsman Lake. The lake sits in a meadow at the base of a thousand-foot cliff. Grizzly bears frequent the area, and moose sightings in the meadow occur occasionally. Off-trail travel is prohibited here due to the concentration of grizzly bears. Cutthroat trout and numerous ducks and other waterfowl inhabit Sportsman Lake. ⦙

Harebell
- violet blue flowers
- blooms July–August

GALLATIN MOUNTAINS AND MAMMOTH AREA

The Gallatin Mountain Range runs south–north from Mt. Holmes to the north border of Yellowstone at Electric Peak. The range continues up into Montana as far north as Bozeman. This guide will deal only with the area inside the boundaries of the park. The Gallatin area trails start either from the Mammoth–Norris Road or from U.S. 191 (Gallatin Highway), which runs from Bozeman to West Yellowstone, Montana.

In this area, the Gallatins are a range of 10,000-foot, somewhat rounded, mainly sedimentary peaks. An extensive array of trails offers many choices for journeying up to the higher places of this section of Yellowstone. The Fawn Pass, Bighorn Pass, Mt. Holmes, and Electric Peak trails all provide the hiker with a chance to get a good feeling for the alpine environment. Besides being an important part of the park's trail system, the range is also an essential part of Yellowstone's ecosystem. Each spring, the mountains' melting snows feed major rivers such as the Madison, Gallatin, and Gardner. Each summer, the area is the home for many of the park's transient large mammals. The high meadows are an escape from the insects and, for elk and sheep, a place to feed. The willow-lined streams attract moose, and a herd of bighorn sheep reside on Quadrant Mountain. Each fall, the lower slopes of the mountains host the famous rut of the elk.

The Gallatins are also home to grizzly and black bears. The grasses and forbs favored by the bears grow in the fertile glacial soil of the Gallatins' ridges and valleys. The upper reaches of the range are dotted with whitebark pine, whose seeds are an important fall food source for the bears. The numerous mountain meadows away from roads and trails also provide the seclusion that the grizzly needs. Because of the bears, there are restrictions on some of the hiking trails in this area. On some of these trails, parties of four or more are recommended for day hiking, and four or more people may be required for overnight camping. From past experience it appears that a group this size is less likely to surprise or be attacked by a bear. Off-trail hiking may also be prohibited in some areas. Check at the Mammoth Visitor Center for current regulations. ◈

GRIZZLY LAKE TRAIL   Map #4

Grizzly Lake Trailhead (1 mile south of Beaver Lake Picnic Area on the Mammoth–Norris Road) to:

Grizzly Lake .... 2 miles .... 3 km

Mt. Holmes Trail Jct. 3.5 6

Mt. Holmes Trailhead .... 6 .... 9.5

Grizzly Lake is a fun hike (when the mosquitoes become unbearable, just keep repeating that to yourself). The trailhead is about a mile south of Beaver Lake on the Mammoth–Norris Road at a small, paved pullout. The trail starts out traveling through a meadow in sight of a spectacular forest fire burn. This hillside burned in 1976, and as usually happens, standing dead trees were left in the fire's aftermath. These standing trees spent the next 12 years getting drier and drier. So when the fire of 1988 hit this incredibly dry wood, it erupted into a severe firestorm, leaving an area that looked as if it had been hit by a small atomic bomb. No standing trees were left this time. This relatively small area received an inordinate amount of attention from photographers who needed fire devastation photos.

From the meadow, the trail climbs 250 feet through the burned hillside to the top of a ridge. The trail travels through burned forest and along a meadow that attracts elk and provides beautiful displays of wildflowers. On the descent down the west side of the ridge, there is an impressive view of Mt. Holmes and the Gallatin Range that was greatly improved by the fire of 1988. The trail now drops 300 feet to the shore of Grizzly Lake. The lake is set down in a steep valley, which can keep down the afternoon breezes and hold in the mosquitoes. Straight Creek flows from the north end of the lake and can be crossed on a logjam. This crossing can be tricky when the logs are wet, and is not advised during high water. The Grizzly Lake Trail continues along the west side of Straight Creek through flowering meadows to Winter Creek. At this point, Winter Creek may be crossed on fallen logs or stepping stones, but it varies from year to year so don't count on it. If you have to wade, the water is usually 1- to 2-feet deep after late July. Once across Winter Creek, the Mt. Holmes Trail junction is ¼ mile away. The main trail continues straight ahead (north) at the junction, passing through open, burned forest, and 1.5 miles farther reaches another ford of Winter Creek. The creek may be forded (1.5- to 2-feet deep after late July) or, depending on the year, may be crossed on fallen logs just upstream from the ford. After this last creek crossing, it's 1 mile to the Mt. Holmes Trailhead. ☙

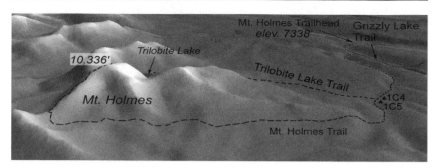

MT. HOLMES TRAIL
(WINTER CREEK TRAIL)   Map #3

Mt. Holmes Trailhead (3 miles south of Indian Creek Campground on the Mammoth–Norris Road) to:

Winter Creek Ford	1 miles	1.5 km
Grizzly Lake Trail Jct.	2.5	4
Trilobite Lake Trail Jct.	4.8	7.7
Summit of Mt. Holmes	10	16

The Mt. Holmes Trail is a good two-day, one-night hike. The trail follows Winter Creek through new lodgepole pine forest (post-1988 fire), up to the open talus slopes of Mt. Holmes. The forest, as well as the higher slopes, may hold patches of snow until early July. A wide assortment of wildlife may be spotted on this trail: black bears, grizzly bears, moose, elk, pine martens, and blue grouse. Look for ravens, hawks, rosy finches, pikas, and marmots above tree line.

The Mt. Holmes Trail starts out in the trees but soon opens up into a nice meadow as you make your way to Winter Creek. The creek may be forded (1.5- to 2-feet deep after late July) or, with some scouting upstream, may be crossed on fallen logs. The forest along this trail sustained various degrees of burn during the 1988 fires, mainly in the first 7 miles. The trail continues through burned forest dotted with snags and fallen trees to the junction with the Grizzly Lake Trail. At this junction, take the right fork in the trail. The path climbs up above Winter Creek for the next ¾ mile. At Winter Creek Meadows, you will find an NPS patrol cabin, campsites, and the junction with the Trilobite Lake Trail. Now the trail climbs steadily through forest and another large open area to the saddle between the White Peaks and Mt. Holmes. From the saddle, the trail climbs steeply (1,000 feet in a mile) up the loose rock to the 10,336-foot summit of Mt. Holmes. The view from the top takes in the Gallatin Range to the north, the Absaroka Range to the east, and even the Teton Range to the south. The summit also has a fire lookout that is no longer staffed. ♠

Barrow's Goldeneye

TRILOBITE LAKE TRAIL   Map #3

Mt. Holmes Trailhead (3 miles south of Indian Creek Campground on the Mammoth–Norris Road) to:

Grizzly Lake Trail Jct.	2.5 miles	4 km
Trilobite Lake Trail Jct.	4.8	7.7
Trilobite Lake	7.3	11.7

Trilobite Lake is a beautiful little lake set in the cirque of Mt. Holmes, Trilobite Ridge and Dome Mountain. This trail receives minimal maintenance, so check at the Mammoth Backcountry Office for current conditions. This trip is a good, but long, day hike or an even better overnight trip. Start at the Mt. Holmes Trailhead and follow the Mt. Holmes Trail for 5.5 miles to the big meadows of Winter Creek. Here, you'll find the closest campsite to Trilobite Lake and the junction with the Trilobite Lake Trail. The Trilobite Lake Trail veers off the Mt. Holmes Trail to the northwest, passing the Winter Creek Patrol Cabin on the left, and climbs about 700 vertical feet in the next 2.5 miles. The tread of this trail can be hard to find, so as you hike, be on the lookout for bright orange markers and, if possible, bring along a map and compass or GPS. The trail travels through forest that was burned to varying degrees in the 1988 fires and past a big blow-down from the spring of 1989. There are non-native brook trout in the lake. ❧

Bighorn Pass Trail–EAST

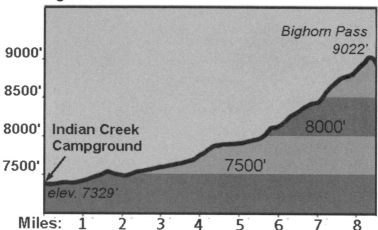

Bighorn Pass Trail–WEST

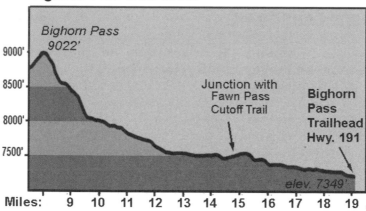

BIGHORN PASS TRAIL

Map #3

Bighorn Pass Trailhead (at Indian Creek Campground) to:

Indian Creek	2.5 miles....	4 km
Panther Creek	4.5	7.2
Bighorn Pass	8.5	14
Fawn Pass Cutoff Trail Jct.	15	24
Bighorn Pass Trailhead on U.S. 191 (milepost 20.5)	19	30

The Bighorn Pass Trail crosses the Gallatin Mountain Range as it travels from the Mammoth–Norris Road to U.S. 191 (Gallatin Highway). The scenery varies from grass and willow river valleys, to dense forest, to high meadows. There is also a variety of wildlife, including grizzlies, to be seen along this trail. Because of the high concentration of grizzly bears in this area, off-trail travel is prohibited along sections of the trail. Solo hiking is not recommended. Check at the Mammoth Backcountry Office for current regulations and travel restrictions.

This trail begins on the west side of the bridge on the Indian Creek Campground entrance road. The trail skirts south around the campground, past an outdoor amphitheatre and tent sites, before coming to a trail junction. The Bighorn Pass Trail veers left at the junction and soon emerges into open sagebrush meadows with sweeping views of the Gallatin Range. (By turning right [north] at the junction, you will follow a short nature loop trail—labeled on some maps as "Fisherman's River Walk"—that takes you to the banks of Indian Creek and then heads east, paralleling Indian Creek, before it winds back into the campground.) About 1.5 miles past the junction, the main trail drops down to Indian Creek; be prepared to ford both Indian Creek and, after climbing a small ridge and dropping down again, Panther Creek. Both crossings are usually 1.5- to 2-feet deep after water levels go down in late July. One or both may be impassable during peak runoff. After the fords, the trail runs through a pine, spruce, and fir forest. At about the 6-mile point, the trail will break out of the forest. Look for evidence in this area of a fairly large avalanche that slid off Bannock Peak, north of the trail, in the early spring of 1986. Jumbled piles of trees from the slide litter both sides of the trail. As you near the pass, the trail gets steeper, and climbs 1,100 feet in the last 2 miles. As you hike this section, watch the slopes of Bannock Peak and Quadrant Mountain for bighorn sheep and non-native mountain goats. At the pass there can be a snow cornice lingering on the trail into mid and even late August. From the pass, the view west of the Gallatin River Valley is spectacular and may prompt you to just sit back and absorb the scenery for the rest of the day.

The trail descends steeply from the pass to the Gallatin River and follows it through forest and meadows to the junction with the cutoff trail to Fawn Pass. This cutoff trail allows you to make a loop hike of sorts between the two trails. The Big Horn Pass Trail continues 4 more miles to the Gallatin River. The meadows along the river are popular spots for elk, and subsequently wolves, during the fall. Grizzly bear sightings in this area are also relatively common. The footbridge over the Gallatin River has been closed due to instability so a ford of the river is now required. From the crossing, it is just a few minutes to the trailhead on U.S. 191. ❧

Fawn Pass Trail–EAST

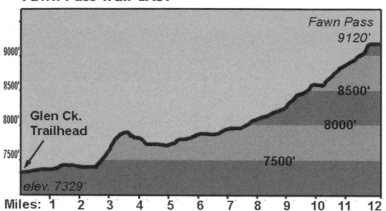

Fawn Pass Trail–WEST

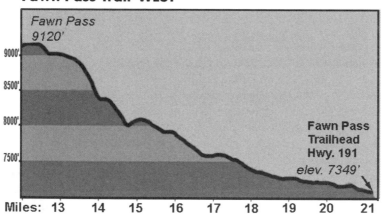

FAWN PASS TRAIL

Maps# 3, 4

Glen Creek Trailhead to:

Snow Pass Jct.	2 miles	3 km
Gardner River footbridge	4	6.5
2nd crossing of Fawn Creek	5.5	9
Fawn Pass	12	19
Bighorn Pass Cutoff Trail	16	26
Fan Creek Trail Jct.	19.5	31
Fawn Pass Trailhead on U.S. 191 (milepost 22)	21	34

The trail starts at the Glen Creek Trailhead, which is about 5 miles south of Mammoth on the Mammoth–Norris Road. The first 2 miles of your route are actually on the Glen Creek Trail, which travels through sage and grass meadows along the base of Terrace Mountain. At about 2 miles, the trail veers northwest and comes to a junction (locally called the Snow Pass junction). Here, the Fawn Pass Trail turns to the southwest (left) and continues through flat sage meadows for the next few hundred yards.

The Fawn Pass Trail now starts climbing over a 500-foot ridge, through meadows and stands of aspen. From this ridge, there are good views of Gardners Hole and the southern portion of the Gallatin Range. This is also an excellent area for spotting elk during late September and October. The trail drops down the ridge's other side to the Gardner River Valley and crosses the Gardner River via a bridge. A short way farther, the trail crosses Fawn Creek by an easy ford that is usually 1.5–2 feet deep after the water levels go down in late July. There is an impressive view of Electric Peak (north) from this area, and moose may be spotted here during the summer.

The trail now climbs gradually through the forest, following Fawn Creek and crossing it once more (knee-deep crossing after mid-July). Soon after the crossing, the trail starts climbing moderately, gaining 1,100 feet in the last 5 miles to Fawn Pass at 9,100 feet. From the open meadows of the pass, there are good views off to the west of the Gallatin River Valley and the Madison Range. Traveling west, the trail descends 1,100 feet in 4 miles down to the cutoff trail to Bighorn Pass. By taking the cutoff trail, a loop hike of sorts can be made of the Fawn Pass and Bighorn Pass trails. The Fawn Pass Trail continues through meadows that hold large numbers of elk from late September through May.

One and a-half miles before reaching U.S. 191, the Fawn Pass Trail meets the Fan Creek Trail. For a beautiful 43-mile loop hike, turn right (northeast) and take the Fan Creek Trail to the Sportsman Lake Trail, then follow the Sportsman Lake Trail to the Glen Creek Trailhead.

From the Fan Creek Trail junction, the Fawn Pass Trail continues to a bridge over Fan Creek and then on to the bridge over the Gallatin River. The trail ends a few hundred yards farther, at milepost 22 on U.S. 191. ❧

SPORTSMAN LAKE TRAIL–EAST   Map #1, 3, 4

Glen Creek Trailhead (5 miles south of Mammoth) to:

Fawn Pass Trail Jct.	2 miles	3 km
Sepulcher Mtn. Trail Jct.	3	5
Cache Lake Trail Jct.	5	8
Electric Pk. Trail Jct.	5.8	9.2
Gardner River	6	9.6
Electric Divide	10	16
Sportsman Lake	14	22.5
Specimen Creek Trailhead on U.S. 191 (milepost 26)	24	38.5

The eastern section of the Sportsman Lake Trail travels from the Mammoth–Norris Road to Sportsman Lake. Whether you hike just a portion or all of this section of trail, you'll find the scenery interesting and varied. The trail takes you through sage and grass meadows and stands of Douglas fir along Glen Creek, across the clear Gardner River, up and over the rocky meadows of Electric Divide, and finally down through a burned forest to Sportsman Lake.

Elk and bighorn sheep may be seen near Electric Divide during the summer, and moose near Sportsman Lake and in Gardners Hole. Hiking along Glen Creek in the fall is an excellent way to spot elk. Early in the morning during rutting season, the bulls will be out in the meadows bugling, sparring, and just generally putting on a great show. The Sportsman Lake Trail also goes through some prime grizzly bear habitat near Electric Divide, so be certain to take proper precautions. Off-trail hiking is prohibited along the upper sections of this trail. Check at the Mammoth Visitor Center for current regulations and travel restrictions.

The trail starts at the Glen Creek Trailhead, which is about 5 miles south of Mammoth on the Mammoth–Norris Road. The first 2 miles of your route are actually on the Glen Creek Trail, which travels through sage and grass meadows along the base of Terrace Mountain. At about 2 miles, the trail veers northwest and comes to a junction (locally called the Snow Pass junction). Here, the Sportsman Lake Trail continues to head northwest into the draw formed by Glen Creek. About a mile past the Snow Pass junction, the Sportsman Lake Trail reaches the junction with the Sepulcher Mountain Trail (it's about 2 miles and 2,300 vertical feet to the summit of Sepulcher Mountain from here). The Sportsman Lake Trail stays left at the junction and continues on an open hillside, climbing gradually and paralleling Glen Creek, until it enters the forest and leaves the creek. Soon, you will come to the turnoff for Cache Lake. To reach Cache Lake, turn northwest (right) at this junction and hike on this spur trail a little less than 1 mile. About ¾ mile farther, the Sportsman Lake Trail passes the junction with the Electric Peak Trail and then starts to descend to the crossing of the Gardner River (1.5- to 2-feet deep after late July). After the crossing, the trail starts climbing, crosses the river again, and continues uphill through forest to Electric Divide. The divide is about 4 miles and 2,000 vertical feet above the first river crossing.

From the divide, the trail descends steeply, 2,100 feet in 3 miles, to Sportsman Lake. This area was burned to varying degrees by the fires of 1988. The lake, which contains cutthroat trout, sits in a meadow at the base of a 1,000-foot cliff. Moose and elk are frequently spotted in the meadow during the morning and evening. From the lake, the trail continues west to U.S. 191, 10 miles away. This section of the trail is described in the Sportsman Lake Trail–West segment of this book, page 58. ♣

CACHE LAKE TRAIL 🐻   Map #1, 3, 4
(One-way distance: .8 mile, 1.2 km)

Cache Lake is a small mountain lake sitting at the base of Electric Peak and is reached by a 1-mile spur trail through unburned spruce-fir forest from the Sportsman Lake Trail–East. The easiest route into the lake starts at Glen Creek Trailhead and provides a nice variety of scenery. There are no campsites at Cache Lake. ♣

ELECTRIC PEAK TRAIL 🐻   Map #1, 3, 4
(One-way distance: 3.1 miles, 5 km)

This is not a maintained trail, and is only a marked route to assist hikers in navigation. The route is very steep, and some scrambling must be done near the summit. The trail climbs 3,000 vertical feet, and the summit of Electric Peak is about 9 miles from the Glen Creek Trailhead. The view from the summit is superb, and on a clear day you can see everything from the town of Gardiner, Montana, to the Grand Tetons.

The spur trail up Electric Peak leaves the Sportsman Lake Trail–East 5.8 miles from the Glen Creek Trailhead on the ridge above and north of the Gardner River crossing. The route follows the top of this ridge through open meadows until it reaches the southeast ridge of Electric Peak. Follow the southeast ridge on scree slopes until you are stopped by a band of rock about 100 vertical feet below the summit. Traverse down to the left (south) about 50 feet until you come to a break in the wall. Veer right (northwest) through this break and up a gully to regain the southeast ridge. Scramble along the ridge top to the summit. Careful hand and foot placements are important here, as the rock is loose. To descend, you will use the same route. ⚹

SEPULCHER MOUNTAIN TRAIL   Map #3, 4

Glen Creek Trailhead (5 miles south of Mammoth) to:

Sepulcher Mtn. Trail Jct. .... 3 miles......... 5 km

Summit of Sepulcher Mtn.. 5................. 8

Claggett Butte Trail Jct.. 8................. 13

Beaver Ponds Trail Jct. .... 8.7.............. 14

Sepulcher Mtn. Trailhead .... 9.2.............. 15

Glen Creek Trailhead .... 12................ 19

The Sepulcher Mountain Trail can be turned into one of the best loop hikes in the park, providing a little bit of every kind of scenery Yellowstone has to offer. This 9,652-foot peak is named for the strangely shaped formations of volcanic rock near its summit. To some morbid soul, these looked like grave markers, or sepulchers. There are a number of route combinations that will take you to the mountain's summit. The easiest of these starts at the Glen Creek Trailhead and follows the Sportsman Lake Trail to its junction with the Sepulcher Mountain Trail. From the junction, the Sepulcher Mountain Trail climbs 2,300 feet through open meadows that are filled with flowers during June and July. Near the summit mountain goats may be seen. Another route starts at the Sepulcher Mountain Trailhead, between Liberty Cap and the stone house (Judge's house) next to the Mammoth Terraces, and climbs 3,400 feet up the forested slopes of Sepulcher's north face. By using the Snow Pass Trail and Howard Eaton Trail as connecting routes, you can make the Sepulcher Mountain Trail a very interesting loop hike (see map #4 for a clearer picture of this). ⚹

East Slope of Electric Peak.

HOWARD EATON TRAIL–
MAMMOTH TO GLEN CREEK
(One-way distance: 4 miles, 6.4 km)

Map #3, 4, 5

This trail travels through diverse terrain, including the Mammoth Hot Springs and the Hoodoos, and provides the opportunity for a medium-length loop hike from the Mammoth area. The trail starts at the Sepulcher Mountain Trailhead, between Liberty Cap and the stone house (Judge's house) next to the Mammoth Terraces. The Howard Eaton Trail veers left (south) after a couple hundred yards, and begins climbing steeply up toward the Upper Terrace Drive. The trail passes some hot springs, parallels the Upper Terrace Drive, then continues south through limber pine and juniper as it climbs up and away from the hot springs area. About 1.2 miles from the trailhead, the Howard Eaton Trail passes the junction with the Snow Pass Trail. It continues climbing up through the Hoodoos, which are a huge, jumbled collection of limestone boulders that have sheared off and tumbled down from the cliffs to the west. The trail eventually tops out on the shoulder of Terrace Mountain, where there is a good view of the Gallatin Range. The trail has climbed about 1,100 vertical feet from the trailhead. The Howard Eaton Trail now descends to the Glen Creek Trail (or Sportsman Lake Trail-East), about 300 yards from the Glen Creek Trailhead at Golden Gate. To loop back to Mammoth (approximately 5 miles), take the Glen Creek Trail northwest to Snow Pass Junction. &

BUNSEN PEAK TRAIL   Map #3, 4, 5

Bunsen Peak Trailhead to:

Summit of Bunsen Peak .... 2 miles .... 3 km
Bunsen Peak Road Hiking/Biking Trail Jct. 3.8 6
Bunsen Peak Trailhead 6.8 11

The hike up Bunsen Peak is an especially good, short, steep trip. The view from the top is awesome at sunrise. The early sun turns the eastern slopes of nearby Electric Peak a glowing gold. Although it's only about a 1,300-foot climb to Bunsen's summit, the view will make it seem much higher as you stare down the peak's north face and look out to the Yellowstone River Valley 3,000 feet below you.

Bunsen Peak is actually the eroded remains of an ancient volcano's cone. Don't let that keep you from taking the hike—it hasn't erupted in 50 million years. The peak is named for Robert Bunsen, who did early research on geysers. Bunsen Peak has been burned over by forest fires many times in the past, and it happened again in 1988. In its wake, we are left with a classic burn mosaic.

The trail starts at the Bunsen Peak Trailhead, 5 miles south of Mammoth on the Mammoth-Norris Road. Walk up the Bunsen Peak Road a very short distance and watch for the trail sign on the left, just a few feet off the road. If you walk over and face the trail sign, the Bunsen Peak Trail leads up the slope straight ahead, past the sign. The trail climbs through sagebrush and burned pine and fir. There is NPS radio-relaying equipment near the top of Bunsen Peak. Once at the summit, it is possible to follow the trail down the backside (east side) of the peak to the Bunsen Road Hiking/Biking Trail. From the Bunsen Road you can either go down to Osprey Falls or loop back to the Bunsen Peak Trailhead. 🐾

OSPREY FALLS TRAIL   Map #4
(One-way distance: 4.6 miles, 7.4 km)

To reach Osprey Falls, start at the Bunsen Peak Trailhead, which is about 5 miles south of Mammoth on the Mammoth–Norris Road. Follow the old roadbed, which is now a hiking/biking trail, for approximately 3 miles to the turnoff for the Osprey Falls Trail. From here it is about 1.5 miles to the falls. The trail starts right at the rim of Sheepeater Canyon and drops 800 vertical feet down a series of switchbacks to the canyon bottom. Sheepeater Canyon was named for the Sheepeater Indians, a band of the Shoshone tribe that frequented this region of the park. Once at the bottom of this narrow, deep canyon, the trail follows the Gardner River up to the base of Osprey Falls. Don't approach too closely the cliffs at the base of the falls—the rock is wet and loose. Osprey Falls is a memorable sight: the Gardner River plunges over a 150-foot drop directly in front of you while the vertical cliffs of the canyon tower above your head. ❧

LAVA CREEK TRAIL

Map #4, 5

Lava Creek Trailhead to:

Footbridge at Gardner River	0.75 miles	1.2 km
Confluence of Lava Creek & Gardner River	2	3.5
Undine Falls	4.25	6.5
Lava Creek Picnic Area Trailhead	4.3	6.7
Blacktail Creek Trail Jct.	6.75	10.8
Blacktail Creek Trailhead	7.2	11.6

The Lava Creek Trailhead is 0.4 mile north of the entrance to the Mammoth Campground on the Mammoth–Norris Road. From the trailhead, the trail descends 200 feet to a suspension bridge over the Gardner River and then follows the Gardner River upstream to the mouth of Lava Creek. Look for signs of beaver working in this area. The trail now follows Lava Creek upstream, with the bottom of the rock walls of Mt. Everts on your left. As you approach Undine Falls, you enter a forest, and the trail begins to climb steeply. Undine is a beautiful double falls, picturesque enough to have once graced the cover of *National Geographic*. Once above the falls, you can continue to follow the trail another few hundred yards until you see a short, marked cutoff trail to the east side of the highway bridge across Lava Creek. This trailhead is across the highway from the Lava Creek Picnic Area.

If you want to continue east and follow the Lava Creek Trail to Blacktail Creek Trailhead, do not take the cutoff to the bridge and picnic area. Instead, continue to follow the Lava Creek Trail as it veers northeast (and may be shown on some maps as the Howard Eaton Trail) through open meadows and past Blacktail Ponds to the Blacktail Creek Trail junction. These last 3 miles of the trail are almost entirely within sight and sound of the main road. ❧

BEAVER PONDS TRAIL
(One-way distance: 5 miles, 8 km)

Map #3, 4, 5

The Beaver Ponds Trail travels through stands of Douglas fir and aspen and through meadows of grass, sage, and other flowering plants to a series of ponds dammed by (you guessed it) beavers. Unfortunately for us, the beavers go about most of their above-surface activity in the early morning and late evening. Consequently, most people miss seeing nature's answer to the Army Corps of Engineers as the beavers repair and improve their log dams and lodges. Due to the lower elevation here, the scenery along the trail is often most interesting in late spring or during the fall. Because the snow leaves earlier and comes later, the larger animals migrate here and stay from October to June. Chances of seeing them at this time are excellent. The flowers (such as bitterroot and primrose) are already blooming in May and June, and in the fall, the aspen leaves turn a golden yellow. Another good reason to hike this trail in the spring or fall is to avoid the trail's hot and dry conditions during the summer. Black bears are frequently spotted in this locale, so make noise while hiking. Pronghorn also frequent the lower portions of this trail during the summer, but the same noise that scares bears usually scares pronghorn too.

One of the park's few short loop trails, the Beaver Ponds Trail starts at the Sepulcher Mountain Trailhead, between Liberty Cap and the stone house (Judge's house) next to the Mammoth Terraces. The trail travels up the Clematis Creek drainage gulch, gaining about 400 feet in ½ mile, until it hits the junction with the Sepulcher Mountain Trail. Here, the Beaver Ponds Trail turns right (north) and continues climbing to a good vantage point. The ponds are about 1.5 miles farther, for a total of 2.5 miles from the trailhead. From the ponds, the trail travels through sagebrush for 2 miles to the Old Gardiner Road. Along this section there are good views of the steep, bare slopes of Mt. Everts to the east and prominent Sheep Mountain to the north. The trail continues to follow the old road until it ends behind the Mammoth Hot Springs Hotel. ❧

FAN CREEK TRAIL   Map #1, 2, 3

Fawn Pass Trailhead (milepost 22, U.S. 191) to:

Fan Creek Trail Jct. .... 1.5 miles ...... 2.5 km
Sportsman Lake Trail Jct. .... 8 .... 12.8

The Fan Creek Trail is a relatively new fishing access trail, and won't be shown on topographic maps put out before 1980. To reach the Fan Creek Trail, use the Fawn Pass Trailhead on U.S. 191 and follow the Fawn Pass Trail for 1.5 miles to a trail junction. At the junction, the Fan Creek Trail turns northeast (left) and heads up through the meadows of Fan Creek. Moose may be seen in the willows along the creek. A trail reroute was completed in 2010 that moved the ford of Fan Creek. Campsite WC2 now is reached via a spur trail. The crossing of Fan Creek can be thigh to waist deep until early July. About 4.5 miles up the creek, the North and East Fork of Fan Creek converge. The trail follows the North Fork until it reaches the junction with the Sportsman Lake Trail.

From this junction, it is about 3 miles to Sportsman Lake. It is common to see evidence of both wolves and bears in this area.

The Fan Creek Trail can be combined with other trails to make a long loop hike over the Gallatin Range. By using the Sportsman Lake Trail, Fawn Pass Trail, and the Fan Creek Trail, the distance will be 43 miles if you start at Glen Creek Trailhead on the Mammoth–Norris Road or 42 miles if you start at the Fawn Pass Trailhead on U.S. 191.

Off-trail hiking is prohibited along the East Fork of Fan Creek. Check at an NPS ranger station or visitor center for details. &

BACON RIND CREEK TRAIL
(One-way distance: 2 miles, 3 km)

Map #1

The Bacon Rind Creek Trail starts at a service road at milepost 22.5 on U.S. 191. Unlike the other trails in the area, this trail starts on the west side of the highway. This easy trail travels through meadows and forest edge along Bacon Rind Creek to Yellowstone's west boundary. Willows in the meadows provide food for beaver, moose, and elk, and grizzly bears roam the area as well. From the park boundary, the trail heads up toward the high peaks of the Lee Metcalf Wilderness Area. Check at a US Forest Service ranger station for information on this trail. &

Western Fringed Gentian
- bluish purple flowers
- blooms late June–September
- in wet soil, especially near hot springs

LOWER YELLOWSTONE RIVER AREA

The area around the lower Yellowstone River—between Tower Fall and Gardiner, Montana—is one of relatively low elevation. While most of Yellowstone Park is about 7,000–8,000 feet above sea level, most of the lower Yellowstone is between 5,000–6,000 feet. The difference in temperature, plant life, animal distribution, and rock formation is very noticeable.

Because this area is lower, summer comes earlier and winter later. Stands of aspen, cottonwood, Douglas fir, limber pine, and Rocky Mountain juniper grow here instead of the vast and dense lodgepole pine forests of the higher elevations. You'll even see cactus along the lower portions of the Yellowstone River and Rescue Creek trails. When winter comes and the rest of the park is buried in deep snow, the lower Yellowstone River area has relatively little snow. That makes it an attractive wintering spot for Yellowstone's transient mammals. Bison, elk, pronghorn, mule deer, bighorn sheep, and coyotes are densely congregated in this area from November to May. But even though the snow and cold aren't as severe here as in the rest of the park, it's by no means a tropical paradise for those wintering animals. Temperatures are constantly below freezing; the snow crusts and hardens, making grazing an energy-sapping, inefficient chore. With all these hungry animals, there is a lot of competition for the available food. The trees are browsed as far up as the animals can reach, and this obvious "browse line" is evident all year. Despite the cold and crowding, most animals make it—but some don't. They die due to old age or complications caused by lack of food and the cold, just as animals have been doing for thousands and thousands of years. Those that die are food for insects, coyotes, bears, ravens, magpies, and others. Those that survive the weather may be preyed upon by wolves or mountain lions. Parts of the animals that aren't immediately consumed will eventually decompose, and their bodies' elements will be recycled back into the soil, providing nutrients for plants and thus, eventually, other animals. Come spring, the bones and antlers will be all that remain, but these, too, will disappear, as they also decompose or are nibbled away by calcium-seeking rodents (or are stolen by antler hunters).

The rock formations in this area also differ from the predominantly volcanic material that covers most of the rest of Yellowstone. The gneiss and schist exposed here are some of the oldest rocks in the park. Formed during Precambrian times over 2.5 billion years ago, these rocks were originally granite, slate, and sandstone until they were changed and crumpled by heat and pressure. The north face of Hellroaring Mountain exposes a 2,000-foot block of this metamorphic rock, which can be viewed from the Hellroaring Creek Trail. &

Hellroaring Trailhead to Blacktail Creek Trail Jct.

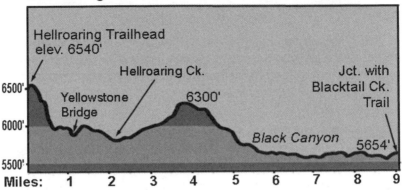

YELLOWSTONE RIVER TRAIL   Map #4, 5, 6

Hellroaring Trailhead to:

Yellowstone River Suspension Bridge	1 miles	1.5 km
Buffalo Plateau/Coyote Creek Trail Jct.	1.5	2.5
Hellroaring Creek Trail Jct.	2	3.2
Hellroaring Creek Ford	2.2	3.5
Hellroaring Creek Stock Bridge	3.5	5.5

Add 3.0 miles to the following distances if you use the Hellroaring Stock Bridge to cross Hellroaring Creek:

Cottonwood Creek	6 miles	9.5 km
Blacktail Creek Trail Jct.	9.5	15
Crevice Creek	11	17.5
Knowles Falls	11.5	18.5
Gardiner, Montana*	18.5	29.5

As of 2012 there was no access to Gardiner from this trail. The U.S. Forest Service is constructing a new trail. Check at the Mammoth Backcountry Office for current status.

The Yellowstone River Trail travels from the Hellroaring Trailhead to Gardiner, Montana. The trail follows the Yellowstone River, passing a variety of interesting features along its 18-mile length. For most of the way, the river flows through the Black Canyon of the Yellowstone. This canyon is over 1,000 feet deep, and in many places the dark canyon walls rise vertically from the water's edge. The western end of the canyon contains Knowles Falls, a 15-foot drop of the Yellowstone River. You'll find that when a river this size drops even a mere 15 feet, the result is still impressive.

Wildlife is abundant here from late fall through early spring. Bison, elk, bighorn sheep, pronghorn, mule deer, and coyotes all congregate in this area during the cold months. By mid-June, these animals move to higher elevations, and they are scarce along the lower Yellowstone until November.

Because this trail goes through some of the lowest elevations in the park, it's a good place to hike when other spots are too cold, wet, or mosquito-infested. This can be a hot hike during the summer, and even during early fall (especially Knowles Falls to Gardiner), so plan to do the majority of your hiking early and late in the day.

During the 1980s, there was a footbridge over Hellroaring Creek near the Hellroaring Ford that has now been removed. This bridge may still be shown on some topographical maps. (See trail description below for details.)

Starting at the Hellroaring Trailhead, 3.5 miles west of Tower Junction on the Tower–Mammoth Road, the Yellowstone River Trail descends a series of switchbacks to a dramatic suspension bridge over the Yellowstone River. The descent is about 600 vertical feet in a mile, which won't seem too important for those going down, but you'll remember each of those 600 feet if you have to trudge up them after a long day of hiking with a full pack. After crossing the suspension bridge, the trail continues through a small draw and into open sage land. Hike past (north of) the Buffalo Plateau/Coyote Creek Trail junction to the junction with the Hellroaring Creek Trail. Here, a serious choice needs to be made.

If you continue 0.2 mile north, just to the west of a small pond, you will come to the ford of Hellroaring Creek. This section of the trail is not marked—the NPS does not want hikers to attempt the ford. Nonetheless, the trail is very evident and easily followed as it heads toward the creek. The ford is filled with big rocks and boulders that cause unstable footing. This is a big creek with fast water, and shouldn't be forded until the water level drops significantly. There have been numerous close calls and even a death here. Once the water goes way down, it is certainly a crossable ford, but that may not happen until August or later. Check at the Tower Ranger Station for conditions if you are thinking about fording Hellroaring Creek. The good news is that you do not have to attempt the ford. There is a stock bridge across Hellroaring Creek 1.5 miles up the Hellroaring Creek Trail to your right (northeast). There is then a trail back down the other side of the creek that rejoins the Yellowstone River Trail near the ford. This will add about 3 miles to your hike, but that's a small price to pay for safety.

Once on the west side of Hellroaring Creek (you may want to fill water bottles at the creek—it is the last water until Little Cottonwood Creek), the trail continues past the junctions with side trails leading to Hellroaring backcountry campsites and climbs mixed open and forested slopes to a ridge above the walls of the

Black Canyon. Here, from about 400 feet above, the view of the Yellowstone River and its canyon is simply inspiring. Gazing out over such a large river so unchanged and unspoiled by humans is a marvelous feeling. The trail gradually descends to Little Cottonwood Creek and then on to Cottonwood Creek. From the creek, the trail follows the river closely, while directly across the water, the immense black walls of the canyon rise prominently.

Three and a-half miles from Cottonwood Creek, the Yellowstone River Trail meets the Blacktail Creek Trail. From this point, the Blacktail Creek Trail heads south, crosses the suspension bridge and climbs 1,100 feet out to the Mammoth–Tower Road. The Yellowstone River Trail heads west from the junction, past Crevice Lake, and on to Crevice Creek. A bridge takes you over this delightful, tumbling stream to the junction with the Crevice Creek Trail. The Crevice Creek Trail climbs 2,000 feet in 2 miles through open sage and grassland to the park's north boundary. During the summer this is a hot, strenuous hike.

After the Crevice Creek Trail junction, the Yellowstone River Trail climbs steeply up, over, and down a ridge to a point downstream from Knowles Falls, where there is a good view of the falls. From the falls, the trail again follows the Yellowstone River until the river enters another narrow stretch of the canyon. The trail climbs up and over this section. Once back by the river, there is a good view upstream of the canyon and of a large cave carved out of the canyon wall across the river from you.

From this point to Gardiner (6 miles away), the trail travels above and away from the river, so make certain to fill your water bottles before starting on this section. Along this final section of trail, the Yellowstone River has shaped some intriguing rock formations, and you'll be treated to a type of scenery most people don't associate with Yellowstone. From Bear Creek, the old NPS trail that formerly ended in Gardiner, MT near the Yellowstone River Bridge has now been abandoned and is not maintained. To exit to Gardiner, one must now hike to the new trailhead near the Eagle Creek Campground on the Jardine Road, approximately 2.6 miles uphill from the Jardine Road/Highway 89 junction in Gardiner. Check at the Mammoth Backcountry Office or Gardiner Forest Service Office for an updated map and current status. ❧

Knowles Falls

Rescue Creek Trail

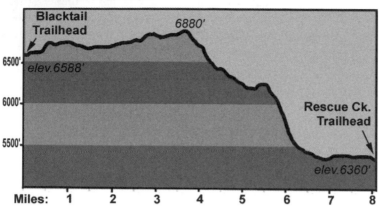

RESCUE CREEK TRAIL

Map #5

Blacktail Creek Trailhead (7 miles east of Mammoth) to:

Lava Creek Trail Jct. .... 0.4 miles...... 0.6 km

Rescue Creek Trail Jct. .... 0.7............. 1

Turkey Pen Peak... 5................. 8

North Entrance Road .... 8................. 12.8

The Rescue Creek Trail travels from the Blacktail Creek Trailhead on the Mammoth–Tower Road to the Rescue Creek Trailhead located about 1 mile south of the North Entrance Station. From the Blacktail Creek Trailhead, the route follows the Blacktail Creek Trail for the first ¾ mile. The Rescue Creek Trail veers off to the left at this point and starts to gradually climb. It follows Rescue Creek upstream for a little over a mile, then climbs moderately up a low, grassy hill. From this point, it's all downhill as the trail descends 1,400 feet in the remaining 6 miles. The trail passes by Turkey Pen Peak and Rattlesnake Butte on its way to the Gardner River footbridge. The vegetation along this pleasant downhill ramble includes sagebrush, aspen, Douglas fir, and a variety of early blooming flowers. Use discretion in choosing a spot to sit down for a rest, or you may inadvertently encounter the prickly pear cactus. From November through May, wildlife viewing is very good, with elk, mule deer, coyote, bighorn sheep, pronghorn, and occasionally even grizzly bears spotted along this section. During the summer, this is a hot, dry hike with Rescue Creek as the only source of water until you reach the Gardner River. Large animals are scarce along this trail during the summer, as are mosquitoes. ❧

Blacktail Creek Trail

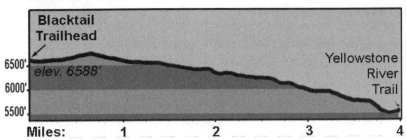

BLACKTAIL CREEK TRAIL   Map #5

Blacktail Creek Trailhead (7 miles east of Mammoth) to:

Lava Creek Trail Jct. .... 0.4 miles...... 0.6 km
Rescue Creek Trail Jct. 0.7 1
Blacktail Suspension Bridge 3.7 6
Yellowstone River Trail .... 4 .... 6.5
Knowles Falls 5.5 9

The Blacktail Creek Trail travels from the Blacktail Creek Trailhead on the
Mammoth–Tower Road to the Yellowstone River and the Yellowstone River
Trail. The trail follows Blacktail Deer Creek as it descends 1,100 feet in 4 miles,
with about 900 of those feet dropping away in the last mile and a-half. The
trail passes down among rolling, grassy hills that bloom with wildflowers
such as bitterroot and wild orchids during June and early July. If you hike this
trail before they hibernate in August, you'll probably also encounter a colony
of Uinta ground squirrels. As the trail nears the river, it enters a Douglas fir
forest and continues down to the Blacktail suspension bridge. After crossing
this large, sturdy suspension bridge, the Blacktail Creek Trail continues a
few hundred yards to the junction with the Yellowstone River Trail. From
this junction, it's about ¼ mile farther to Crevice Lake, and about 1.5 miles to
Knowles Falls via the Yellowstone River Trail. ❧

BUFFALO PLATEAU/
BUFFALO FORK TRAIL

Map #5, 6, 7, 8

Hellroaring Trailhead (3.5 miles west of Tower Jct.) to:

Buffalo Plateau/Coyote Creek Trail Jct.	1.5 miles	2.5 km
Coyote Creek Trail Jct.	2	3.2
Buffalo Plateau Patrol Cabin	9	14.5
Poachers' Trail	10.5	18.5
Buffalo Fork Trail	13	21
Slough Creek Campground	22	35

The Buffalo Plateau/Buffalo Fork Trail offers a wide variety of scenery to go along with a lengthy, strenuous hike. The trail travels from the Yellowstone River/Hellroaring Creek Trail up to the Buffalo Plateau and Buffalo Fork Creek, north of the park boundary. It then descends back into the park and ends at the Slough Creek Campground. The upper portions of this trail were burned in the fires of 1988, but shouldn't detract from your hiking experience if you don't mind better views, and more undergrowth. The area outside of the park also receives more precipitation and stock use than the lower portions of the trail, making for some potentially muddy hiking conditions. From the Hellroaring Creek Trail, you'll climb about 3,000 feet in 7 miles through open sage slopes, stands of Douglas fir, and sub-alpine meadows.

The Buffalo Plateau Trail is easy to follow from the Buffalo Plateau/Coyote Creek Trail junction with the Yellowstone River/Hellroaring Creek Trail. The Buffalo Plateau Trail then splits to the northeast (right) at the junction with the Coyote Creek Trail and continues to the Buffalo Plateau Patrol Cabin near the north boundary; after that it's not so easily followed, as it receives little use. From the cabin, the trail travels about 1.5 miles north to an old, east–west running poachers' trail that is now maintained and well marked by the U.S. Forest Service. Be aware that there are many distinct game and social trails just north of the park boundary that may be confused for the USFS trail. There is one along the divide running north that is actually cleared by hunters, making it even more confusing. A map, compass, and/or GPS are helpful here. Once you find the poachers' trail, it can be hard to follow, especially at first, as it descends 1,900 feet to the scenic meadow along Buffalo Creek and to the junction with the Buffalo Fork Trail. To loop back into Yellowstone, follow the Buffalo Fork Trail south toward the park boundary and cross Buffalo Creek to its east side. The trail climbs above and away from Buffalo Creek and onto the lower slopes of Anderson Mountain. From mid-September through mid-October, this area is an excellent spot for watching elk and listening to them bugle.

The Buffalo Fork Trail descends from Anderson Mountain down to the Slough Creek Valley. At the trail junction, almost in the valley bottom, head south (right) for approximately 2 miles along the marked trail to a ford across Slough Creek opposite the Slough Creek Campground. Slough Creek is moderately swift, rocky, and too high to ford safely before mid-July. It is still a major ford after that (1.5- to 2.5-feet deep). Early season hikers have frequently been stranded on the northwest side of the creek. Once at the campground, the trail ends between campsites #5 and #7. &

HELLROARING CREEK TRAIL   Map #5, 6

Hellroaring Trailhead to:

Yellowstone River Suspension Bridge .... 1 miles .... 1.5 km
Buffalo Plateau/Coyote Creek Trail Jct. .... 1.5 .... 2.5
Hellroaring Creek Trail Jct. .... 2 .... 3.2
Hellroaring Creek Stock Bridge................................. 3.5 .... 5.5
North Boundary of Yellowstone .... 7.1 .... 11.5

The Hellroaring Creek Trail travels from the Mammoth–Tower Road to the park's north boundary and continues into the Gallatin National Forest. The trail follows Hellroaring Creek through sage land and stands of Douglas fir, and past rock outcrops over two billion years old. Pronghorn, elk, mule deer, moose, and bison may all be seen along the Hellroaring Creek Trail from November to June. During the summer, chances aren't very good for seeing large animals, although moose and mule deer are sometimes spotted early in the morning.

The confluence of Hellroaring Creek and the Yellowstone River is a delightful spot. There is the cold, clear, rushing water of the creek, the deep surging river, a sandy beach, and the sheer walls of the Black Canyon of the Yellowstone. Osprey nest in these cliffs, and are frequently seen flying over the river looking for trout. The confluence can be easily reached by following the east side of Hellroaring Creek downstream along the campsite access trail until you reach the Yellowstone River.

The Hellroaring Trailhead is 3.5 miles from Tower Junction on the Mammoth–Tower Road, and is just north of Floating Island Lake. The Hellroaring Creek Trail initially shares the same footprint as the Yellowstone River Trail and descends a series of switchbacks, dropping about 600 feet in a mile to the suspension bridge over the Yellowstone River. The trail then travels through sagebrush, past the Buffalo Plateau/Coyote Creek Trail junction to the Hellroaring Creek Trail junction.

From this junction, the Hellroaring Creek Trail remains on the east (near) side of Hellroaring Creek and heads north up the forested valley of Hellroaring Creek. Hellroaring Mountain looms high above on your left, and Buffalo Plateau rises to your right. About a mile past the junction, a patrol cabin will come into view across the creek. From here it is ½ mile farther to the stock bridge over Hellroaring Creek. The bridge crosses over a calm, deep pool of the creek. Look down while crossing and you may be able to see trout swimming in the clear water below you. Once across the bridge, there is a trail leading south along the west side of the creek back to the Yellowstone River Trail. The Hellroaring Creek Trail continues north through the rocky forested valley to the park's north boundary. The trail continues into the Gallatin National Forest, where several long loop hikes are possible. ♣

COYOTE CREEK TRAIL   Map #5, 6

Hellroaring Trailhead to:

Buffalo Plateau/Coyote Creek Trail Jct. .... 1.5 miles......2.5 km
Coyote Creek Trail Jct. .... 2.................3
North Boundary of Yellowstone................................. 7................11
USFS Hellroaring Trail .... 11..............17.5

Start at the Hellroaring Trailhead (3.5 miles from Tower Junction on the Mammoth–Tower Road), and follow the Yellowstone River/Hellroaring Creek Trail 1.5 miles to the Buffalo Plateau/Coyote Creek Trail junction. Turn right (northeast) here and follow this trail ½ mile to the Coyote Creek Trail junction. Take the left (west) fork and follow the trail through sage meadows and open stands of Douglas fir. The views of the Washburn Range and the Yellowstone River Valley to the south are very nice as you climb up the open hillsides that lead into the spruce-fir-pine forest of the plateau. By the time you reach the north boundary, you will have climbed approximately 1,500 vertical feet from the suspension bridge. It is possible to continue north from the boundary, gradually descending through the forest, to the Gallatin National Forest section of the Hellroaring Creek Trail. This trail can be followed south back to Yellowstone National Park and the Hellroaring Trailhead, making for a loop hike. The section of trail in the Gallatin National Forest receives a great deal of stock use and can be difficult to follow due to numerous unofficial trails. It also receives more precipitation than the lower sections of trail, and can be quite mucky for hiking. ♣

TOWER AREA

T his section is devoted to those trails starting in the vicinity of Tower Junction and Tower Fall. The area offers a number of interesting short hikes, most of which are conveniently located for people staying at the Roosevelt Lodge or the Tower Fall Campground. The main points of interest in the area are Tower Fall, the Grand Canyon of the Yellowstone, and the petrified trees. Good views of the Grand Canyon are available from the Specimen Ridge Trail, the Yellowstone River Picnic Area Trail, and the Agate Creek Trail. The petrified trees are located mainly on Specimen Ridge, away from any maintained trails, although you can see a petrified tree from your car at the Petrified Tree Road.

The elevation and climate of the Tower area is similar to that of the Lower Yellowstone area—lower, warmer, and drier than most of the park. The larger mammals such as bison, elk, pronghorn, mule deer, and bighorn sheep are more abundant here from the fall through the spring than they are during the summer. Moose may be seen at any time throughout the summer, as well as an occasional black bear. Because this area is drier, mosquitoes usually aren't as bad, and they thin out sooner than in other places in the park. ♣

TOWER CREEK TRAIL   Map #5, 6, 14
(One-way distance: 2.8 miles, 4.5 km)

The Tower Creek Trail travels from the Tower Fall Campground up through the forested canyon of Tower Creek. Park in the small parking area opposite the campground registration sign and descend the trail toward the creek from campsite #1. This area was burned by the fires in 1988, and offers a good look at the relationship between a burned area and a stream. Notice how burned trees that have fallen in the stream change the course of the stream and add new eddies and pools. People mainly interested in fishing use this trail, but it also offers a pleasant hike along a rushing mountain stream and the chance to spot kingfishers, water ouzels, and an occasional moose or bear. The bridge over Tower Creek approximately ½ mile up the trail was removed due to deterioration, but a ford of Tower Creek is usually possible by August; use caution when fording. ♣

TOWER FALL TRAIL   Map #5, 6, 14
(One-way distance: 0.5 mile, 0.8 km)

The 132-foot waterfall of Tower Creek is a primary attraction in the Tower area. An easy, one-hundred-yard trail leads to a scenic overlook of the fall. A ½-mile trail down a series of switchbacks leads to an overlook of the confluence of Tower Creek and the Yellowstone River. The trail from here to the base of Tower Fall was closed in 2004 when serious instability obliterated a section of the trail. Until this section of the trail is reconstructed, the base of the fall is no longer accessible. ❧

YELLOWSTONE RIVER
PICNIC AREA TRAIL   Map #5, 6, 14
(One-way distance: 2 miles, 3 km)

This short, easy trail travels from the Yellowstone River Picnic Area (1.5 miles east of Tower Junction on the Northeast Entrance Road) to the Specimen Ridge Trail. A spectacular view of the Grand Canyon and the Yellowstone River awaits those who take this often-overlooked hike. The trail parallels the canyon for most of its 2 miles, and bighorn sheep can occasionally be seen during fall and early summer. As tempting as it is to make this a loop with the eastern portion of the Speciman Ridge Trail, there really is no trail from the Speciman Ridge Trailhead back to the picnic area other than walking on the road, which has no shoulder. ❧

AGATE CREEK TRAIL   Map #5, 6, 14
(One-way distance: 6.7 miles, 10.7 km)

The Agate Creek Trail provides panoramic views of the Washburn Range and access to a remote section of the Grand Canyon of the Yellowstone. The trail starts at the Specimen Ridge Trailhead (2.5 miles east of Tower Junction.) and follows the Specimen Ridge Trail for the first 2.4 miles. Bison are often seen grazing along the south slopes of Specimen Ridge in late summer. After veering south off the Specimen Ridge Trail, the Agate Creek Trail contours around the Quartz Creek drainage through open terrain, then drops steeply down about 1,100 feet to the confluence of Agate Creek and the Yellowstone River. The confluence is a beautiful spot and worth the long hike. ❧

LOST LAKE TRAIL

Map #5, 6

Roosevelt Lodge to:

Tower Fall Trail Jct. .... 0.6 miles...... 1 km
Lost Lake .... 0.8.............. 1.3
Petrified Tree .... 1.7.............. 2.7
Tower Ranger Station... 4.................. 6.5

The Lost Lake Trail starts behind Roosevelt Lodge at Tower Junction and leads up through the forested hillside until it comes to a trail junction. The trail to the left (southeast) leads eventually to Tower Fall. The Lost Lake Trail continues to the right (west), and reaches Lost Lake in 0.2 mile. Waterfowl are frequently seen in the lake, and beaver are occasionally spotted. From the lake, the trail contours around the hillside down to the Petrified Tree parking area, where you may view a petrified tree behind an iron fence. (Without this fence, this tree would probably be no more than a Petrified Stump, due to years of plundering by thoughtless specimen gatherers.) To loop back to Tower Ranger Station, follow the trail at the southeast end of the parking lot. This trail climbs up to open sage hilltops with good views of the Buffalo Plateau. This is also a good area to look for hawks during spring and fall migrations. The trail then descends to the Tower Ranger Station area. Follow the orange trail markers across the maintenance area parking lot and cross Lost Creek on the small footbridge to follow the trail back to Roosevelt Lodge. 🦌

ROOSEVELT LODGE TO TOWER FALL CAMPGROUND
Map #5, 6, 14
(One-way distance: 3.5 miles, 5.7 km)

The trail from Roosevelt Lodge toward Tower Fall Campground is currently an out-and-back trail. The footbridge over Tower Creek was removed due to deterioration in 2006 but the creek can usually be waded by August. For hikers from the Roosevelt Lodge area looking for a pleasant local hike with a good blend of views and a variety of terrain, start behind Roosevelt Lodge on the trail to Lost Lake. Follow the Lost Lake Trail up the hill for approximately 0.6 mile to a trail junction. Lost Lake is to the right (west), and the path toward Tower Fall Campground is to the left (southeast). Turning left, you will reach an overlook of Lost Creek Falls after another 0.6 mile. The trail continues east through forest another 0.4 mile, where a heavily used horse trail will veer off to the north, down to the Roosevelt corral. You'll want to continue heading east.

The next stretch of trail travels along the side of a ridge through meadows and aspen groves with tremendous views of the surrounding area. As the trail nears Tower Creek, watch for an expected reroute that cuts back upstream to join the Tower Creek Trail approximately ½ mile from Tower Fall Campground. Before hiking this trail, inquire at the Tower Ranger Station for the status of the anticipated reroute. 🦌

GARNET HILL TRAIL   Map #5, 6

Tower Junction Parking Area to:

Yancey's Hole Cookout Area	1.6 miles......	2.6 km
Yellowstone River/Hellroaring Creek Cutoff Trail Jct.....	3.5..............	5.5
Tower Junction	7.5..............	12

The Garnet Hill Trail is a good loop hike traveling through a variety of terrain without a great deal of elevation loss and gain. The trail also provides access to the Yellowstone River/Hellroaring Creek Trail. On sunny summer days, the last stretch of this trail can be pretty hot and dry. To access the trail, park at Tower Junction, in the parking area just east of the gas station, and walk west along the road toward the Tower Ranger Station. At the ranger station flagpole, turn north (right), walk across the highway, and cross open sage flats for about 75 yards to the concessionaire's Stagecoach Road. Follow the Stagecoach Road west about 1.5 miles to the Yancey's Hole cookout area. The trail register is to the north (right) of the hitch rail. Follow the trail along Elk Creek for approximately 2 miles, through meadows where mule deer are often spotted during spring and fall. When you reach the junction with the cutoff to the Yellowstone River/Hellroaring Creek Trail, you may want to take a ½-mile side trip to the suspension bridge over the Yellowstone River; if so, turn left (northwest) and follow the trail across Elk Creek and down to the suspension bridge. The Garnet Hill Trail continues to the right (northeast) at the cutoff junction and contours around Garnet Hill, through forest, until it breaks out into the open sage hills of Pleasant Valley. Follow the trail east to the Northeast Entrance Road and walk about ¼ mile back to your car at Tower Junction. 🦌

Dipper
- on rocks in fast streams
- flies low and fast
- bobs up and down

SPECIMEN RIDGE TRAIL   Map #5, 6, 14

Specimen Ridge Trailhead (2.5 miles east of Tower Jct.) to:

Grand Canyon of the Yellowstone	1 miles	1.5 km
Agate Creek Trail Jct.	2.4	3.8
Summit of Amethyst Mountain (9,614 feet)	10.1	16.2
Lamar River Ford	16	26
Soda Butte/Lamar River Trailhead	17.5	28

The Specimen Ridge Trail travels from the Specimen Ridge Trailhead (2.5 miles east of Tower Junction on the Northeast Entrance Road) to the Soda Butte/Lamar River Trailhead. This trail offers sub-alpine meadows filled with wildflowers and sweeping vistas of the park. Although the trail runs near petrified trees, you can't actually see them from the Specimen Ridge Trail.

The Specimen Ridge Trail is not as easily followed as most trails in this book. Because most of it is above tree line, it is marked with posts and rock cairns. Both of these are subject to the effects of wildlife and severe weather and are frequently knocked down. The tread on the hiking trail may be faint or nonexistent, while wildlife trails may be much more prominent and easily mistaken for the real trail. Please try to stay on the maintained trail. In forested areas, cut logs are a clue that will help distinguish the foot trail from wildlife trails. Over the years, this trail has consistently provided rangers with lost hikers on whom they can practice their search and rescue skills. Take a map and compass or a GPS unit and know how to use them.

Starting from the west, the Specimen Ridge Trail climbs moderately through sagebrush to the edge of the Grand Canyon of the Yellowstone. This spot provides a fine view, upstream, of the Yellowstone River and the magnificent canyon it has carved for itself. From the edge of the canyon, the trail climbs more steeply, about 600 feet in the next 1.4 miles, to the junction with the Agate Creek Trail. The Specimen Ridge Trail continues to climb through sage and grass meadows where elk are often spotted feeding during early morning. As the trail ascends, you'll notice the difference in vegetation, not only in the trees, but in the flowering plants, as well. When the summit of Amethyst Mountain is reached, you will be at the trail's highest point (which is the highest point in the immediate area, in case you're lost and need to regain the trail), and will have gained about 3,400 feet in elevation from the trailhead.

From the summit of Amethyst Mountain, the Specimen Ridge Trail descends steeply, about 400 feet through meadows to the relatively "flat" ridge of the Mirror Plateau. Hikers have had problems in this area in the past when they have lost the trail and continued south along this open plateau instead of following the trail as it veers northeast and descends steeply to the Lamar River. The trail drops 2,600 vertical feet through intermittently burned forest and meadows, where grouse are often encountered and where there are good views of the Soda Butte and Amphitheater valleys. At the Lamar River, a knee- to thigh-deep ford is required (it can be over waist deep and not passable before mid-July). Once across the river, the trail travels through sagebrush to the Lamar River Trail, which you'll follow to the Soda Butte/Lamar River Trailhead on the Northeast Entrance Road. ♣

PETRIFIED TREES

Probably the easiest access to the petrified trees of Specimen Ridge is from a large pullout on the Northeast Entrance Road a few hundred yards west of the Lamar River Bridge and about five miles east of Tower Junction. The parking area is marked with an unnamed sign that simply reads "TRAILHEAD". The route to the trees is unmarked and not well maintained. From the parking area, follow an old road about 100 yards until the trail veers off to the south and soon starts climbing. You'll be following the ridge that is just west of the west fork of Crystal Creek. The right (west) side of this ridge is forested, and the left (east) side is open meadows. Near the top of this ridge, just inside the forest on the right side, you will find some standing petrified trees. This is a very steep hike, and there is no maintained trail. You must climb about 800 vertical feet in 1.5 miles. Be careful not to knock any rocks down on other hikers, and keep a watchful eye for rock fall from above. Another danger on this trail is lightning. Try to do this hike in the morning, before the afternoon thunderstorms arrive.

Check at Tower Ranger Station for a detailed map showing the locations of the petrified trees. Remember, it is unlawful, and bad etiquette, to remove anything from the petrified trees. Petrified wood is not a renewable resource. ♣

NORTHEAST CORNER

The northeast corner of Yellowstone National Park contains wide, open, Slough Creek Valley, the forested valley of Pebble Creek, and the rugged mountains that surround the two. Trails follow both of these valleys, and the Bliss Pass Trail makes a strenuous, but scenic, connecting route between them. This area is best enjoyed after late July, when the snow has left the passes, the mosquitoes have thinned out in the forest, and the streams have subsided and become easier to cross. ❧

SLOUGH CREEK TRAIL   Map #7,8

Slough Creek Trailhead to:

First Meadow	2 miles	3 km
Bliss Pass Trail Jct.	8	13
North Boundary of Yellowstone	11	17.5

The Slough (pronounced "slew") Creek Trail travels from Slough Creek Campground to the park's north boundary, following Slough Creek through a beautiful, broad, grassy valley most of the way. The valley is bordered by scenic peaks, including the prominent Cutoff Mountain. The best time to see wildlife along this trail is during the fall (late September and October), when the elk gather in the valley and surrounding low ridges for the mating season and coming winter. On fall mornings and evenings, the bugling of bull elk can be heard as they challenge far-off rivals. During the summer, moose and trumpeter swans are occasionally seen in the valley. Sandhill cranes are frequently seen and heard. Bear activity has increased in the valley since the reintroduction of wolves in 1995. Wolves often chase elk, their primary food source, into Slough Creek. This hunting strategy has proven to be very efficient at providing wolves, and opportunistic bears, with necessary calories. Hikers and anglers should be alert for fresh carcasses and bear activity in or near Slough Creek. Packs containing food should be worn or kept within an arm's reach to keep them secure from bears.

Slough Creek is a very popular backcountry area with fishermen, horse groups, day hikers, and backpackers. Advance reservations are recommended for backcountry campsites. Traffic on the Slough Creek Trail includes the horse-drawn wagon that travels between the trailhead and Silver Tip Ranch. The wagon is a little piece of living history, and the only method by which the ranch is allowed to transport their supplies for this 11-mile stretch through the park. Horses may be easily spooked by hikers carrying fishing rods or walking sticks. Step well off the road and stand quietly to allow the wagon or other horse parties to safely pass.

The Slough Creek Trail starts from the gravel road leading to Slough Creek Campground and is reached about ½ mile before the campground. From the trailhead, the Slough Creek Trail climbs gradually through stands of Douglas fir up to an open area where there is a good view of Cutoff Mountain to the northeast. The trail then descends to the broad, open valley of Slough Creek, known as the First Meadow.

The Slough Creek Trail continues up the valley, leaving the creek as it climbs a 200-foot ridge and then descends the other side to what is known as the Second Meadow. The trail again nears the creek at the junction with the Bliss Pass Trail. The Slough Creek Trail continues north through grassy meadows and forest to the park's north boundary. The Silver Tip Ranch (privately owned) is just north of the boundary, in Gallatin National Forest. There are many trails branching off the Slough Creek Trail north of the park that provide opportunities for long loop hikes. For trails in this area, check with the U.S. Forest Service office in Gardiner, Montana. &

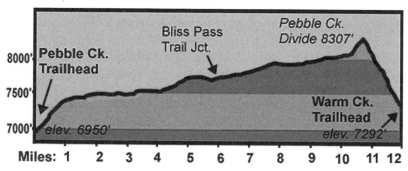

Pebble Creek Trail

PEBBLE CREEK TRAIL   Map #7,8

Pebble Creek Trailhead (200 yards east of Pebble Creek Bridge on the Northeast Entrance Road) to:

Bliss Pass Trail Jct. .... 6.6 miles...... 10.5 km
Upper Meadows... 9.5.............. 15.2
Warm Creek Trailhead .... 12.............. 19

The Pebble Creek Trail travels through a glacial valley lined with rugged peaks rising to over 10,000 feet. The valley is mostly forest, with lodgepole pine, Engelmann spruce, and sub-alpine fir. There are some extensive meadow areas in the upper Pebble Creek valley. These meadows contain blooming cinquefoil, geranium, lupine, and other flowers during July and early August. Elk are occasionally seen coming down into these meadows to feed during summer evenings, and moose may be seen feeding on the willows along the banks of Pebble Creek. Mosquitoes may be quite numerous along Pebble Creek until early August, but shouldn't be bad enough to deter you from hiking through this scenic valley.

The trail travels from Pebble Creek Trailhead to the Warm Creek Trailhead. Starting from the Warm Creek Trailhead is the shortest way to get to the scenic upper valley of Pebble Creek, although this route does require a steep 1,100-foot climb.

On the west side, the trail starts at either Pebble Creek Campground or Pebble Creek Trailhead. The two trails join together after a short distance. The trail then climbs 500 feet on a series of switchbacks to a small meadow. Most people will rest here while taking in the spectacular view of the Thunderer to the southeast. The trail then parallels Pebble Creek through the forest above until about 3 miles from the trailhead, where it makes two crossings of the creek in about a mile. These crossings can be 3 feet deep and very swift before early July. Later in the summer, Pebble Creek subsides to about 1.5- to 2-feet deep.

From the crossings, the trail climbs up and away from the creek for another 3 miles until it meets the Bliss Pass Trail alongside a lovely little meadow. Farther on, the Pebble Creek Trail makes another crossing and then enters the upper meadows. From the meadows, there are good views of Cutoff Mountain (west), Wolverine Peak (north), and Sunset and Meridian peaks (east). These peaks are a summer range for bighorn sheep and mountain goats. The trail turns south and makes another crossing of Pebble Creek at the east end of the meadows. It then climbs about 200 feet to a ridge top where there is an excellent view of the sheer north face of Abiathar Peak. The trail now winds down through forest, dropping 1,100 feet in 1.5 miles to the Northeast Entrance Road. Along this last section of the trail, there is a very nice view of the valley of Soda Butte Creek and Barronette Peak to the west. This impressive peak was named after "Yellowstone Jack" Baronett, a mountain man, guide, army scout, assistant superintendent of the park, and builder of the first bridge over the Yellowstone River. The trail meets the road near Warm Creek Trailhead, which is about 1.5 miles from the Northeast Entrance Station. ❧

BLISS PASS TRAIL
Map #7,8, 9

From Pebble Creek Trail Junction (6.6 miles from Pebble Creek Trailhead and 5.5 miles from Warm Creek Trailhead) to:

Bliss Pass	1.8 miles	2.9 km
Slough Creek Trail Jct.	6.8	10.9
Slough Creek Trailhead	14.8	23.7

This trail travels from the Slough Creek Trail, over 9,350-foot Bliss Pass, to the Pebble Creek Trail. From the Pebble Creek side, the Bliss Pass Trail gains 1,400 feet. From the Slough Creek side, it rises 2,700 feet. The scenery from either side is impressive.

This trail may be started at either Pebble Creek Trailhead, Warm Creek Trailhead, or Slough Creek Trailhead. Starting from the junction with the Pebble Creek Trail, the Bliss Pass Trail immediately fords Pebble Creek. This ford is usually calf deep after mid-summer, but may be knee to thigh deep and swift during June snow melt. From the crossing, the trail ascends through a meadow where the trail may be hard to follow. If so, look for the orange markers at the edge of the forest to the north. From the meadows, the trail climbs steeply through timber to the pass.

After the pass, the trail descends, steeply in some spots, through forest and meadow to the Slough Creek Trail. From this point, it's 8 miles of relatively level hiking to the Slough Creek Trailhead. ♣

TROUT LAKE TRAIL
Map #9, 10
(One-way distance: 0.5 mile, 0.8 km)

This trail is used mainly by anglers, and only on a day-use basis, as there are no backcountry campsites at Trout Lake. The trail starts from a small pullout about 1.5 miles southwest of Pebble Creek Campground on the Northeast Entrance Road. The trail climbs about 150 feet through stands of Douglas fir to the lake. Waterfowl are occasionally spotted, as are the lake's large rainbow, cutthroat, or rainbow-cutthroat hybrid trout when they rise to feed on the surface. Back in the 1880s, the fish in Trout Lake were an important food source for the people of nearby Cooke City, Montana. As you might suspect, the angling techniques were anything but sporting. Spears, nets, and gunpowder were all employed to illegally harvest Trout Lake's trout. Unfortunately, at that time, there was no National Park Service, and the people administering Yellowstone National Park had neither the personnel nor the power to prevent this poaching. Fortunately, things today have changed. ♣

LAMAR RIVER AREA

As the title of the section suggests, the Lamar River is the central part of this huge wilderness area. The valley of the Lamar River is the area's main route of travel by both animals and people. In early summer, bison and elk move up the valley from their wintering grounds to the high meadows where they seek new plant growth and an escape from the hordes of biting insects. The wolves follow the bison and elk and hunt them, summer and winter, in this area. Most hikers traveling in this area will also follow the Lamar River for a portion of their hike as they, too, seek the high mountain meadows and the wildlife that live there.

Much of the Lamar area was burned to varying degrees by the fires of 1988. As in other burned areas of the park, vegetation in the Lamar area is growing back. Hiking through this area offers an excellent, though prolonged, opportunity to view the cycle of regrowth after a fire. In spite of frequent trail clearing by rangers, it is a distinct possibility that you will have to scramble over some downed trees across the trail. Extensive blow-downs after big windstorms may cover the trail with trees and make route finding a little more challenging. ❧

LAMAR RIVER TRAIL   Map #10, 11

Soda Butte/Lamar River Trailhead (on Northeast Entrance Road about 4 miles west of Pebble Creek Campground) to:

Cache Creek Trail Jct.	3.1 miles	5 km
Miller Creek Trail Jct.	9.2	14.7
Cold Creek Jct.	16	26.8

The Lamar River Trail travels from the Lamar Trailhead to the junction with the Mist Creek Pass Trail and the Frost Lake Trail. The trail serves mainly as a connecting route for the numerous side trails heading to the high meadows, lakes, and mountain passes of the park's east boundary. Along this trail, the most intense burns during the fires of 1988 occurred near the confluences of the Lamar River with Cache Creek and, about 6 miles farther south, with Miller Creek.

Upstream from Cache Creek to the end of the Lamar River Trail, the Lamar Valley is a narrow, forested canyon; it is much different in appearance from the lower valley near the road, which is open, wide, and covered with sage and grass. Consequently, the majority of the Lamar River Trail is not a place to witness spectacular displays of wildlife, although animals are still seen occasionally throughout the summer. Elk and bison winter in the valley downstream from Cache Creek, and may be spotted there between October and early June. In summer, they move up the valley to the higher elevations along open ridge tops above the valley floor, with only an occasional old bull bison lingering behind.

Hikers will start this trail at the Soda Butte/Lamar River Trailhead, which is signed and provides a bridged crossing of Soda Butte Creek. Horse parties will start at a parking area 0.7 mile west of the Soda Butte/Lamar River Trailhead, and must ford the creek. Leaving from the trailhead and crossing the Soda Butte Creek Bridge, the Lamar River Trail travels across flat meadows and soon passes the cutoff trail to the horse-use trailhead and the junction with the Specimen Ridge Trail. Farther on, the trail passes the junction with the Cache Creek Trail, then descends about 200 feet to Cache Creek. Expect the crossing of Cache Creek to be anywhere from calf deep to knee deep after mid-July. Before that time, the crossing may be too deep and swift to cross safely.

From Cache Creek, the Lamar River Trail parallels the Lamar River, crosses Calfee Creek, meets the Miller Creek Trail junction, and then crosses Miller Creek (both fords are shallower than Cache Creek). The trail travels through green forest, burned forest, wildflowers and meadows. It climbs up and over some steep side hills that provide nice views of the river, along with an elevated pulse rate. Remember that the reason for hiking this stretch of trail is to enjoy the wild, rushing Lamar River. Take time to sit along its banks and feel its serenity—unless you're in a hurry to reach your campsite before dark, in which case just take a quick photo over your shoulder and leave the serenity for later. ♣

CACHE CREEK TRAIL   Map #7, 9, 10

From Lamar River Trail Junction (3.1 miles from Lamar River Trailhead) to:

Thunderer Cutoff Trail Jct. .... 11 miles .... 17.5 km
Republic Pass .... 16.5 .... 26.4
Cooke City .... 21.5 .... 34.5

From the junction with the Lamar River Trail, the Cache Creek Trail travels through sagebrush for the first mile then enters an area of intense burn from the fires of 1988. After about 2 miles, Death Gulch and Wahb Springs can be seen on the other side of Cache Creek. Death Gulch is accurately named. It contains a small thermal area that gives off an irrespirable gas that has killed everything from sparrows to bears. In fact, Wahb Springs is named after the bear in Ernest Thompson Seton's story, "Biography of a Grizzly." In Seton's story, when Wahb knew his time was up, the huge old grizzly came to this deadly gulch to die.

The Cache Creek Trail continues to parallel the creek through the forest and over numerous small side streams. Near the confluence with South Cache Creek, the trail climbs up and away from Cache Creek and continues to the junction with the Thunderer Cutoff Trail. From this junction, the Cache Creek Trail continues about 0.2 mile to Cache Creek Patrol Cabin. About ½ mile farther, the trail makes a shallow crossing of Cache Creek and then parallels an unnamed fork of the creek for about 3 miles. At this point, the Cache Creek Trail turns north and follows a tributary of the unnamed fork. There is also a trail that continues along the unnamed fork that vanishes after about a mile, so don't get on that trail by mistake.

The Cache Creek Trail continues following the tributary, becoming steeper as it moves upstream. About 1 mile from Republic Pass, the trail leaves the tributary and climbs directly to the pass. From Cache Creek Patrol Cabin, the trail has climbed about 2,300 vertical feet to the 10,000-foot pass. The view from the pass is startling. Rugged, snow-streaked mountains appear on all sides, presenting a scene most people wouldn't think to associate with Yellowstone. Grizzlies frequent the area near Republic Pass, so be alert. From Republic Pass, a Forest Service trail continues about 5 miles down to the old Irma Mine road, which comes out on U.S. 212 at the east end of Cooke City. A topographic map will be helpful in negotiating this last section of trail. ❧

The Thunderer and Soda Butte Creek from Pebble Creek Divide.

THE THUNDERER CUTOFF TRAIL   Map #7, 9, 10

The Thunderer Trailhead (1 mile north of Pebble Creek Campground on the Northeast Entrance Road) to:

Pass (a.k.a. Chaw Pass) .... 4 miles .... 6.4 km

Cache Creek Trail Jct. .... 5.5 .... 8.8

Republic Pass .... 11 .... 17.6

Cooke City 17 27

The Thunderer Cutoff Trail travels from the Northeast Entrance Road to upper Cache Creek by climbing 1,900 feet up and over the saddle between the Thunderer and Peak 10,300 Feet (unnamed peak designated by altitude). This trail is a good first leg of a semi-loop hike for either Republic Pass or the Cache Creek Trail.

From the trailhead, you must immediately cross Soda Butte Creek, which is about 1.5- to 2-feet deep after mid-July. Once across the creek, the trail winds through an open stand of lodgepole pine where there is an exceptional view of the sheer north face of the Thunderer. The trail soon begins to climb moderately, but steadily, to what is known locally as Chaw Pass.

Unfortunately, only occasional glimpses of spectacular Amphitheater Valley are available from the trail due to the trees, although there are good views to the east of the ridge tops above Cache Creek. From the pass, the trail descends about 1,000 feet in 1.5 miles to the junction with the Cache Creek Trail. From this junction, it's 5.5 miles to Republic Pass, or 14.1 miles down Cache Creek to the Soda Butte/Lamar River Trailhead. ❧

MILLER CREEK TRAIL   Map #10

From Lamar River Trail Junction (9.2 miles from Lamar River Trailhead) to:

Canoe Lake Trail Jct.. 7.5 miles...... 12 km
Hoodoo Basin Trail Jct. .... 8.5.............. 13.5
Bootjack Gap .... 12.5............ 20
Crandall Ranger Station... 28.5............ 45.5

The Miller Creek Trail travels from the Lamar River Trail to the park's east boundary at Bootjack Gap. The trail follows Miller Creek through pine, spruce, and fir forest, some of which was burned in the fires of 1988. The fire burned very intensely on the lower section of the trail, leaving almost a complete burn. The upper reaches of the trail burned less intensely, which resulted in more of a mosaic burn pattern. The Miller Creek Trail provides access to two very scenic spur trails: the Canoe Lake Trail and the Hoodoo Basin Trail.

From the junction with the Lamar River Trail, the Miller Creek Trail climbs up and away from Miller Creek and continues above the creek almost the entire way to the Canoe Lake Trail junction. The trail travels through burned forest, lodgepole pine forest, and occasional meadows. Look for elk in these meadows during the morning and evening. In the first 7 miles, the trail gains only about 700 feet in elevation.

From the junction with the Canoe Lake Trail, the Miller Creek Trail descends to the shore of Miller Creek at an NPS patrol cabin. (Here, the Hoodoo Basin Trail veers off to the southeast across Miller Creek.) From the patrol cabin, the Miller Creek Trail climbs moderately for about 3 miles through spruce, fir, and pine forest. It then climbs more steeply through whitebark pine forest for the last mile to the park boundary at 9,200-foot Bootjack Gap. The trail gains about 1,500 feet in the 4 miles from the patrol cabin to the pass. From the gap, there is a great view to the east of the Absaroka Range and its foothills in the Shoshone National Forest.

A USFS trail continues into Shoshone National Forest, following Papoose Creek Trail up and down for 18 miles to Crandall Ranger Station on the Sunlight Basin Road. Topographic maps are a must for this section of trail. ❧

HOODOO BASIN TRAIL
Map #10
(One-way distance: 11 miles, 17.5 km)

The Hoodoo Basin Trail travels from the Miller Creek Trail (8.5 miles from the Lamar River Trail and 17.7 total miles from the Soda Butte/Lamar River Trailhead) to the park's east boundary. Starting from the Miller Creek Trail, the Hoodoo Basin Trail immediately crosses Miller Creek. This crossing is usually calf deep after mid-July. After the crossing, the trail climbs through forest and meadows to the saddle of Parker Peak at 9,600 feet. At this point, you will have come 4.5 miles from Miller Creek and climbed 2,100 vertical feet. The view of the Lamar area and the Mirror Plateau is superb, but don't get so caught up in the scenery that you forget about grizzlies. They feed in these high meadows throughout the summer.

Upon leaving the Parker Peak saddle, the trail descends into the Hoodoo Basin, named for its oddly shaped volcanic rock formations. After descending about 400 feet, the trail climbs back up about 500 feet to open meadows where elk and grizzly bear are occasionally spotted. The trail again descends about 200 feet into another valley, then climbs back out to the park's east boundary. From this point, the trail climbs steadily as it parallels the boundary through picturesque meadows for 3 miles. It's hard to surpass the view available from these meadows; high peaks, open ridge tops, and forested valleys surround you. The Hoodoo Basin Trail ends when it again joins the park boundary at 10,470 feet. It's possible to continue on a Forest Service trail down to Sunlight Creek and the Sunlight Basin Road in Shoshone National Forest. Topographic maps of Sunlight Peak and Dead Indian Peak should be consulted for hikes in this area. 🐾

CANOE LAKE TRAIL
Map #10
(One-way distance: 4 miles, 6.5 km)

The Canoe Lake Trail starts from the Miller Creek Trail (7.5 miles from the Lamar River Trail and 16.7 total miles from the Soda Butte/Lamar River Trailhead) and climbs up to Canoe Lake and the park's east boundary. Parts of this trail were burned in the fires of 1988. The trail climbs about 1,900 feet, mainly through forest, to the meadows surrounding Canoe Lake. These meadows attract both bear and bison, and are actually along one of the bison's main routes of summer movement. If you're fortunate enough to catch a glimpse of these huge, shaggy beasts sprinting along a high alpine ridge, it's guaranteed to be a sight you won't soon forget. The park boundary is just a short distance above Canoe Lake. A Forest Service trail descends from the park boundary down to Timber Creek and out to Crandall Ranger Station (approx. 18.5 miles from Canoe Lake), which is reached from the Sunlight Basin Road in the Shoshone National Forest. Ernest Hemingway visited, and wrote about, the Timber Creek and Crandall Creek areas during the 1930s. He obviously loved the place and longingly described the mountains, grizzlies, elk, and bighorn sheep in an article called "The Clark's Fork Valley, Wyoming" for the February 1939 issue of *Vogue*. It's refreshing to see how his descriptions remain accurate today. In his understated style, Ernie was right: it's "good country." &

FROST LAKE TRAIL   Map #10, 11
(One-way distance: 5.5 miles, 9 km)

The Frost Lake Trail travels from the Cold Creek junction on the Lamar River Trail (16 miles from the Soda Butte/Lamar River Trailhead) to the park's east boundary near Frost Lake. The trail starts at the Cold Creek junction, where the Lamar River Trail and the Mist Creek Pass Trail meet. This junction is on the south side of the Lamar River. From the junction, the Frost Lake Trail parallels the south side of the Lamar River for just under a mile through scenic meadows before it turns uphill and starts climbing up a broad ridge through an area burned in 1988. The trail climbs gradually at first and then more steeply as it switchbacks up to the open plateau of the east boundary of the park. From this plateau there is a superb view of Castor Peak and Little Saddle and Saddle mountains, and a glimpse of Yellowstone Lake. There is no marked trail to Frost Lake, but it isn't difficult to find by following the park boundary.

From the east boundary, there is a very scenic, 13-mile Forest Service trail that travels through the North Absaroka Wilderness Area of the Shoshone National Forest. This trail descends to the North Fork of the Shoshone River and comes out to "civilization" at Pahaska Tepee on the highway to Cody, Wyoming, 2 miles east of Yellowstone's East Entrance Station. &

Shooting Star
- violet flowers
- blooms May–August
- early spring food for elk

PELICAN VALLEY AREA

T his section of the backcountry includes Pelican Valley and the headwaters of Pelican and Broad creeks. The trails here reach out over Pelican Valley, to backcountry lakes and thermal features, to the top of Pelican Cone, and over Mist Creek Pass to the Lamar area.

While Pelican Valley proper is a wide, open meadow, most of the rest of the area is forested. Much of this forest was burned in the fires of 1981, 1988, and 1994. Overnight camping is allowed at designated campsites outside of Pelican Valley. 🐾

PELICAN VALLEY RESTRICTIONS

- Closed to hiking until July 4 each year.
- Closed from 7 PM to 9 AM each day.
- No off-trail travel on the first 2.5 miles of the Pelican Valley Trail.

PELICAN VALLEY TRAIL   Map #11, 12

Pelican Valley Trailhead to:

Pelican Creek Bridge	3.4 miles	5.4 km
Astringent Creek/Broad Creek Trail Jct.	5	8
Pelican Creek Ford	6.6	10.6
Upper Pelican Creek Trail	6.7	10.8
Pelican Cone Trail	7.1	11.4
Raven Creek	7.7	12.3
Mist Creek Pass Trail	8.9	14.2
Pelican Creek Bridge	12.7	20.3
Pelican Valley Trailhead	16.1	25.8

This trail travels from the Pelican Valley Trailhead to the Pelican Creek bridge and then makes a loop around the edge of Pelican Valley. Because this is a large, open valley without much shade, it can get pretty warm here on sunny summer days. I think the best time to hike in Pelican Valley is on cloudy, rainy, or even snowy days, when wildlife is more likely to be visible. You may see moose wading in the creek, an eagle or sandhill cranes soaring overhead, a grizzly bear loping along the edge of the forest, or even wolves trotting along the banks of Pelican Creek. Don't count on seeing all of this in one day, but don't be surprised if you do. Big bull bison are almost always out in the valley and should be given a wide detour. (Remember, big, gaping puncture wounds leave unsightly scars.)

The newest additions to Pelican Valley's viewable wildlife are the wolves. In the summer, they hunt Pelican Valley's elk herd and make frequent kills. The wolves are sometimes chased off of their elk kills by opportunistic grizzly bears. You may see these wolf-killed elk carcasses near the trails. Be cautious around these carcasses, and don't approach them. Grizzlies could be actively feeding on the kill and are very aggressive in defending their food.

The Pelican Valley Trailhead is located on a spur road just north of Indian Pond, 3 miles east of Fishing Bridge. From the trailhead, the Pelican Valley Trail heads north across sage land and then arcs northeast through intermittently burned forest before emerging from the woods to a nice view of Pelican Valley. The Absaroka Mountains run along the eastern skyline and Pelican Cone rises to the north. The trail passes a small hydrothermal area and eventually descends to Pelican Creek and goes through some short, wet, muddy sections where fantastic displays of flowering elephant heads can be seen in mid-summer.

The Pelican Creek bridge is a nice place to sit, eat lunch, and take in the scenery. If you are continuing on to Mist Creek Pass, you will want to stay on the south side of Pelican Creek—do not ford the creek. If you are heading to Wapiti Lake or Pelican Cone or are continuing on to hike the Pelican Valley loop, go ahead and cross the creek. The bridge is in disrepair and is not useable. The crossing is an easy one: 1.5–2 feet deep. Follow the trail up the hill through the meadows. The trail continues through meadows to a bridged crossing of Astringent Creek, then makes its way to the junction with the Astringent Creek/Broad Creek Trail.

From the Astringent Creek/Broad Creek Trail junction, the trail parallels the forest edge and stays in meadows that are favorite grazing areas for grizzlies. Look for bear scat in the patches of clover near the trail. The trail will eventually drop back down to a ford of Pelican Creek. This is a relatively easy ford, and is usually no higher than knee deep after mid-July. Right after the ford of Pelican Creek, the trail meets the junction with the Upper Pelican Creek Trail (which goes uphill to the left).

The Pelican Valley Trail veers to the right and stays in the meadows. The tread of the trail from here to the Pelican Springs Patrol Cabin can be difficult to discern—be sure to have a map handy and be prepared to navigate without

Bull elk near Turbid Lake.

orange trail markers. The trail arrives shortly at a small, unnamed creek that comes down from Pelican Cone. This is probably the best drinking water in the valley. (At least it's cold and clear—water treatment is up to you.) At this creek, the Pelican Cone Trail heads uphill into the forest. The Pelican Valley Trail continues through the meadows to Raven Creek, where there are nice views of Mt. Chittenden and the Absaroka Range.

Raven Creek is slow and deep. It can be waist deep or deeper if you hit one of the big holes. By scouting around, you should be able to find a shallower crossing, but expect deep water until mid-July. The trail continues through meadows and past a little pond where ducks and mergansers raise their young each summer. Near an inactive thermal area, the trail passes through forest and goes over rolling hills to Pelican Springs Patrol Cabin and the junction with the Mist Creek Pass Trail.

The Pelican Valley Trail heads back down the valley from the patrol cabin, crossing Pelican Springs Creek on a bridge. The trail continues through meadows, up and over rolling hills, across Russell Creek (knee to calf deep), more meadows, and then two more bridged crossings of an unnamed creek. There is a small waterfall that is not visible from the trail about 30 yards downstream of the bridge on this creek.

The trail continues down valley, following the edge of the forest until it descends back to the Pelican Creek bottom in a wet meadow. The trail tread may be hard to find here, but just continue paralleling the creek and you will eventually hit the trail again. This soon leads you back to the Pelican Creek bridge and the route on which you started the hike. &

UPPER PELICAN CREEK TRAIL   Map #10, 11, 12

Pelican Valley Trailhead to:

Pelican Creek Bridge ....3.4 miles .....5.5 km
Pelican Creek Ford ....6.6..............10.6
Upper Pelican Creek Trail ....6.7..............10.8
Mud Pot...11.7............18.7
Jct. with Cutoff Trail to Astringent Ck./Broad Ck. Trail ...12.7............20.3
Wapiti Lake..16.8............26.9

The Upper Pelican Creek Trail starts at the Pelican Valley Trailhead, located on a spur road just north of Indian Pond, 3 miles east of Fishing Bridge Junction. Do not confuse this trail with the Pelican Creek Nature Trail, which starts about 1 mile east of Fishing Bridge. The Upper Pelican Creek Trail takes you through diverse scenery as it follows Pelican Creek through open grass and sedge meadows, past mud pots and hot springs, and through the lodgepole pine forests to Wapiti Lake. This entire area receives a great deal of bear use. Be cautious, as the rolling hill-type terrain of this trail can make it easy to surprise a bear. To reach the Upper Pelican Creek Trail, you can start either from Wapiti Lake (see Wapiti Lake Trail in Canyon Area section) or from Pelican Valley.

From the Pelican Valley Trailhead, take the Pelican Valley Trail to the junction with the Upper Pelican Creek Trail. From the junction, the trail veers uphill to the left and into the trees. The trail goes up and down short, steep ravines for the next ½ mile or so. There are many game trails in this area, so be certain to look for trail markers to be sure you are on the right route. The trail eventually drops back down to the meadows above Pelican Creek and more or less parallels the creek until it arrives at the Mushpots.

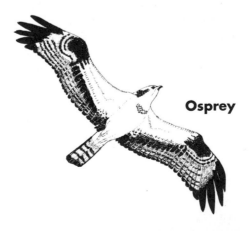

Osprey

The Mushpots are a collection of mudpots, fumaroles, and hot springs. Near these thermal features are patches of clover growing alongside the trail. This is a favorite feeding area for bears, as you can tell by the numerous piles of scat. From the thermal area, the trail continues to follow Pelican Creek upstream through rolling hills and wet meadows, crossing the creek repeatedly (all easy, knee-deep crossings), until the trail enters the forest and begins climbing away from the creek. Here, you will pass close to a large, impressive mud pot off the trail to the east. The trail eventually emerges from the forest and descends to the meadows of Pelican Creek for yet another creek crossing and then climbs up the opposite bank to the junction with the cutoff trail to Broad Creek. (It is possible to follow this trail back to Pelican Valley via the Astringent Creek/Broad Creek Trail; see page 108.)

The Upper Pelican Creek Trail continues upstream along the west bank of the creek for the next ¼ mile and then makes another crossing. From this point, you hike upstream through meadows above the creek and then finally make the last crossing of Pelican Creek about ½ mile farther. The last 4 miles of trail travel through meadows and intermittently burned forest to Wapiti Lake. Because of numerous game trails in this last section, it is again important to watch for trail markers and signs to confirm that you are on the right trail. Wapiti Lake is surrounded by forest, not very scenic, and contains no fish. The best thing that can be said for it is that it's very remote. ❧

PELICAN CONE TRAIL 🐻   Map #11, 12
(One-way distance: 12.1 miles, 19.3 km)

The shortest route to Pelican Cone starts at Pelican Valley Trailhead and follows the Pelican Valley Trail for 6.7 miles to the ford of Pelican Creek and then to the junction with the Pelican Cone Trail. (Fill your water bottles at the creek at the start of this trail.) The trail climbs through mostly burned forest (1994 fire) the entire way, gaining about 1,600 feet in the 4 miles to the top. The far-reaching view from the top includes the Teton Range and Yellowstone Lake to the south, Mt. Washburn to the northwest, and the skyline of the Absaroka Range to the east. There is a fire lookout on the summit that is no longer staffed. ❧

BEARS AND WOLVES IN PELICAN VALLEY

Pelican Valley is excellent habitat for grizzly bears. A variety of vegetation upon which to graze, the carcasses of winter-killed bison to scavenge, and a busy elk calving area to exploit all attract grizzly bears to the area. To allow the bears some undisturbed use of Pelican Valley, the NPS has placed travel restrictions on the valley. As mentioned earlier, the valley is closed to all travel before July 4 each summer. On and after July 4, Pelican Valley is open at 9 AM and closes at 7 PM, giving the bears a predictable time period each day to venture into the open valley and feed. This closure is strictly enforced because it directly protects the bears. This is not a safety closure. Violators of this regulation can displace grizzly bears from prime habitat.

One of the most interesting new relationships in Yellowstone is the one between wolves and grizzlies. While grizzly bears are excellent predators of elk calves, wolves using the Pelican Valley are more efficient predators of adult elk and bison. The elk calving season is relatively short lived, so, to supplement their meat supply before and after calving season, the grizzlies began taking over the carcasses of elk and bison that the wolves have killed. This has now become routine and some grizzly bears have adapted to exploiting this new source of protein, going so far as to follow the movement of the wolf pack in anticipation of the next kill. When the wolves make their kill, they may have initial, uncontested access to their carcass, but once a grizzly, or grizzlies, show up, the ownership of the carcass is up for grabs–with the bears usually winning. As many as 9 separate grizzlies have been seen on a single wolf kill in Pelican Valley. &

Wolf following grizzly bear in Yellowstone National Park.   NATIONAL PARK SERVICE PHOTO

ASTRINGENT CREEK/BROAD CREEK TRAIL 🐻
(TERN LAKE TRAIL)　　　　　　Map #11, 12

Pelican Valley Trailhead (on spur road 3.5 miles east of Fishing Bridge Jct.) to:

Astringent Creek Trail	5 miles	8 km
White Lake	9	14.5
Tern Lake	10	16
Jct. with Cutoff Trail to Upper Pelican Creek Trail	11.6	18.7
Fern Lake Cutoff Trail (to Canyon)	12	19.2
Wapiti Lake	14.7	23.5

This trail travels from the Pelican Valley Trailhead to Wapiti Lake by way of Astringent Creek and Broad Creek. The entire trail is fairly level and offers no long-ranging vistas, as it is mainly down in the forest. White Lake, Tern Lake, and Fern Lake are all passed on the way. These lakes and their meadows are good spots for viewing wildlife. Swans, Canada geese, a wide variety of ducks, great blue herons, sandhill cranes, and bald eagles are all seen here, along with moose and elk. Bears are also present, but are not seen as frequently. Much of this area was burned by natural fires during the 1980s and 1990s, and presents a real mosaic of burn and regrowth. Mosquitoes can be quite numerous on the upper portions of this trail. The lower section of this trail is part of the Pelican Valley Bear Management Area and is closed to travel from 7 PM to 9 AM each day.

To reach the start of the Astringent Creek/Broad Creek Trail, you must follow the Pelican Valley Trail for 5 miles until you come to the trail junction just northeast of the crossing of Astringent Creek. After leaving the Pelican Valley Trail, the Astringent Creek/Broad Creek Trail heads north along the meadows of Astringent Creek. There are two bridged crossings of Astringent Creek along this section. After 3.5 miles, the trail leaves Astringent Creek and crosses a low ridge to White Lake and the drainage of Broad Creek. Only a small portion of White Lake is visible from the trail. In 1984, a Swiss woman was attacked and killed by a grizzly bear while camped in this area.

At 11.6 miles, you'll meet the cutoff trail to the Upper Pelican Creek Trail (1 mile away to the east). From this junction, the Astringent Creek/Broad Creek Trail enters the forest and soon comes to another trail junction. (Here, the Fern Lake Cutoff Trail heads west, across Broad Creek, to Fern Lake, ½ mile away, and Ponuntpa Hot Springs, 1.5 miles away and an occasional wintering spot for bison. The Fern Lake Cutoff Trail eventually joins the Wapiti Lake Trail and can be followed back to Canyon Village.) The main trail continues to follow Broad Creek through meadows and forest to the junction with the Wapiti Lake Trail. To reach Wapiti Lake, turn right (east) and follow this trail as it climbs about 300 feet in the ½ mile to the lake. From Wapiti Lake, you may loop back to Pelican Valley by way of the Upper Pelican Creek Trail. (See page 105.) 🐾

MIST CREEK PASS TRAIL   Map #10, 11, 12

Pelican Valley Trailhead (on spur road 3.5 miles east of Fishing Bridge) to:

Pelican Creek Bridge .... 3.4 miles ...... 7.4 km

Pelican Springs .... 7.4 .... 1.7

Mist Creek Pass .... 9.2 .... 14.8

Lamar River Trail 17 27

Soda Butte/Lamar River Trailhead   33   53

This trail travels from Pelican Valley up to Mist Creek Pass and down to the Lamar River. To reach Mist Creek Pass from this side, you must take the Pelican Valley Trail up to the junction with the Mist Creek Pass Trail. Much of the forest along this route was burned during the fires of 1988.

From the trailhead, the trail follows the Pelican Valley Trail to the Pelican Creek bridge. To reach the Mist Creek Trail, stay on the trail on the east side of Pelican Creek (don't cross the bridge). This section of trail is often overgrown and hard to follow through the marshy meadow. Just keep paralleling the creek and the trail will become visible again once you reach drier ground. The trail then goes over rolling hills and across small streams, one of which may have to be waded. At Pelican Springs Patrol Cabin there is another junction. (The trail to Pelican Cone goes left, or west, here.) The Mist Creek Pass Trail goes straight ahead, northeast. After climbing about 600 feet through 2 miles of burned forest, you will arrive at Mist Creek Pass. The trail descends to Mist Creek Meadows, where there are some pretty campsites and where elk are occasionally seen early and late in the day. From the meadows, the trail descends gradually through burned forest to the meadows of the Lamar River. Here you must cross the Lamar River, which is knee deep after late July, to gain the Lamar River Trail on the river's east side. The Soda Butte/Lamar River Trailhead (on the Northeast Entrance Road) is 16 miles away. 🐾

TRAILS TO TURBID LAKE   Map #11, 12, 32

Turbid Lake is a small lake with discolored water from thermal activity, surrounded by forest burned in 2003 by the East Fire. In order to protect grizzly bear habitat, the western end of the old Turbid Lake Road is closed, and no hiking is allowed on or off the road in that area. However, there are two hiking trails to Turbid Lake that travel outside of the bear management closures.

The first route is 3 miles long and starts from the Pelican Valley Trailhead. Follow the Pelican Valley Trail for about 2 miles through open sage land, forest, and out into the open spaces of Pelican Valley. Look for a trail junction sign (the trail itself is very faint) that will direct you south (right), through meadows and burned forest. As you hike toward Turbid Lake, keep an eye out for bright orange trail markers to stay on the path, and make plenty of noise to avoid surprising a bear.

The second route (about 5 miles long) starts directly across the highway from the parking area for Nine Mile Trailhead (Thorofare Trailhead). The East Fire of 2003 completely changed the scenery along this path; what once was a thick, mature spruce-fir forest is now an exposed area subject to scorching summer sun, burned trees lying across the trail, and, on the plus side, open views and breezes off the Yellowstone Lake. If you want a hike that includes abundant wildflowers and you don't mind uninterrupted sights and sounds of highway traffic for the first ½ mile, by all means, use this trail. The start of this route to Turbid Lake may be marked on the north side of the highway only by an orange trail marker. The trail first travels northwest for less than a ¼ mile, then makes a sharp right turn at the remains of an old corral, and traverses around the side of Lake Butte. The trail crosses the Lake Butte Road, and continues on through burned forest to Turbid Lake. There is a great deal of bear activity in this area, and a man was mauled by a grizzly here in 1986. ♠

STORM POINT TRAIL   Map #12, 13
(One-way distance: 1.0 mile, 1.6 km)

This is a scenic, short trail out to Storm Point, a windy rock outcropping on the lakeshore that offers a wide, spectacular view of Yellowstone Lake. Occasionally, the trail can be closed due to grizzly bear activity; check at the Fishing Bridge Visitor Center or Bridge Bay Ranger Station before leaving for the trailhead.

The trail starts at the Indian Pond parking area, 3 miles east of Fishing Bridge and directly across from the spur road to the Pelican Valley Trailhead. The trail travels through open meadows above Indian Pond, where goldeneye ducks, Canada geese, and occasionally even loons can be seen. Be certain to give a wide berth to the big bull bison that frequently graze in these meadows. Once down near the lake, the trail veers to the right and heads into trees. The trail meanders through mixed spruce-fir forest until it reaches a barren thermal area. Look for bison wallows and the resident yellow-bellied marmots as you hike this open stretch of trail to Storm Point. Stevenson Island and the massive Mt. Sheridan are prominent landmarks to the south. The early explorer David Folsom, who visited the shores of Yellowstone Lake in 1869, described his impressions of the lake this way: "Nestled among the forest-crowned hills which bounded our vision, lay this inland sea, its crystal waves dancing and sparkling in the sunlight as if laughing with joy for their wild freedom."

It is possible to take a different route (about 1 mile in length) back to the parking area by following the trail west along the shoreline and then through the lodgepole pine forest to the big meadows near the start of the trail. There is minimal tread and no trail marking in this last meadow, but the East Entrance Road and the parking area are visible as soon as you emerge from the trees. ♣

HOWARD EATON TRAIL–
FISHING BRIDGE TO CANYON   Map #13, 14, 15

Fishing Bridge Trailhead (east side of Fishing Bridge) to:

LeHardy's Rapids .... 4 miles......... 6.5 km
Buffalo Ford .... 6................. 8
Sour Creek .... 11.5............. 18.4
Wrangler Lake Trail .... 13............... 20.8
Wapiti Lake Trailhead... 15............... 24

The Howard Eaton Trail travels from Fishing Bridge to the Grand Canyon of the Yellowstone. It is part of the old Howard Eaton Trail system that follows the route of the present day Grand Loop Road. Much of this trail travels through Hayden Valley, which is some of the park's best wildlife habitat. Unfortunately, most of this stretch of trail is also within sight and sound of the main road. The first couple miles of the north and south end of the trail are probably the most worthwhile sections to hike, as they both offer interesting terrain away from the highway. As of 2012, the northern end of the Howard Eaton Trail has been frequently closed due to grizzly bear activity, wolf denning, or both. Because of this, the trail tread may be very faint or indiscernible north of Sour

Creek. Check at the Canyon Visitor Center or Bridge Bay Ranger Station for the current status of this trail. Both ends of the Howard Eaton Trail have been the scenes of grizlly bear attacks so take the proper precautions.

The Fishing Bridge Trailhead is about 100 yards east of the Fishing Bridge on the East Entrance Road. From the trailhead, the Howard Eaton Trail closely parallels the Yellowstone River for a short stretch, then veers to the right and travels alongside a service road for a few hundred yards until it heads left, away from the service road, and angles towards the river. The next mile of trail travels through open meadows, where a variety of wildlife, including bears, may be encountered. The Yellowstone River is nearby and offers an excellent spot for viewing waterfowl such as white pelicans, swans, and goldeneye ducks. Continuing north through forest, you'll reach a good overlook of LeHardy's Rapids. Farther north, the trail passes Buffalo Ford, or more correctly, Nez Perce Ford, which was used by the Nez Perce Indians in their escape from the U.S. Cavalry in 1877. Bison herds now use it routinely. The trail then passes by some riverside thermal features opposite the Mud Volcano area. From this point on, the trail enters the open meadows of Hayden Valley and can be difficult to follow. Good navigation skills, a map and compass, and GPS may be needed. This stretch of trail also can be hot and dry during the summer, with a surprising amount of up and down hiking.

Just south of Sour Creek, the trail reaches a junction that may or may not be marked. The mileage to the end of the trail is roughly equivalent for the two trail options. The right fork leads to junctions with the Wrangler Lake Trail and the Wapiti Lake Trail, and eventually ends at the Wapiti Lake Trailhead. The Howard Eaton Trail veers to the left (west) at the trail junction and crosses Sour Creek (an easy, knee-deep ford after mid-July). The hard-to-follow trail then continues through the meadows of Hayden Valley and along the edge of the forest until it arrives at the Wapiti Lake Trailhead. This trailhead is located at the Chittenden Bridge Picnic Area, which is the first turnoff east of Chittenden Bridge on the South Rim Drive. ❧

CANYON AREA

Although the Grand Canyon of the Yellowstone is the main point of interest in the Canyon area, it really doesn't receive very extensive coverage by true "backcountry" trails. Yet, there are many short walkways that lead up to, around, and into this spectacular canyon. These walkways are described in a leaflet that also explains the area's interesting geology. The leaflet is available at all park visitor centers. The only backcountry trails that offer good views of the canyon are the Glacial Boulder Trail, the Seven Mile Hole Trail, and the Clear Lake/Ribbon Lake Loop Trail. The remaining trails in the Canyon area take you through a variety of terrain, from forested lakes to large open meadows and even to the top of Mt. Washburn. Grizzly bears inhabit much of the area, and elk and bison are frequently seen. ♣

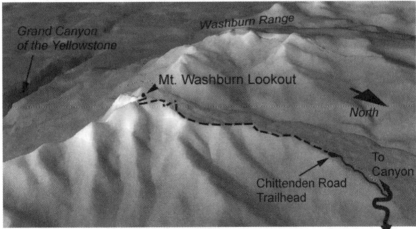

Mt. Washburn Trail from Chittenden Road

MT. WASHBURN TRAILS   Map #14, 15

Dunraven Pass Trailhead to Mt. Washburn Lookout .... 3.2 miles ... 5.1km
Chittenden Road Parking Area to Mt. Washburn Lookout .. 3 .... 4.8

If you have time to take but one short hike in Yellowstone, make it Mt. Washburn. During the summer, wildflowers and bighorn sheep abound on the mountain's slopes. The bighorns migrate from their lowland winter range to this high spot to spend the summer. They seem to accept the presence of hikers, and often feed surprisingly close to the trail. They are not visible from the trail every day, but when they do make an appearance, camera memory cards fill up quickly as hikers point and shoot with reckless abandon. Nowhere else in Yellowstone can amateur photographers get such close-ups of bighorn with their point-and-shoot cameras. Ravens, marmots, and golden-mantled ground squirrels are also frequently seen here. The view from the summit of Mt. Washburn is tremendous; it will seem as if the whole park is below you. With the help of your map, you'll be able to spot the Grand Canyon of the Yellowstone, Yellowstone Lake, the Teton Range, Hayden Valley, Electric Peak, and maybe even some vapor rising from the geyser basins along the Firehole River.

There are two 3-mile-long trails to the top of Mt. Washburn, and both start from the Canyon–Tower Road. The southern trail begins at the Mt. Washburn Trailhead at the Dunraven Pass parking area; the northern trail leaves from the Mt. Washburn North Trailhead at the Chittenden Road parking area. Both trails to the summit climb about 1,400 feet.

In recent years, there have been a few points of misunderstanding about the Mt. Washburn hike that, with any luck, will be clarified here.

- From the south, the Mt. Washburn Trail starts at the Dunraven Pass parking area, and not at the Dunraven Road Picnic Area a few miles south.

- If you arrive to park at the Dunraven Pass parking area and find the lot full, be aware that there is no room to park on the shoulder of the road. Consider either parking at one of the two pullouts just north of Dunraven Pass or driving to the trailhead at Chittenden Road, where there is usually more space, and starting your hike from there.

- Due to heavy use of this area, the delicate alpine vegetation is being severely trampled, and numerous false trails have been started. Please help reduce this source of visual, as well as physical, impact by staying on the old road that serves as the main trail.

- Don't feed the bighorn sheep. Feeding does not benefit the sheep, and the sight of a bighorn with a pickle in its mouth certainly is not what most people hike up Mt. Washburn to see. ❧

WASHBURN SPUR TRAIL   Map #14, 15, 16

Glacial Boulder Trailhead (on Inspiration Point Road) to:

Seven Mile Hole Trail Turnoff .... 3 miles .... 5 km
Washburn Hot Springs .... 4.8 .... 7.7
Summit of Mt. Washburn .... 8.5 .... 13.5
Mt. Washburn Trailhead (Dunraven Pass) .... 11.5 .... 18.5

To reach the Washburn Spur Trail, start at the Glacial Boulder Trailhead on the road to Inspiration Point. Follow the Seven Mile Hole Trail (the first 2 miles may also be called the Glacial Boulder Trail) until you reach a junction where the Seven Mile Hole Trail turns off to the right and the Washburn Spur Trail goes left. The trail passes through Washburn Hot Springs (mud pots) and continues through a large meadow, where there is a good view of Mt. Washburn above and wildflowers below. From this point, the trail climbs about 2,000 feet in the 2.5 miles to the top. There are very good views to the south most of the way up, and especially when you reach the top of Mt. Washburn's east ridge. Grizzly bears frequent this area, so stay alert.

The Washburn Spur Trail is the most difficult and least traveled of the three trails up Mt. Washburn. An enjoyable way to hike this trail is to take the trail from Dunraven Pass parking area up to the summit of Mt. Washburn and then hike the Washburn Spur Trail down to Canyon Village. Due to the steepness of this trail, it's much easier to enjoy the spectacular view while strolling downhill than while puffing uphill. &

Bighorn Sheep: horns help estimate age

1.5-year-old male or mature female   3-year-old ram   10- to 16-year-old ram

GLACIAL BOULDER TRAIL   Map #14, 16
(One-way distance: 2 miles, 3 km)

The Glacial Boulder Trail offers a good view of the Grand Canyon of the Yellowstone, although not quite as good as the views from Inspiration Point (which you can drive to). The trail also provides access to the Seven Mile Hole Trail. There are some short stretches of steep uphill and downhill, but the trail is generally level as it parallels the canyon rim for most of its 2 miles. It is also out of sight of the view into the canyon much of the way.

The trail starts at Glacial Boulder, which is about 2 miles from Canyon Village on the road to Inspiration Point (which is off the North Rim Drive). The Glacial Boulder is a 500-ton hunk of 600+ million-year-old gneiss sitting on top of 600,000-year-old rhyolite. About 15,000 years ago, during the last ice age, a glacier plucked the older rock from an exposed bed of gneiss at least 40 miles away and left it right here, on top of the younger rhyolite. A local custom among hikers is to try and scale the 15-foot-high rock before starting out on the trail. Try it, but no fair using the trees. &

SEVEN MILE HOLE TRAIL   Map #14, 16
(One-way distance: 5.5 miles, 9 km)

The Seven Mile Hole Trail provides the hiker with a different type of view of the Grand Canyon. This trail leads you from the Glacial Boulder Trailhead to the bottom of a section of the canyon that is broad, mostly forested, and very impressive. Because the trail leads to the Yellowstone River, it's popular with anglers. The Yellowstone River is the only source of water along the trail, so be certain to bring plenty of water with you. Because this stretch of the river is downstream from human developments at Fishing Bridge and Canyon Village, if you do drink from the Yellowstone River, it would be a good idea to treat your water.

The trail follows the Glacial Boulder Trail along the rim of the canyon, through lodgepole pine forest, for the first 2 miles. Three miles from the start of the trail, you will reach a trail junction. The Washburn Spur Trail splits off to the left, while the Seven Mile Hole Trail continues on ahead and soon begins the descent into the canyon. The trail drops about 1,400 feet in 1.5 miles, sections of which are fairly steep. Take it easy on the descent, and save your leg muscles for the climb back out. The old cliché about this trail, "5 miles in and 35 out," can feel very accurate. The descent takes you by both dormant and active hot springs. Once down at the river, look for ouzels fluttering around the rocks and osprey soaring overhead. &

CLEAR LAKE/
RIBBON LAKE LOOP TRAIL
Map #14, 16, 17

Wapiti Lake Trailhead to:

Clear Lake	1.5 miles	2.5 km
Lily Pad Lake	2	3
Ribbon Lake	3	5
Wapiti Lake Trail Jct.	3.5	6
Wapiti Lake Trailhead	6	10

The Clear Lake/Ribbon Lake Loop Trail is an easy, relatively level, 6-mile trail that offers the opportunity to see a variety of wildflowers, some charming backcountry lakes, and possibly even a moose or grizzly bear. Take the necessary precautions for encountering bears and check the status of the trail at an NPS backcountry office before hiking here.

The Clear Lake/Ribbon Lake Loop can be reached from three different trailheads, all on the South Rim Drive (approximately 2 miles south of Canyon Village on the Canyon–Lake Road). After turning onto South Rim Drive, you will immediately cross the Yellowstone River on the Chittenden Bridge. The first right turn after the bridge leads to the Chittenden Bridge Picnic Area, where the Wapiti Lake Trailhead is located. The trail description and mileages below are for a start from this trailhead.

A bit farther along the South Rim Drive on the left, you will reach Uncle Tom's parking area and the Clear Lake Trailhead. This trail leaves the parking area, crosses the South Rim Drive, and gradually climbs up through meadows for about 0.7 mile to meet the Clear Lake/Ribbon Lake Loop Trail near Clear Lake.

If you continue on South Rim Drive until it ends, you will arrive at the Artist Point parking area. At the east end of this lot, you can follow the trail along the South Rim (past the overlook to Artist Point) to a junction, where you can turn south and reach the Clear Lake/Ribbon Lake Loop Trail (about 1 mile from the parking area).

From the Wapiti Lake Trailhead, the Clear Lake/Ribbon Lake Loop Trail climbs an open grassy hillside and then reaches a trail junction. Turn north (left) at this junction and you will reach Clear Lake in about ½ mile, passing one more trail junction just before the lake—stay to the right at this junction. The trail skirts the east shoreline of this hot spring-fed lake and proceeds through terrain dotted with thermal features—depending on the water level, hot springs, fumaroles, and mudpots can be viewed. The trail continues into a forested area and arrives at a junction. Turning left at the junction will take you past Lily Pad Lake and out to the Artist Point parking area, while the main trail to Ribbon Lake heads to the right. The trail now climbs a forested ridge and then descends to Ribbon Lake and an unnamed lake to the east. At Ribbon Lake, a spur trail to the left continues to backcountry campsites 4R1 and 4R2. Between the two campsites, a trail cuts off north, up a little hill, to a very nice view of the canyon. The start of Silver Cord Cascade is visible early in the season when the water level is high, though the best—and only safe—view of Silver Cord Cascade is from the Glacial Boulder Trail on the north rim.

From Ribbon Lake, the Clear Lake/Ribbon Lake Loop Trail turns south along the western shore of Ribbon Lake, passes a small lake on the right, and soon comes to the junction with the Wapiti Lake Trail. After the junction, the Clear Lake/Ribbon Lake Trail is actually following Wapiti Lake Trail west as it descends through forest, past another small lake, to the junction with the Sour Creek Trail. The Sour Creek Trail heads off to the south (left), leading to the Wrangler Lake Trail and the Howard Eaton Trail, while the Clear Lake/ Ribbon Lake Loop Trail continues west (right). The trail now climbs up the open, grassy hillside, past the turnoff to Clear Lake (stay left at the turnoff) and returns to the Wapiti Lake Trailhead. ♣

WRANGLER LAKE TRAIL   Map #14, 16
(One-way distance: 4 miles, 6.5 km)

As of 2012, this trail had been closed for three seasons due to wolf denning in the area. Check at the Canyon Visitor Center for its current status. The Wrangler Lake Trail starts at the Wapiti Lake Trailhead on the South Rim Drive. Follow the Clear Lake/Ribbon Lake Loop Trail as it climbs through open meadows where bison are often seen. After approximately ¾ mile, the trail to Clear Lake will veer off to the left near the top of a hill. Follow the right fork of the trail up, over, and down a hill and then up another. The trail to Wrangler Lake heads off to the right in the clump of trees at the top of this hill. For the next ½ mile, the Wrangler Lake Trail goes down through lodgepole pine forest and grassy meadows and over a small warm stream to another junction. Wrangler Lake Trail turns east through sage meadows to Sour Creek, where it makes two knee-deep crossings of this slow-moving creek and its tributary. Once across the creek, the trail heads south through the woods to Wrangler Lake. The lake is almost completely surrounded by trees, and its shoreline is quite marshy. As you might guess, mosquitoes can be a real problem here. ♣

Bighorn rams

WAPITI LAKE TRAIL   Map #11, 12, 14, 16
(One-way distance: 15.5 miles, 25 km)

The Wapiti Lake Trail travels from the Wapiti Lake Trailhead through stands of pine, spruce, and fir to Broad Creek and Wapiti Lake. This is a hike for lovers of remote, dense forest. Far-ranging panoramic views are not a part of the scenery for the majority of this trail. In recent years the first few miles of this trail have seen heavy use by wolves and grizzly bears and may be closed accordingly. Take the necessary precautions for encountering grizzlies and check at an NPS backcountry office for the current trail status.

The Wapiti Lake Trail starts out through open meadows that often hold elk, bison, and occasionally a bear. The trail then climbs gradually through the forest for 12 miles to a wooded pass at 9,000 feet. There is a trail junction at the pass; stay left to continue on the Wapiti Lake Trail. (The Fern Lake Cutoff Trail, described in the following paragraph, goes to the right.) The trail makes its way through narrow meadows for about ½ mile, and then descends for 2 miles into a steep canyon to Broad Creek, passing through areas of forest that burned in the 1988 fires. The crossing of Broad Creek, near backcountry campsite 4B3, is usually less than knee deep. The trail then parallels Broad Creek for 1 mile through marshy meadows and reaches another trail junction. To the right is the Astringent Creek/Broad Creek Trail, which follows Broad Creek and passes backcountry campsites 5B2 and 5B1. To stay on the Wapiti Lake Trail, turn left and follow the trail uphill as it travels through a forest and climbs about 300 feet in elevation. The trail reaches its namesake—the tree-lined shores of Wapiti Lake—½ mile from the last trail junction. To continue on to Pelican Valley, follow the Upper Pelican Creek Trail description on page 105 (in reverse). A note about backcountry campsites 4B1, 4B2, and 4B3: Off-trail travel is required to reach these sites. At one time there was a fairly easy social trail along the western edge of the Broad Creek meadow, but that route is now strewn with downed trees and quite overgrown; hiking or horseback riding to these sites requires a certain amount of bushwhacking.

The Fern Lake Cutoff Trail begins at the 9000-foot pass on the Wapiti Lake Trail (see above paragraph); it leads to Fern Lake and the Astringent Creek/Broad Creek Trail. From the pass, the cutoff trail descends to an overlook with a good view of the Absaroka Range to the east, then drops steeply down into the meadows of upper Sour Creek, near Ponuntpa Springs (a hydrothermal area). The trail then climbs up over a low ridge, descends past Fern Lake, and drops down to Broad Creek. The 1988 fires burned sections of this cutoff trail—be prepared, especially early in the hiking season, to find downed trees across the trail. The crossing of Broad Creek and the outlet of Fern Lake are easy and shallow after mid-July. Once across Broad Creek, the cutoff trail reaches a trail junction with the Astringent Creek/Broad Creek Trail. Heading to the right (south) will take you to Pelican Valley, while turning left (north) will lead you past backcountry campsites 5B1 and 5B2 to the Wapiti Lake Trail. ♣

Sandhill Crane

- found in meadows and marshes
- gray body, dark wing tips, white cheek patch

GREBE LAKE TRAIL   Map #17
(One-way distance: 3 miles, 5 km)

Grebe Lake and Wolf Lake make up the headwaters of the Gibbon River, the start of one of the longest waterways in the world. The Gibbon flows into the Madison River, which flows into the Missouri River, which flows into the Mississippi River. So when the water from Grebe Lake finally mingles with the salt water of the Gulf of Mexico, it's traveled over 3,500 miles.

The waters of Grebe Lake are home for the arctic grayling, a rare native fish of Yellowstone. This is one of the few spots left in the country, outside of Alaska, that has a viable population of these beautiful fish. Grebe Lake is also a summer home for a variety of waterfowl, including ducks, loons, California gulls, and, recently, nesting trumpeter swans. The swans' nesting success has been helped by early season area closures to limit disturbances from hikers. The lake is almost completely surrounded by meadows that are growing spots for a number of summer wildflowers. These meadows are usually damp throughout the summer, which means you may encounter numerous mosquitoes, at least until early August. Luckily, there's usually an afternoon breeze blowing across the lake that keeps the bugs at bay until evening. Grizzly bears are sometimes seen in this area during early summer, so be certain to check at the Canyon Visitor Center for the latest bear information. Moose and deer can also be spotted throughout the summer at dawn and dusk.

The Grebe Lake Trail starts from Grebe Lake Trailhead, which is approximately 4 miles west of Canyon Junction on the Canyon–Norris Road. This trail, which follows an old fire road almost the entire way, is the shortest and driest route into Grebe Lake. The first mile of the trail winds through meadows near the edge of a forest. The remainder of the trail passes through a dense lodgepole pine forest that was heavily burned during the fires of 1988. Once at the lake, the trail follows the shoreline through meadows. At the east end of Grebe Lake, the trail meets the Howard Eaton Trail. By following the Howard Eaton Trail west, you can travel to Wolf Lake (2 miles away), Ice Lake, and Norris Campground. By taking the Howard Eaton Trail to the east, you can reach Cascade Lake (2 miles away) and Canyon Village. ♠

TRAILS TO CASCADE LAKE   Map #14, 16, 17

Cascade Lake Trailhead on
Canyon–Tower Road to Cascade Lake .... 2.2 miles ...... 3.5 km
Cascade Creek Trailhead on
Canyon–Norris Road to Cascade Lake 2.5 4

Cascade Lake is a small lake sitting at the base of the Washburn Range. Cascade Creek flows out of the lake and through grassy meadows and stands of willows. The willows provide food and building materials for beavers. In years past, there has been a beaver lodge on the south shore of Cascade Lake and a lodge and dam on Cascade Creek. Cascade Lake and its meadows are also home to numerous waterfowl, otter, coyotes, moose, and bears. Much of this area was burned during the fires of 1988.

There are two short trails to Cascade Lake. The shorter and more enjoyable is the trail that starts at the Cascade Lake Trailhead, about 0.3 mile south of the Cascade Lake Picnic Area (about 1 mile north of Canyon Junction on the Canyon–Tower Road). This trail to Cascade Lake brings you out through open meadows and over small spring creeks. The wildflower display here can be quite spectacular during mid-summer. After approximately 1.2 miles, this trail joins the Cascade Creek Trail and continues on to Cascade Lake. The total distance to Cascade Lake is 2.2 miles.

The Cascade Creek Trail starts at the Cascade Creek Trailhead, about ½ mile west of Canyon Junction on the Canyon–Norris Road. This trail follows Cascade Creek through burned forest to Cascade Lake. The advantage to this trail is that the trailhead is an easy walk from Canyon Village. The total distance of this trail to Cascade Lake is 2.5 miles. ☙

OBSERVATION PEAK TRAIL 🐻   Map #17
(One-way distance: 3 miles, 5 km)

The trail to Observation Peak climbs about 1,400 feet in three miles. Although it's not shown on pre-1980 maps, the trail provides a very nice view of Grebe Lake, Hayden Valley, and the Central Plateau. There are very impressive displays of wildflowers and the opportunity to occasionally see bears. The Observation Peak Trail starts at the northwest corner of Cascade Lake, and can be reached by way of any of the three trails to Cascade Lake. The trail that starts at the Cascade Lake Trailhead provides the shortest access to the Observation Peak Trail (2.2 miles). The trail travels mainly through open meadows and whitebark pine forest. ☙

ICE LAKE TRAIL AND
HOWARD EATON TRAIL   Map #17

Ice Lake Trailhead (3.5 miles east of Norris on the Norris–Canyon Road) to:

Ice Lake	0.3 miles	0.5 km
Wolf Lake	4	6.5
Grebe Lake (west shore)	5	8
Cascade Lake	7.5	12
Cascade Creek Trailhead	10.4	16.7

This whole area is a part of the Solfatara Plateau, which sits at about 8,000 feet above sea level. This plateau is a relatively flat lodgepole pine forest, much of which was burned in the fires of 1988. Ice Lake is penned in by this forest, while Wolf Lake is surrounded by open marshy meadows. Wolf Lake is home for a variety of waterfowl. Sandhill cranes and herons can often be spotted here, especially along the lake's shoreline away from the trail, and, in recent years, loons have been spending the summers here. Moose may also be seen in this area. As with Grebe Lake, grayling and rainbow trout inhabit the waters of Wolf Lake.

From the Ice Lake Trailhead, it's only a couple minutes' easy walk to Ice Lake. Here, you join the Howard Eaton Trail. (If you turn west, the trail will take you to Norris Campground.) To reach Wolf Lake, continue east on the Howard Eaton Trail along Ice Lake's north shore. From Ice Lake, the trail climbs gently through lodgepole pine forest to the meadows of Wolf Lake. There are two easy crossings of the Gibbon River in this section of trail. Here, the Gibbon resembles a creek more than a river. There are two more easy crossings in the meadow east of Wolf Lake.

From Wolf Lake, the trail continues east through meadow and forest to the west shore of Grebe Lake. The Howard Eaton Trail continues around the north shore of Grebe Lake until it comes to a junction with the Grebe Lake Trail. To reach Cascade Lake, stay on the Howard Eaton Trail as it continues east through marshy meadows. From Cascade Lake, you will be an easy 2.5-mile walk away from one of two trailheads. ◆

WOLF LAKE CUTOFF TRAIL   Map #17
(One-way distance: 1 mile, 1.6 km)

This short trail provides a shortcut to Wolf Lake, and a nice view of Little Gibbon Falls. Park at the big pullout about ¼ mile east of the Ice Lake Trailhead on the Canyon–Norris Road. Walk across the road from the pullout, and you will see the orange markers as they lead you through the burned forest and on to a good view of Little Gibbon Falls. The trail continues on to the Howard Eaton Trail, from which it is a little over 2 miles to Wolf Lake. ◆

NORRIS AREA

The main point of interest in the Norris area is Norris Geyser Basin, one of the hottest and most changeable basins in the park. The basin is covered by a network of short trails and walkways that take you past an amazing variety of thermal features. A description of these walkways and an explanation of the features are covered in a leaflet available at the Norris Geyser Basin Museum.

As for the backcountry trails, the Solfatara Creek Trail and the trail to Ice Lake start at Norris Campground, making them convenient hikes for campers in the area. The other two trails, Monument Geyser Basin Trail and Artist Paint Pot Trail, both provide an interesting look at off-the-beaten-track hydrothermal areas. ❧

SOLFATARA CREEK TRAIL   Map #3, 17, 18

Norris Campground to:
Whiterock Springs .... 3.5 miles...... 5.5 km
Mammoth–Norris Road
(¾ mile south of Beaver Lake Picnic Area) .... 6.5.............. 10

From the Norris Campground, the trail travels through the forest paralleling Solfatara Creek (the trail to Ice Lake forks east after ¾ mile.) During the summer, the meadows along Solfatara Creek are an excellent place to spot elk, as well as a variety of wildflowers such as Indian paintbrush, glacial lilies, wild strawberries (fruit in late July), and sticky geraniums. Once past Whiterock Springs, the trail begins to climb gradually up to Lake of the Woods (which is actually a few hundred yards north of the trail). The trail then descends, about 400 feet in a mile, and passes by Amphitheater Springs and Lemonade Creek. There are often bright emerald-green algae growing in Lemonade Creek, which make the creek look much more like limeade than lemonade. Either way, don't drink the water, as the sulfur springs feeding this little creek give it a taste unlike either of the aforementioned beverages. This trail ends at a short service road off the Mammoth–Norris Road, 5.5 miles south of Indian Creek Campground. One final note: the Solfatara Trail is within sight of utility lines for much of its length. ❧

HOWARD EATON TRAIL– NORRIS CAMPGROUND TO ICE LAKE   Map #17, 18

Norris Campground to:
Ice Lake .... 4.5 miles ...... 7 km
Wolf Lake... 8.5 14
Grebe Lake 9.5 15
Cascade Creek Trailhead........................... 15 24

From Norris Campground, the trail to Ice Lake begins by paralleling Solfatara Creek for about ¾ mile. The Ice Lake Trail then veers east, crosses the creek, and continues through the intermittently burned forest to a large meadow. This meadow is often a feeding spot for elk during summer evenings and mornings. From the meadow, the trail climbs about 300 feet in the remaining 1.5 miles to Ice Lake. Although this small lake has been stocked with over 3 million fish since 1905, it is barren of fish today. Rainbow trout, cutthroat trout, and grayling have all been stocked, but the absence of a constantly flowing inlet and outlet stream for spawning has precluded a self-sustaining fish population. The Howard Eaton Trail continues from Ice Lake to Cascade Lake, making a Norris-to-Canyon hike possible. Refer to the description of the Ice Lake Trail and Howard Eaton Trail (Canyon Area) for more information. ♠

MONUMENT GEYSER BASIN TRAIL   Map #19
(One-way distance: 1 mile, 1.5 km)

This short, steep trail starts at the Gibbon River Bridge, 5 miles south of Norris Junction on the Norris–Madison Road. The trail climbs 500 feet in elevation, mainly through lodgepole pine forest burned in the 1988 fires. Monument Geyser Basin has a variety of thermal features, including mud pots, sulphur pools, steam vents, and some interestingly shaped geyser cones. ♠

ARTIST PAINT POT TRAIL   Map #19
(One-way distance: 0.3 mile, 0.5 km)

The trailhead for Artist Paint Pot is located about 4 miles south of Norris
Junction, on the east side of the road in Gibbon Meadows. This interesting,
short trail winds through a lodgepole pine forest where harebell can be found
blooming from July through mid-August. The relatively level path leads to a
variety of thermal features. The main attraction among these is the mud pot
located at the top of the hill, where the trail begins to loop back around. This
thermal area also contains some small geysers, hot pools, and steam vents. This
is a worthwhile hike. 🦌

MISTAKEN IDENTITIES

Immature Golden Eagle
- white areas restricted to base of flight feathers and tail
- relatively long tail, distinct terminal band on tail

Immature Bald Eagle
- large amounts of white on underwing linings and belly
  in a wide variety of combinations

CENTRAL PLATEAU AREA

The Central Plateau area, which includes Nez Perce Valley, Hayden Valley, and the Central Plateau, is contained, for the most part, within the perimeter of the Grand Loop Road's southern half. A combination of geologic, natural, and cultural history makes this section of Yellowstone well worth exploring.

About 640,000 years ago, the hot spot under Yellowstone caused a cataclysmic volcanic eruption. A huge explosion ejected subterranean molten rock and ash as far away as California. With so much material gone, including missing sections of the Washburn and Red mountains, the empty chamber underground collapsed, creating one of the world's largest crater-like calderas. This giant caldera measured well over 1,000 square miles and was at least 1,000 feet deep. Over the ensuing several hundred thousand years, lava oozed up through cracks in the ground, partially and unevenly filling in this vast hole. The caldera is still visible from high vantage points, like the top of Mt. Washburn or Observation Peak. The Central Plateau is in the middle of the caldera and was formed by these later flows of molten rock. In this area of Yellowstone, you'll notice plenty of lodgepole pines—they have an affinity for the silica-rich soil provided by the volcanic rhyolite.

Hayden Valley, too, was once exposed volcanic rock, until more recent geologic processes intervened. Evidence suggests the valley was covered, at least once, by the waters of an enlarged Yellowstone Lake. This larger version of the present

Bison herd in Upper Hayden Valley.   NATIONAL PARK SERVICE PHOTO

lake, formed by an ancient rock and ice dam, left fine-grained lake sediments behind when it drained from Hayden Valley. More recently, Hayden Valley was blanketed by glaciers. When the glaciers retreated, about 14,000 years ago, they deposited a layer of glacial till. Along with the lake sediments, the glacial till—a mixture of clay, sand, and other sediments of various sizes—impedes water percolation, which means fewer lodgepole pines and, instead, an abundance of grasses, sedges, and forbs.

Bison, grizzly bears, and wolves are all attracted to Hayden and Nez Perce valleys. The bison graze on the valleys' lush plant growth in spring, summer, and fall. Come winter, many of them move to lower elevations along the Firehole River, but some stay on, feeding on the snow-covered vegetation in the valleys. Grizzly bears, too, depend on the valleys' plants, especially yampa, clover, and biscuitroot. Grizzlies will also supplement their diet with meat, particularly during the spring. During this time, bears may chase down newborn elk calves or feed on winter- or wolf-killed bison carcasses.

One of the most fascinating aspects of the reassimilation of wolves into the Yellowstone ecosystem is the beneficial effect their presence has had on the grizzlies. In places like Hayden Valley, where the summer elk herd migrates out of the valley to lower elevations in cold weather, wolves resort to hunting the year-round resident bison during the winter. Taking down a bison is a technical, labor-intensive, and dangerous endeavor—wolves may suffer injuries or even die during the process. Grizzlies have learned to capitalize on the wolves' predatory habits without having to, quite literally, lift much more than a sharpened toenail. When these clever—and hungry—opportunists emerge from their dens, they chase wolves off a bison carcass and claim it for themselves. This strategy is particularly valuable now that the harvest of whitebark pine nuts—once an important autumn food source for the grizzlies— is low. While this behavior benefits the grizzlies, it is less than ideal for the wolves; the grizzlies' poaching creates stress on the wolves and may contribute to lower wolf pup production.

As far as human history is concerned, in 1877, the Nez Perce Creek area was the site of a somewhat unfriendly meeting between a band of Nez Perce Indians and some early Yellowstone tourists. The Nez Perce, led by Chief Joseph, had entered the park while attempting to escape the U.S. Cavalry. A radical band of the tribe attacked and captured a group of tourists who were camping in the Nez Perce Creek area. During the attack, one of the tourists, George Cowan, was shot in the head and left for dead. As it turned out, not only did George survive and manage to escape, even after another Indian shot him in the hip, but when the bullet was finally removed from his skull, he had it made into an ornament for his watch. And if that wasn't enough excitement, Mr. Cowan later had a creek in Nez Perce Valley named Cowan Creek in his honor. ❧

CYGNET LAKES TRAIL
Map #17, 19
(One-way distance: 4.5 miles, 7.2 km)

The Cygnet Lakes Trail starts at a pullout on the south side of the Norris–Canyon Road, approximately 5.5 miles west of Canyon Junction. The trail travels through intermittently burned forest to the expansive meadows of the Cygnet Lakes. Moose, deer, and a variety of waterfowl may be seen in these meadows. This is a day-use-only area; no overnight camping is allowed. The trail is not maintained past Cygnet Lakes. ♣

MARY MOUNTAIN TRAIL–WEST 🐻
(NEZ PERCE CREEK TRAIL)
Map #19, 22

Mary Mountain West Trailhead to:

Nez Perce Creek	2 miles	3 km
Magpie Creek	4	6.4
Mary Lake	11	18
Trailhead on Canyon–Lake Road	20	32

The western portion of the Mary Mountain Trail travels from the trailhead on the Old Faithful–Madison Road (about 6 miles south of Madison Junction) to Mary Lake. The trail follows Nez Perce Creek through lodgepole pine forest and meadows most of the way. Bison are often seen in this area during spring (late April, May, and early June), and this is an especially good time and place to view bison cows with their newborn calves. Grizzlies might also be spotted in the valley during the spring months. Because of the high concentrations of grizzly bears in the surrounding area, no overnight camping is allowed along any portion of this trail.

From the trailhead, the trail follows an old road to the bridge over Nez Perce Creek. The trail then travels intermittently through forest and meadows to the crossings of Magpie Creek and Cowan Creek (both can be crossed on logs). About ½ mile before reaching Magpie Creek, the trail takes a slight northward turn and skirts the tree line of a meadow. Be sure to keep an eye out for orange trail markers to avoid following one of the bison trails by accident. Near Cowan Creek, the trail goes through some meadows that remain soggy all summer long. Once past these meadows, the trail enters a lodgepole pine forest and climbs 900 feet, very steeply in spots, to Mary Lake. Mary Lake is a tree-lined lake that holds no fish but is home to a variety of waterfowl. ♣

MARY MOUNTAIN TRAIL–EAST   Map #19
(One-way distance: 9 miles, 14 km)

Due to the heavy use of this area by grizzly bears, the NPS advises hikers to stay on the trail, travel in groups of 3 or more, and carry pepper spray. This trail starts at a large pullout about ¼ mile north of Alum Creek on the Canyon–Lake Road (on the north end of Hayden Valley). For the first 4 miles, the route parallels the tree line along the edge of the meadow of Hayden Valley and follows Alum Creek. There are small thermal areas and a variety of water birds (mallards, sandpipers, killdeer, herons, and ouzels) to be seen along this stream. Don't count on Alum Creek for drinking water: one taste will tell you why. About 4 miles from the road, the trail crosses Violet Creek and begins to gain elevation as the trail makes its way to the west end of Hayden Valley (it is no longer paralleling the tree line). There are many bison trails in this area, so be certain to follow the trail with the orange markers. Because there are no trees along this section of the trail, the trail markers must be placed on posts. The posts are frequently used as scratching aides by the bison, and are consequently likely to be on the ground and not visible until you step on them. A topographic map would be beneficial for this section of trail.

Once you're out of Hayden Valley and atop the forested Central Plateau, you will soon pass Highland Hot Springs and arrive at lodgepole-lined Mary Lake. Mary Lake doesn't hold any fish, but there are often coots and other waterfowl swimming here.

It's not unusual for people to hike the entire Mary Mountain Trail, East and West sections (20 miles), in a day. It's a good, long, day hike, but actually the most interesting sections of the trail are the first 4 miles on either side. Because of the high concentrations of grizzly bears in this area, there is no overnight camping allowed along any portion of this trail. 🐾

ELEPHANT BACK TRAIL   Map #13
(Roundtrip distance: 3.6 miles, 5.8 km)

The Elephant Back Trail climbs about 800 vertical feet from the trailhead at 7,800 feet to the overlook at 8,600 feet. The trail starts at Elephant Back Trailhead approximately 1 mile south of Fishing Bridge Junction on the road between Lake Village and Fishing Bridge. The trail starts by paralleling the road south for about 50 yards and then veers up into the trees. The trail passes the old Lake Village water source pipe and then passes under the power line. After the power line, the trail climbs steadily through lodgepole forest. Deer are frequently seen in this area. About a mile from the trailhead, you will come to a trail junction. Both sides lead to the top and will join at the overlook. The left path is the shorter route to the top, about 0.8 mile away. From the overlook on top, there is a sweeping panorama that takes in Pelican Valley to the left, Yellowstone Lake and its islands straight in front of you, and the Absaroka Range rising above the lake as far as you can see. 🐾

MADISON VALLEY AREA

The Madison Valley contains three trails: Harlequin Lake Trail, Purple Mountain Trail, and Gneiss Creek Trail. The first two are relatively short hikes starting near the Madison Campground, while the latter is a longer hike starting about 7 miles west of the campground.

From the junction of the Firehole and Gibbon rivers to the Gneiss Creek Trailhead, the Madison Valley is more like a canyon than a valley. Its steep walls of volcanic rock rise almost vertically from the banks of the Madison River. Downstream from the Seven Mile Bridge Trailhead (where the Gneiss Creek Trail starts), the Madison Valley is a broad, flat plain covered with grass, sage, and aspens. Much of the Madison area was burned to varying degrees in the fires of 1988. 🐾

HARLEQUIN LAKE TRAIL   Map #20
(One-way distance: .5 mile, .8 km)

This short trail starts about 1.5 miles from the Madison Campground on the West Entrance Road. The hike passes through a burned lodgepole pine forest to the small lake, which is usually home for a variety of waterfowl—but not harlequin ducks as the name might imply. Large numbers of mosquitoes have also found a home here and can be quite thick until late July. 🐾

PURPLE MOUNTAIN TRAIL   Map #20
(One-way distance: 3 miles, 5 km)

Calling this a mountain is a bit optimistic; nonetheless, the hike to the top does seem like a long one. The trail climbs 1,500 vertical feet through intermittently burned forest to a pretty good view of the Gibbon River Valley. The best thing about this trail is that it starts close by Madison Campground, about ¼ mile north of Madison Junction on the Norris–Madison Road. Parking is on the opposite (south) side of the Norris–Madison Road. 🐾

GNEISS CREEK TRAIL 🐻   Map #20, 21

Seven Mile Bridge Trailhead to:

Cougar Creek	4 miles	6.5 km
Maple Creek	7	11
Gneiss Creek	9	14.5
Campanula Creek	12	19
Trailhead on U.S. 191	14	22.5

The Gneiss Creek Trail travels through the flat Madison Valley, among stands of Douglas fir and aspen, and across clear, willow-lined creeks. Elk spend the fall, winter, and spring in this area and can sometimes be seen in large numbers. The bigger meadows along the trail attract herds of grazing bison. The area is also good wolf and grizzly habitat—take the proper precautions for avoiding bears. Remember that grouse are also abundant in this area, and may occasionally explode out of a clump of brush beside the trail and fly away in front of you. To hikers treading cautiously along this trail thinking that a grizzly could be lurking behind any tree, this sudden surprise could cause heart failure—or at least require a change of pants. Stream crossings are all easily waded after June, but beware that biting flies can be very unpleasant from mid to late summer. Because of the limited forest cover, this hike can be a hot and sunny one in July and August, and can feel like a very exposed place during a summer lightening storm. The trail's abundant deciduous vegetation makes it a great hike in the fall, when autumn colors are on display.

The Gneiss Creek Trail starts from the Seven Mile Bridge Trailhead, about 7 miles west of Madison Junction on the West Entrance Road. The trail follows the Madison River along the steep cliffs of its north shore for 1 mile, and then leaves the river and heads north through the forest. The trail reaches a junction 1.5 miles from the trailhead; stay left to remain on the main path (the spur trail to the right leads to an NPS patrol cabin). About 4 miles in, at the Cougar Creek crossing, bison trails become obvious and finding the tread of the actual hiking trail can be a challenge. Trail markers cannot be counted on to guide you— burned trees and posts, normally used for the bright orange trail markers, are perfect scratching stations for the bison and don't stay standing for long. Be sure to bring a map or GPS if you're hiking this trail for the first time. The trail continues through sage meadows, aspen groves, and fir forest for the remainder of the hike. The only significant hill climbing along this route takes place after crossing Campanula Creek, when the trail gains about 200 feet in elevation in ½ mile. The trailhead on U.S. 191 is located at Fir Ridge Cemetery, milepost 9. 🐾

FIREHOLE VALLEY AREA

The valley of the Firehole River is probably best known for its hydrothermal areas, which contain the largest concentration of geysers anywhere in the world. There are three main thermal areas along the river. From the north to south they are the Lower, Midway and Upper geyser basins. Old Faithful is located in the Upper Geyser Basin. Each of these areas has an abundance of short walkways that offer a close look at a variety of amazing hydrothermal features. A leaflet describing the Upper Geyser Basin and its many walkways is available from the Old Faithful Visitor Center. If you are staying in the Old Faithful area and don't have a car, you'll be happy to know that all of the trailheads in this section can be accessed from the Upper Geyser Basin by using boardwalks, winter ski trails, and asphalt walkways. These access routes aren't all described, but I will tell you which ones to use, and they are labeled on the maps.

The backcountry trails in the Firehole Valley travel not only to thermal features, but also to waterfalls, lakes, and meadows. Some of the more spectacular of these are Lone Star Geyser, Fairy Falls, and Mystic Falls. There are bison and elk that spend the entire year near the Firehole Valley, wintering in the vicinity of the geyser basins and spending their summers feeding in places such as Buffalo Meadows and Little Firehole Meadows. With the reintroduction of wolves to Yellowstone in the mid-1990s, the elk population in the Firehole Valley has declined from an estimated population of 600–800 to about 150–200 individuals. While it is still possible to view elk, this valley is now a good place to occasionally glimpse wolves, mostly in the late fall and winter. ♣

LONE STAR GEYSER TRAIL   Map #22, 24, 25

Lone Star Trailhead* to:

Lone Star Geyser	2.5 miles	4 km
Bechler River Trail Jct.	6.7	10.7
Shoshone Lake	8.5	13.5

The Lone Star Trailhead is located just south of Kepler Cascades, 3.5 miles from the Old Faithful overpass on the Old Faithful–West Thumb Road. This route is also a partially paved bike trail as far as Lone Star Geyser. No bicycle travel is allowed beyond Lone Star Geyser or off of the paved path—if you want to continue past the geyser on foot, a bike rack has been installed at the end of the paved path for you to lock up your bike. The level trail follows the Firehole River the entire way and is an easy, pleasant hike. Lone Star Geyser erupts about every 3 hours from its 12-foot cone. The eruptions can be up to 45 feet high and are followed by a roaring steam phase. The Shoshone Lake Trail continues from Lone Star Geyser up to Grants Pass and down to a junction with the Bechler River Trail and Shoshone Lake. &

Lone Star Trailhead can also be reached on foot from the Old Faithful area by using the Kepler Cutoff Ski Trail (about 1.7 miles), which starts at the Mallard Lake Trailhead.

HOWARD EATON TRAIL TO LONE STAR GEYSER
Map #22, 23, 24, 25
(One-way distance: 3.1 miles, 5 km)

This trail starts about 0.9 mile east of the Old Faithful overpass on the south side of the Old Faithful–West Thumb Road, at the Howard Eaton Trailhead. Walk a short distance up the service road and look to your left for the Howard Eaton Trail. This route leads up, over and down a 500-foot, forested hill to Lone Star Geyser. This trail is longer, much steeper, not as scenic, and thus, less traveled than the other trail to Lone Star Geyser. &

FERN CASCADES SEMI-LOOP TRAIL
(One-way distance: 1.7 miles, 2.7 km)
Map #22, 23

This short trail starts in the Old Faithful housing area (from the Old Faithful Ranger Station, follow the service road southwest, cross the entrance and exit roads, and then cross the main road to the housing area) and ends near the start of the Howard Eaton Trail to Lone Star Geyser. The Fern Cascades Trail travels entirely through forest, and climbs and descends about 200 feet. Fern Cascades are pretty, but not very impressive. A short detour to the west is required to look down into the little canyon and see the cascades. Although it's a great ski trail in the winter, I'd only recommend it in the summer to people staying in the Old Faithful area who don't have a car, and who have hiked all the other trails in the area. Most of this trail was heavily burned in 1988. &

OBSERVATION POINT LOOP TRAIL   Map #23
(Roundtrip distance: 2 miles, 3 km)

Although not really a backcountry trail, this is one of the best short trails in the park. It provides a great overlook for viewing an eruption of Old Faithful, a walk past interesting thermal features and a good look at the Firehole River. Before starting on the trail, check at the Old Faithful Visitor Center for the next scheduled eruption of Old Faithful, and time your hike accordingly. The trail starts at the Old Faithful Visitor Center and follows the Geyser Hill Trail around Old Faithful Geyser and across the Firehole River. On the north side of the river, the Observation Point Trail starts climbing steadily along switchbacks (160 vertical feet) to Observation Point. From the overlook, the trail descends about 0.3 mile down to Solitary Geyser, then continues on down to the Geyser Hill Trail, and back to the visitor center. 🐾

MALLARD LAKE TRAIL   Map #22, 23

Mallard Lake Trailhead (southeast of Old Faithful Lodge cabins) to:

Mallard Creek Trail Jct.	3.2 miles	5.1 km
Mallard Lake	3.4	5.5
Old Faithful–Madison Rd. and Jct. with trail back to Old Faithful	7.5	12
Morning Glory Pool	10.4	16.7
Old Faithful Visitor Center	11.8	19

The trailhead for the Mallard Lake Trail is located between the cabins of the Old Faithful Lodge and the Firehole River. There is a small bridge across the river at this spot. From the bridge, the trail climbs gradually through a lodgepole pine forest, passing Pipeline Hot Springs, which contains some small mud pots. After 2.5 miles, the trail winds through an open rocky area. The cliffs on either side of the trail are composed of rhyolite, as is the entire Central Plateau upon which the Mallard Lake Trail rests. From the junction with the Mallard Creek Trail, it is 0.2 mile to Mallard Lake. The lake is surrounded by lodgepole pine. Waterfowl can usually be seen swimming and diving in its cold waters.

If you continue on the Mallard Creek Trail, you'll climb steeply to a good overlook of Mallard Lake and the Mallard Creek Canyon. Much of this area was burned during the 1988 fires. Approximately 2 miles farther down the trail you'll descend into the canyon of Mallard Creek. Here, the creek is a lovely little warm water cascade. The trail then ascends to the top of the north side of the canyon. From this point, there is a view to the west of the Twin Buttes. Near the 7.4-mile point, you'll come to a junction. The trail to the right leads to Fairy Falls about 3 miles away. The trail to the left leads to Old Faithful. The trail to Old Faithful will parallel the road south (following the power lines part of the way) until it hits the old road back to Morning Glory Pool. From Morning Glory, you follow the asphalt trail, passing Riverside and Castle geysers, back to the Old Faithful Visitor Center. &

Castle Geyser

STOCK ACCESS TO MYSTIC FALLS, SUMMIT LAKE & FAIRY CREEK TRAILS

For stock access to these trails, use the trailhead located about 0.1 mile south of the Biscuit Basin parking area in a small pullout on the west side of the Old Faithful-Madison Road. The stock access trail prevents stock users from having to go through the geyser basin. This trail joins up with the main trail near its start at the back end of the geyser basin. ♣

MYSTIC FALLS TRAIL   Map #22, 23

Trailhead at Biscuit Basin Parking Area* to:

Fairy Creek Trail Jct. (east)	.3 miles	.5 km
Mystic Falls	1.1	1.8
Top of Mystic Falls	1.3	2.2
Fairy Creek Trail Jct. (west)	1.8	2.9
Scenic Overlook	2.3	3.7
Biscuit Basin Parking Area	3	4.8

Mystic Falls is an impressive, 70-foot drop of the Little Firehole River as it comes off the Madison Plateau into the Firehole River Valley. The trail to the falls starts at Biscuit Basin parking area (on the Old Faithful-Madison Road). Follow the boardwalk to the back end (west side) of the geyser basin, where the Mystic Falls Trail branches off from the boardwalk. The trail travels through a dense, young lodgepole pine forest, all new growth after the fires of 1988. After about ¼ mile, the longer loop trail to Mystic Falls (which is also the Fairy Creek Trail) branches off to the right and heads uphill. Keep left for the shorter (0.7 mile) and more scenic approach to Mystic Falls. From the base of Mystic Falls, the trail climbs a series of switchbacks to an excellent view at the top of the falls. If you want to make this a loop hike (at this point it's only about 0.4 mile farther than going back the way you came), continue on this trail until it meets the Fairy Creek Trail. At this junction, turn right and descend to an overlook; here it is possible to view a faraway eruption of Old Faithful. Continue downhill through a series of switchbacks to loop back to the boardwalk and parking area at Biscuit Basin. ♣

Biscuit Basin can also be reached on foot from the Old Faithful area (2.3 miles), by following the Upper Geyser Basin Trail northwest past Castle Geyser and Morning Glory Pool, and then continuing on the Artemisia Trail to Biscuit Basin.

SUMMIT LAKE TRAIL   Map #22, 23
(One-way distance: 7.5 miles, 12 kilometers)

The Summit Lake Trail starts at Biscuit Basin parking area (on the Old Faithful-Madison Road) and follows the Mystic Falls Trail for about ¼ mile. After branching south from that trail, the Summit Lake Trail crosses the Little Firehole River, then climbs 600 feet in 1.5 miles to the Madison Plateau. The trail continues to climb gradually, gaining 700 more feet in the remaining 6 miles to the lake. Much of this area was burned during the 1988 fires. Summit Lake is almost completely surrounded by trees except for a small meadow. Should you choose to continue hiking past Summit Lake, one-half mile west of the lake is the continental divide. Here, there are some interesting and seldom-visited thermal features, as well as good views of Idaho's Centennial Range. The backcountry office at the Old Faithful Ranger Station frequently receives updates on the conditions of this trail from CDT hikers, so feel free to stop by for the latest report. ❧

FAIRY CREEK TRAIL
(LITTLE FIREHOLE MEADOWS TRAIL)   Map #22, 23

Trailhead at Biscuit Basin Parking Area to:

Mystic Falls Trail Jct. .... 0.3 miles .... .5 km
Little Firehole Meadows 5.5 9
Imperial Geyser 10.2 17
Fairy Falls .... 11 .... 18.6
Fairy Falls Trailhead (south of Midway Geyser Basin) .... 13.5 .... 21.6

The Fairy Creek Trail travels from Biscuit Basin to Little Firehole Meadows, past Imperial Geyser and Fairy Falls, to the Fairy Falls Trailhead, 1 mile south of Midway Geyser Basin. The highlight of this trail is Fairy Falls (which can also be reached by two shorter routes: one starts at the Fairy Falls Trailhead, and the other leaves from the Freight Road Trailhead on Fountain Flat Drive).

Starting from the Biscuit Basin parking area (2 miles north of Old Faithful on the road to Madison Junction), the Fairy Creek Trail follows the Mystic Falls Trail for about ¼ mile until reaching a trail junction where the Fairy Creek Trail continues uphill to the west (right). The Fairy Creek Trail climbs steeply—400 vertical feet—up open, rocky slopes. From these slopes, it's possible to watch Old Faithful Geyser erupt in the distance to the southeast. The trail continues to climb through lodgepole pine forest for 2 more miles. It then descends to the Little Firehole River just downstream from a lovely waterfall. From this point, the trail follows the river upstream, about ½ mile, to Little Firehole Meadows.

The Little Firehole Meadows are a summering spot for bison. You may occasionally see bison from the trail, but they're often feeding on parts of the meadow that aren't visible from the beaten path. Even if you don't see the bison themselves, you're certain to see evidence of their presence, such as droppings (careful where you step...) and trees that have had the bark stripped and whole branches removed by the bison's horning.

The Fairy Creek Trail follows the eastern edge of the meadows about ¼ mile and then reenters the forest. From Little Firehole Meadows, the trail descends gradually until it reaches the edge of the Madison Plateau where it drops about 400 feet in ½ mile. In this area, the trail may be hard to follow, due to the heavy burn and numerous game trails. Look for trail markers to be certain you are on the trail (this is a popular place to get lost). Once at the bottom of the plateau, the trail passes Imperial Geyser, which is a large pool of boiling water that is almost constantly erupting. A short way past Imperial Geyser, the trail branches. The trail to the left heads north along Fairy Creek to Fountain Flat Drive. The other trail travels to Fairy Falls and the trailhead 1 mile south of Midway Geyser Basin. (See "Trails to Fairy Falls" section.) 🐾

TRAILS TO FAIRY FALLS   Map #22, 23

The 200-foot drop of Fairy Creek makes Fairy Falls one of Yellowstone's highest waterfalls; you'll need a wide angle lens to get it all in one photo. The small stream of water coming off the plateau above seems to descend in delicate slow motion. This spectacular falls can be reached by two different short trails. Both trails can also be done as an 8-mile loop hike by combining the two routes.

The longer (3.8 miles), but more scenic, route to Fairy Falls is via the Imperial Meadows Trail. It starts at the Freight Road Trailhead (at the Ojo Caliente parking area, at the south end of Fountain Flat Drive). From the trailhead, you will cross the Firehole River by bridge and hike south along the old road for a total of about 1 mile. At this point the Imperial Meadows Trail turns right (west) off the old road. The Imperial Meadows Trail soon enters the meadows of Fairy Creek, passes a trail junction to Sentinel Meadows (stay left at the junction), and continues through wet meadows. There is one bridged crossing of Fairy Creek. The trail continues on to a junction with the Fairy Falls Trail and the Fairy Creek Trail. Here you have two choices. Turn right (west) on the Fairy Creek Trail to go to Imperial Geyser. Turn left (southeast) to see Fairy Falls.

The shorter route (2.5 miles) to Fairy Falls starts from the Fairy Falls Trailhead (1 mile south of Midway Geyser Basin parking area on the Old Faithful–Madison Road). This route follows the south end of the old Freight Road for about 1 mile and then turns west, traveling through young lodgepole forest for another 1.5 miles to Fairy Falls.

The Fairy Falls Trailhead can also be reached on foot from the Old Faithful area (4.4 miles) by using the Upper Geyser Basin Trail to reach Morning Glory Pool, then taking the Artemisia Trail to the power line path, then continuing past the Mallard Creek trail junction, and heading on to the Fairy Falls Trailhead (on the west side of the road). ♠

SENTINEL MEADOWS TRAIL   Map #22, 23

Freight Road Trailhead to:
Sentinel Meadows... 1.5 miles...... 2.4 km
Loop hike back to Freight Road Trailhead................... 4.5.............. 7.2

Sentinel Meadows has a small thermal area that contains a feature called Queen's Laundry. In 1881, under the orders of Yellowstone's second superintendent Philetus Norris, work was begun on a bathhouse at this spring. As it so happened, Norris was replaced as superintendent before the bathhouse was finished, and work never resumed on this building. This structure's logs have been preserved by the mineral-laden water of the hot spring and today this uncompleted bathhouse still remains, although quite dilapidated, as the first government building constructed in any national park solely for the use of the public.

Sentinel Meadows is an occasional feeding spot for bison from October through early June. Sandhill cranes have been observed nesting in this area in June and may be spotted, and heard, throughout the summer in the vicinity of the meadows.

The Sentinel Meadows Trail starts at the Freight Road Trailhead (at the south end of Fountain Flat Drive). From the trailhead you will hike south along the old Freight Road, passing Ojo Caliente Hot Spring and crossing the Firehole River by bridge. Once across the bridge, the trail turns right (west) off the old road and travels 1.5 miles to Sentinel Meadows. The Sentinel Meadows Trail turns south and then east as it circles back to the old Freight Road. Before the trail heads south, however, there is an unofficial spur trail that continues directly west and leads to Queen's Laundry. By hiking the full loop of the Sentinel Meadows Trail, then briefly joining the Imperial Meadows Trail to reach the old Freight Road, and finally heading north to the original trailhead, you will travel 4.5 miles. Be forewarned, though: finding the official Sentinel Meadows Trail once it loops south and east is tricky. There are numerous bison trails that are easy to mistake for the hiking trail, and the orange trail markers are often placed on burned snags that don't always withstand the wind. It is easy to lose the trail and hard to find it again. However, it is also easy to see the old road across the open meadows, so meandering across the open flats is one reliable way to get back to the old Freight Road. Once back on the old road, turn north (left) to return to the trailhead. &

SPRING CREEK TRAIL   Map #22, 24, 25
(One-way distance: 4.5 miles, 7.2 km)

This is mainly a winter ski trail, and is not maintained for summer use. It's wet and boggy. Be prepared to get your feet wet if you take this trail, although it is a nice walk along a relatively lush stream bank. The trail can be started at the Divide Trailhead 6.7 miles east of Old Faithful on the Old Faithful-West Thumb Road. The trail follows the Divide Trail for approximately 0.3 mile as it climbs gradually. The Spring Creek Trail then branches off to the right (west), follows an old roadbed on and off, and climbs some short uphill sections. (The trail can also be accessed from the Spring Creek Picnic Area, which is located one mile west of the Divide Trailhead. Look for the orange trail markers to the right/ north of the vault toilet in the parking area.) The trail then stays close to Spring Creek, passing through some interesting rock formations, and eventually joins the Lone Star Geyser Trail after crossing a footbridge over the Firehole River. It is now about 1.5 miles out to Lone Star Geyser Trailhead (to the right). &

DIVIDE TRAIL   Map #24, 25, 26
(One-way distance: 1.7 miles, 2.7 km)

The Divide Trail starts at the Divide Trailhead and parking area 6.7 miles east of the Old Faithful intersection on the Old Faithful–West Thumb Road. The trail climbs 700 vertical feet, first through lodgepole pine forest with thick mats of grouse whortleberrry, and then through spruce-fir forest, to the site of a former lookout tower. There is a nice view of Shoshone Lake and DeLacy Meadows about halfway up the trail, but no real view from the top due to the trees. The lookout tower has been removed. &

MISTAKEN IDENTITIES

Golden-Mantled Ground Squirrel
- head and body 6 to 8 inches long
- no stripe on side of face

Least Chipmunk
- head and body 3²/3 to 4½ inches long
- 3 stripes on face

GRIZZLY BEAR INFLICTED HUMAN FATALITIES IN YELLOWSTONE'S BACKCOUNTRY, 1872 TO 2015

Date	Location	Victim/Activity	Number in party	Bear
August 2015	Elephant Back Trail	Male, day hiking	One	Female grizzly with 2 cubs
August 2011	Mary Mountain Trail, Hayden Valley	Male, day hiking	One	Grizzly bear, gender unknown
July 2011	Wapiti Lake Trail, Hayden Valley	Male, day hiking	Two	Female grizzly with 2 cubs
October 1986	Otter Creek, Hayden Valley	Male, photo-graphing bear	One	Female grizzly
July 1984	White Lake near Pelican Valley	Female, backpacking	One	Grizzly bear, gender unknown
June 1972	Old Faithful area	Male, camping near trail	One	Female grizzly
1872-1972	No known fatalities in Yellowstone's backcountry			

SHOSHONE LAKE AREA

Shoshone Lake, Yellowstone's largest backcountry lake, has attracted backcountry travelers and explorers for hundreds of years. During this time, it's had many names. It was called Snake Lake by the mountain men of the fur-trading era who referred to the Shoshone Indians as the "Snake" Indians; Madison Lake by those who erroneously thought it drained into the Madison River; DeLacy Lake in honor of the first man to map the lake as flowing into the Snake River; and finally Shoshone Lake to acknowledge the earliest name used by the fur trappers.

Shoshone Lake and its shoreline are home to a variety of finned, furred, and feathered creatures. Its cold, deep waters hold brown, brook, and lake trout. These non-native species were introduced into this formerly fishless lake during the 1890s. Water birds gather on and around the lake to feed on these fish and other aquatic animals and plants. Ospreys, California gulls, Barrow's goldeneye, mallards, scaups, common mergansers, coots, spotted sandpipers, and American avocets can be spotted in this area. Sandhill cranes may or may not be seen, but they're often heard for miles as they call out in a voice that's described as a low, loud, musical rattle. Moose are common to the area, and elk and deer are occasionally seen in shoreline meadows. If you're lucky, you may spot a weasel chasing shorebirds across a beach, or otters frolicking and fishing in the lake. Mosquitoes can be amazingly numerous from late June to late July. Insect netting on tents and mosquito repellent are necessities here.

On Shoshone Lake's west shore is Shoshone Geyser Basin, which has a number of interesting active thermal features. Osborne Russell described walking through Shoshone Geyser Basin in his journal, kept during the 1830s. He wrote, "On a near approach we could hear the water bubbling underground some distance from the surface. The sound of our footsteps over this place was like thumping over a hollow vessel of immense size...." It's quite a feeling to walk through a spot and experience the same thing that someone else experienced 170 years earlier.

Shoshone Lake is one of Yellowstone's most popular backcountry areas, not only with day hikers and backpackers, but also with canoeists and kayakers (I highly recommend advance reservations for campsites during July and August). The lake can be reached via a variety of routes. The shortest routes are the Dogshead Trail and the DeLacy Creek Trail. There are also a series of trails that circumnavigate the lake. These trails open up the possibility of numerous loop or semi-loop hikes.

Trail names can be a little confusing here, but I have attempted to use the same names that the NPS uses on their trail signs. The "true" Shoshone Lake Trail starts at Lone Star Geyser Basin, travels to Shoshone Lake and Shoshone Geyser Basin, then follows the west and south shorelines (although not historically accurate, this section is sometimes called the South Shoshone Trail) until it ends at the Dogshead Trailhead. The "true" DeLacy Creek Trail starts at the DeLacy Creek Trailhead, goes to the east shore of the lake, and then travels south along the east shore (this section is sometimes called the East Shore Trail) to the Dogshead Trail junction. I know we'll all feel better about ourselves, and avoid embarrassment, by using the proper nomenclature. ❧

SHOSHONE LAKE TRAIL 🛡️ Map #22, 24, 25, 26, 29

Lone Star Trailhead (just south of Kepler Cascades on the Old Faithful–West Thumb Road) to:

Lone Star Geyser	2.5 miles	4 km
Grants Pass	6	9.5
Bechler River Trail Jct.	6.7	10.7
Horse Bypass Trail Jct.	7.7	12.8
North Shoshone Lake Trail Jct.	8.8	14
Shoshone Geyser Basin Trail	8.8	14
Moose Creek	15	24
Lewis Channel Trail Jct.	18	28.8
Dogshead Trailhead	22.5	35.8

Starting from the Lone Star Trailhead, the Shoshone Lake Trail follows the bike path along the Firehole River to Lone Star Geyser. From the geyser, the trail crosses the Firehole River by bridge and then follows the river past hot springs, through a forest, and out into a meadow where elk and bison are occasionally seen during spring and fall. The trail then re-enters the forest and climbs moderately (300 feet) to Grants Pass. From the pass, the trail descends to the junction with the Bechler River Trail. The Shoshone Lake Trail continues down towards the lake, crossing Shoshone Creek by informal bridge (two logs side by side), and meeting the Horse Bypass Trail (this 2-mile trail skirts around the Shoshone Geyser Basin and joins back up with the Shoshone Lake Trail farther south).

From the north Horse Bypass Trail junction, the Shoshone Lake Trail continues along Shoshone Creek and then comes to the junction with the North Shoshone Lake Trail. After this junction, the Shoshone Lake Trail crosses a large bog on a footbridge and then comes to another junction. To the left, a spur trail (260 yards long) goes to a landing spot for canoes and kayaks on Shoshone Lake. The spur trail passes by some interesting thermal features and provides easy access to the lakeshore. To the right (south), the Shoshone Lake Trail continues through the geyser basin. Please stay on the trail through this section, both for your safety and to limit damage to the fragile thermal features and delicate soil.

The trail travels through the geyser basin for a mile and then meets the south Horse Bypass Trail junction. From this point, the trail heads down towards the lakeshore and provides a nice view of the west end marsh and Shoshone Lake—but be prepared to wade through up to 10 inches of standing water if you're using this trail before August. (This section of trail from the Shoshone Geyser Basin to the junction with the Lewis Channel Trail may also be referred to as the South Shoshone Trail.) From the west lakeshore, the trail starts climbing through the spruce and fir forest to a ridge-top at about 8,300 feet. This 500-foot climb and subsequent 400-foot descent to Moose Creek is an indication of this trail segment's nature—up and down. In recent years there have been minor trail re routes to ease the grade of the trail, but you still will actually gain and lose about 1,400 feet in elevation between the west shore and the Lewis Channel Trail junction. Traveling alongside the meadows of Moose Creek is the scenic highlight of this area—there are good wildflower displays and a chance to see deer or moose in the evenings or mornings.

After a shallow crossing of Moose Creek, the Shoshone Lake Trail climbs up and down another forested ridge (200-foot elevation gain and loss). This is followed by another climb (200 feet) up through a 1988-burned area to a ridge top at 8,060 feet. From here, you descend steeply to the Lewis River Channel. The crossing of the channel is about 1.5- to 2-feet deep after mid-July. One-quarter mile farther is the Lewis Channel Trail junction, followed soon after by the junction with the Dogshead Trail—both trails lead to the Dogshead Trailhead, but the Dogshead Trail is the shortest route out. You also may choose to continue on around the lake via the DeLacy Creek Trail. ♣

DELACY CREEK TRAIL   Map #24, 25

DeLacy Creek Trailhead to:

Shoshone Lake	3 miles	5 km
North Shoshone Lake Trail Jct.	3	5
Lewis Channel	7.5	12
Dogshead Trailhead (via Dogshead Trail)	11	17.5

The DeLacy Creek Trail is the shortest route to Shoshone Lake. The DeLacy Creek Trailhead is located 8 miles east of Old Faithful on the Old Faithful–West Thumb Road.

The trail starts out through forest, with DeLacy Creek winding alongside. After about a mile, the trail leaves the forest and enters the open meadows of the creek. Both coyotes and moose are commonly seen in these meadows, along with sandhill cranes, mallards, and other waterfowl. The trail continues to follow the edge of the forest and meadows all the way to the shoreline of Shoshone Lake and the junction with the North Shoshone Lake Trail. At the lakeshore, the trail heads south along the east shore. The trail follows the shoreline through a mixed pine-spruce-fir forest, providing frequent views of Shoshone Lake, including a particularly nice one about 100 feet above the lake. The DeLacy Creek Trail ends at the Dogshead Trail junction, where you can either go out to out to Dogshead Trailhead or continue around the lake via the Shoshone Lake Trail. &

NORTH SHOSHONE LAKE TRAIL   Map #24, 25
(One-way distance: 8.4 miles, 13.4 km)

This trail travels from the Shoshone Geyser Basin area to the DeLacy Creek Trail, roughly following the north shore of Shoshone Lake. The western section of the trail is almost entirely forested, offers very few views of the lake, and gains and loses about 900 feet in elevation (in a series of 200-foot climbs and descents). The eastern section, near the mouth of DeLacy Creek, is much more scenic. The only creek crossing is that of DeLacy Creek, which can usually be crossed on a log jam or easily waded at the creek's mouth. &

DOGSHEAD TRAIL   Map #24, 25, 29
(One-way distance: 4 miles, 6.4 km)

The Dogshead Trail is the shortest route in to Shoshone Lake from the South Entrance Road. It leaves from the Dogshead Trailhead (about ½ mile north of Lewis Lake on the west side of the South Entrance Road) and travels through forest burned by the fires of 1988. From the trailhead, it initially follows an old service road for about 1.3 miles and then becomes an actual trail at the Dogshead Creek crossing (usually dry by mid-summer). The trail climbs gradually about 200 vertical feet up and over a forested ridge (good views of Mt. Sheridan and Shoshone Lake), and then down to the junction with the Shoshone Lake Trail (left) and DeLacy Creek Trail (right). ♣

LEWIS RIVER CHANNEL TRAIL   Map #24, 25, 29
(One-way distance: 6.5 miles, 10.5 km)

The trail starts just west of the Dogshead Trailhead (about ½ mile north of Lewis Lake on the west side of the South Entrance Road). It follows the Lewis River channel and provides a longer, but more scenic, route than the Dogshead Trail to Shoshone Lake. From the trailhead, the Lewis River Channel Trail goes west, toward the north shore of Lewis Lake. This first mile is extremely wet, with sections of standing water, until it dries out in late June or early July. Look for huckleberry bushes in this area, usually ripening in late August and through September. From the lakeshore, the trail heads west toward the Lewis River channel and follows it for about the last 3.5 miles to Shoshone Lake. This scenic section of trail is used mainly by fishermen, but is quite worthwhile even if you don't have a rod and reel. The trail ends at the junction with the Shoshone Lake Trail. By following this trail north, you can join the Dogshead Trail and loop back to the Dogshead Trailhead. ♣

BECHLER RIVER & FALLS RIVER AREA

The Bechler area of Yellowstone is also called the Cascade Corner, a fitting name for an area that contains over half of all the park's waterfalls. Fed by creeks and rivers coming off the Madison and Pitchstone plateaus, many of these falls drop over 100 feet. The highest is Union Falls, at 250 feet. Although not as high, Cave Falls, Colonnade Falls, Ouzel Falls, Dunanda Falls, and the many others in this area are all magnificent sights.

The Bechler River and Falls River area is lower and wetter than most of Yellowstone. The park's weather usually comes from the southwest, and much of the moisture from these systems is dropped when the clouds hit the southwest corner of the Yellowstone Plateau (Bechler Meadows and the Pitchstone Plateau). Consequently, the vegetation in Bechler consists of more than just lodgepole pine. You may fine Douglas fir, aspen, and willows in Bechler Meadows; Engelmann spruce, huckleberry, raspberry, thimbleberry, ferns, and mosses in Bechler Canyon; and buffalo berry, gooseberry, and mountain ash along Falls River and Mountain Ash Creek. Even though the area is wet most years, during the drought of 1994 a major forest fir hit the Bechler area and burned 8,400 acres. The fire moved from the west boundary near Robinson Creek to north of Bechler Meadows (near Dunanda Falls), and then continued west along the north rim of Bechler Canyon.

Wildlife viewing opportunities in the area are varied. Both black and grizzly bears, wolves, moose, mule deer, elk, sandhill cranes, and great blue herons are some of the more impressive animals seen in the Bechler River and Falls River areas. Black bears have frequented the berry patches in Bechler Canyon for years, and, since 1994, grizzly bear sightings also occur regularly. The cranes, herons, wolves, and moose are typically seen in Bechler Meadows, while the deer and elk may be seen just about anywhere.

The large amount of precipitation in the Bechler area can cause high stream crossings, muddy trails, and swampy meadows before mid-July. Since most of the major trails have significant stream or river crossings, the most enjoyable time to hike here is during late August and September. By this time, the meadows have dried up, the streams have gone down, and the mosquitoes have thinned out. If you're willing to gamble, you can even try visiting Bechler in October. It's easy to get campsites, mild sunny days are possible, and stream crossings are at their lowest. Of course, you could also get a huge winter storm and end up cursing whomever it was that suggested hiking in October.

Many of the trails in the Bechler area start from either the trailhead at the Bechler Ranger Station or the trailhead at Cave Falls. Driving east from Ashton, Idaho, is the shortest route—26 miles—to these trailheads. In Ashton, turn east off U.S. 20 onto Main Street/Route 47 and follow signs toward Marysville and then Cave Falls Road. The road eventually turns to dirt, but is usually passable in a regular, two-wheel drive vehicle. After you cross the Wyoming State Line, look for the left-hand turnoff for the Bechler Ranger Station. From this turnoff, it is 1.5 miles to the ranger station. To reach the trailhead at Cave Falls, continue on the Cave Falls Road, past the turnoff for the ranger station, for approximately 3 more miles. At Cave Falls, the road branches; the lower loop heads to the base of Cave Falls, while the upper loop leads to the trailhead for the Bechler River Trail and to a trail to the Cave Falls overlook. Parking is located on the west side of this loop, near the outhouse. This is a popular day-use area and has limited parking space and no parking for trailers.

Other trailheads in the Bechler area are most easily accessed by way of Grassy Lake Road (also known as Reclamation Road or Ashton–Flagg Ranch Road). Grassy Lake Road may be accessed either in Ashton, Idaho, or, more commonly, just north of Flagg Ranch, about 2 miles south of Yellowstone's South Entrance gate on U.S. 89. It is a gravel road and conditions change monthly and yearly. In its best condition, the road may be driven in regular passenger vehicles, though the higher the clearance, the better. Check at a visitor center in Ashton or at the Yellowstone's South Entrance Ranger Station for current conditions. ❧

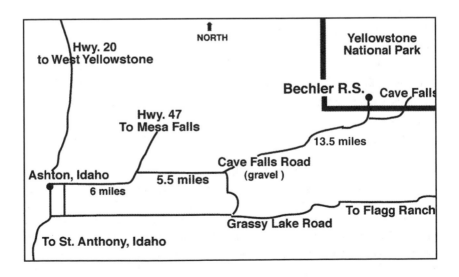

Bechler R.S. to Lone Star Geyser Trailhead–South Section

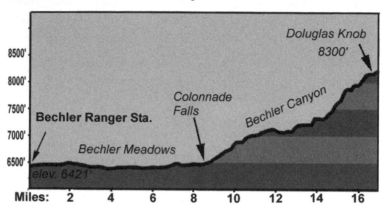

BECHLER RIVER AND
BECHLER MEADOWS TRAILS

Map #24, 25, 26, 27

Bechler Ranger Station to:

Bechler River Cutoff Trail	0.1 miles	0.16 km
Boundary Creek Trail Jct.	1.6	2.6
Boundary Creek	3.5	5.6
Bechler Ford	5.5	8.8
Colonnade Falls	8.6	13.8
Three Rivers Junction	14	22.4
Douglas Knob	17	27.2
Shoshone Lake Trail Jct.	23.5	37.6
Lone Star Geyser	27.6	44.1
Lone Star Geyser Trailhead	30	48

The Bechler (pronounced "bek-ler") River Trail provides access to the most spectacular display of waterfalls and cascades found anywhere in Yellowstone. Cave Falls, Bechler Falls, Colonnade and Iris falls, Ragged Falls, Twister Falls, and others are all located along this spectacular trail. The trail also travels through Bechler Meadows, which is excellent wildlife habitat, especially for moose, wolves, mule deer, cranes, and herons. Bechler Meadows can be quite mucky, and mosquitoes quite numerous, through the end of July. From Bechler Meadows, the trail travels through the lush forest of Bechler Canyon up to the Madison Plateau, then joins the Shoshone Lake Trail, travels over Grants Pass and down to the Firehole River and past Lone Star Geyser.

From the south, there are two starting points for the Bechler River Trail. The longer route starts from the Cave Falls Trailhead (at the end of the Cave Falls Road, 26 miles east from Ashton, Idaho). There is limited parking at Cave Falls, and no trailers are allowed (see introduction to the Bechler area for detailed driving directions). This route follows the Bechler River past Bechler Falls and is the true Bechler River Trail. The shorter route starts at the Bechler Ranger Station and uses the Bechler Meadows Trail to reach the upper stretch of the Bechler River Trail. This is also the most convenient route because of the ample parking and proximity to the ranger station, and is the route for which distances are listed on the previous page.

The actual Bechler River Trail starts at the end of the Cave Falls Road and is marked by a trail sign. Park on the west side of the road's upper loop and look for the trailhead on the southeast side of the loop. The trail travels upstream, past Bechler Falls, to Rocky Ford, where it makes an unbridged crossing of the Bechler River. Rocky Ford is usually thigh deep after the water goes down in mid-July. The ford contains blocky rocks that can make for tricky footing— cross 30 feet downstream from the actual trail crossing. From the ford, the Bechler River Trail continues about another ¾ mile to the junction with the Mountain Ash Creek Trail. The Bechler River Trail continues north (left) at this junction and travels along the east side of the river until it joins the Bechler Meadows Trail near the Bechler Ford. This route is longer, although arguably more scenic, and the ford of the river, at Rocky Ford, is more difficult than on the standard route described below.

From Bechler Ranger Station, the Bechler Meadows Trail travels through lodgepole pine forest and meadow, crosses Boundary Creek by way of a suspension bridge, and comes to the Bechler River Ford. The crossing of the Bechler River is pretty straightforward here, with good footing on the river bottom, but should not be attempted before the river starts going down later in July. This is a scenic spot, with the river and meadows in the foreground and the Teton Range as a backdrop.

From the Bechler Ford, the trail leaves the river and soon joins the Bechler River Trail. The path now winds through lodgepole pine forest and meadows for about 1 mile until it again reaches the river and enters the Bechler Canyon. From this point, the trail follows the river past Colonnade and Iris falls. Past Iris Falls, the trail makes two crossings of the Bechler River in about 1.5 miles. The first crossing can be difficult because of tricky footing and a deep pocket of water—if you cross at the trail. There is an easier crossing 30 feet downstream from the trail. Orange diamonds mark either side of the river crossing and you may notice riffles indicating shallower water. Once across this ford, you may want to leave your wading shoes on, as there are numerous side springs that need to be crossed before you reach the next ford of the Bechler River (which you should be able to cross right at the trail).

Bechler R.S. to Lone Star Geyser Trailhead–North Section

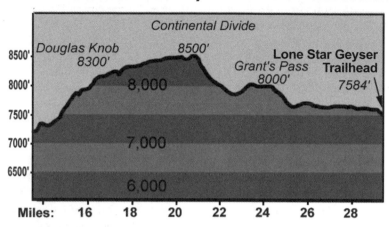

Three Rivers Junction is the confluence of Phillips Fork, Gregg Fork, and Ferris Fork, and is a popular camping area. The Bechler River Trail crosses the Ferris Fork just below Ragged Falls. Because of runoff from hot springs upstream, the water in this creek is warm. After crossing Ferris Fork, the Bechler River Trail climbs a short distance to a bluff that provides a good view of Ragged Falls. Once past the bluff, the trail breaks out into a little clearing where you will see the Ferris Fork Trail heading to the right (east) past a hitch rail (leave your horses here if you take a side trip along the Ferris Fork Trail—no stock are allowed on this short trail). The Ferris Fork Trail goes upstream along the Ferris Fork about ½ mile, passing some interesting thermal features along the way. Recent changes in the thermal activity have caused areas of hot, unstable ground close to, and on, this trail. Watch your footing and don't assume that it is safe just because you are on a trail.

From the clearing, the Bechler River Trail reenters the forest and continues climbing 600 feet in 2 miles along the Gregg Fork, crossing it once about ¼ mile above Twister Falls. From Twister Falls, the trail climbs about 300 more feet up to the base of Douglas Knob. After passing Douglas Knob, the trail goes through the meadows of the Littles Fork, where moose might be spotted. From these meadows, the trail climbs gradually through forest up to the Continental Divide. The trail then descends into a small valley and climbs out the other side over another section of the Continental Divide. From this ridge, the Bechler River Trail heads downhill, losing about 700 feet in elevation in the 2 miles to the junction with the Shoshone Lake Trail. From this junction (you're now actually following the Shoshone Lake Trail out to the trailhead), the trail makes a short easy climb up to Grants Pass, which will be your third crossing of the Continental Divide. It's all downhill from here, as the trail descends through forest to the Firehole River and follows it out past Lone Star Geyser to the Lone Star Trailhead. ❧

BOUNDARY CREEK TRAIL   Map #26, 27

Bechler Ranger Station to:

Boundary Creek .... 5 miles......... 8 km
Dunanda Falls .... 8 .... 12.8
Buffalo Lake... 16 .... 25.7

Starting from Bechler Ranger Station, this trail actually follows the Bechler Meadows Trail for the first 1.6 miles. After branching left off the Bechler Meadows Trail, the Boundary Creek Trail continues through forest and past intermittent meadows and ponds until it emerges in Bechler Meadows, crossing Bartlett Slough. The slough can be kind of scary looking, as you may not be able to see the bottom, and during high water it may be up to 4-feet deep. Yet, once the water goes down in July, it is actually a simple crossing with a nice, hard bottom, easy footing, and slow water. Moose are often spotted in this area. A mile from Bartlett Slough, the trail crosses Boundary Creek, requiring a knee-to thigh-deep ford after water levels go down in July.

Once across Boundary Creek, the trail follows the creek upstream through meadows where sandhill cranes and great blue herons are occasionally seen. After crossing Boundary Creek you may want to leave your wading shoes on, as there are numerous small creek crossings before reaching Dunanda Falls. After following Boundary Creek about a mile, the trail leaves the creek and travels upstream along one of its tributaries. The Boundary Creek Trail follows this meandering stream for about 1 mile, makes a bridged crossing, and heads through the forest to Silver Scarf Falls. From Silver Scarf Falls, a spur trail leads about 200 feet west to the brink of Dunanda Falls. Both of these falls are quite impressive, but Silver Scarf Falls does lose much of its water by the end of the summer. Remnants of the 1994 fires are visible from this area.

From Silver Scarf Falls, the trail travels up through the forested canyon on Boundary Creek and gains about 400 feet in the first 2 miles past the falls. The trail continues to climb, but more gradually, as it follows Boundary Creek (crossing it up to three times) to a large meadow. This section of trail along Boundary Creek and up to Buffalo Lake has a variety of interesting features, including thermal areas, grottos, a talus slope (with pikas), and a scenic canyon. You will also hike through about 1.5 miles of burned forest from the 2000 fire. Very few people hike in this part of the Bechler area. The trail eventually leaves the creek and travels northwest through the forest to Buffalo Lake, a small, meadow-lined lake that is home to a wide variety of waterfowl, including grebes, scaups, mallards, and cranes. Moose are also commonly seen in this area.

It is possible, but not advised, to continue on to the West Boundary Trail. There is an old clear-cut right up to the boundary. It has grown back as a thick, dog hair lodgepole forest. The trail is not cleared and may be hard to follow. There is little of scenic interest along the route. ♣

WEST BOUNDARY TRAIL   Map #26, 27

Bechler Ranger Station to:

Robinson Lake .... 2 miles......... 3.2 km
Robinson Creek .... 4 .... 6.5
West Boundary .... 9 .... 14.5

Technically, the West Boundary Trail travels from Bechler Ranger Station up to the West Entrance at West Yellowstone, Montana, but in actuality only a short portion of that is consistently marked and maintained by the National Park Service. And not coincidentally, the marked and maintained portion is also the most interesting for hiking.

From Bechler Ranger Station, the trail travels through relatively level coniferous forest to Robinson Lake and then drops down into the canyon of Robinson Creek. The next 5 miles in this intimate little canyon, with its rushing creek, a pretty cascade, and lush vegetation, are the highlight of the trip. You'll also notice the effects of the 1994 fire in parts of the canyon. Consistent trail marking and maintenance ends where the trail meets the west boundary. It is possible to continue north on the West Boundary Trail all the way up to Buffalo Lake, or even Summit Lake, by using a map and compass and following the clear-cut that borders much of the boundary in this area, but this is not recommended as the scenery is very similar to other areas that are served by maintained trails. ♣

TRAILS TO BECHLER FALLS   Map #26, 27

Cave Falls Trailhead to Bechler Falls
(Roundtrip distance: 2.6 miles, 4.2 km)

Cave Falls T.H.–Bechler Falls–Bechler R.S.–Cave Falls T.H. Loop
(Roundtrip distance: 7.3 miles, 11.6 km)

The easiest way to get to Bechler Falls is from the trailhead at the end of the Cave Falls Road. Once you reach the falls you can retrace your steps to the trailhead or you can make a longer loop hike out of it. Either way this is a pleasant hike that takes you past Bechler Falls and provides some nice views of the Bechler River along the way. Starting at the Cave Falls Trailhead, head upstream along the Bechler River Trail, passing the confluence of the Bechler and Falls rivers and then continuing up to Bechler Falls. At this point you can either return to the Cave Falls Trailhead or continue another mile upstream to a junction with the Bechler River Cutoff Trail. Take this cutoff trail through relatively level forest for 1.5 miles to the Bechler Ranger Station. From the Ranger Station you will head south along the South Boundary Trail, fording a small stream within the first ½ mile of the trail. The trail remains relatively flat for the next 1.5 miles, passing through lodgepole pine forest, and then descends to parallel the Cave Falls Road and reaches Cave Falls and back to the Cave Falls Trailhead. ♠

TRAILS TO UNION FALLS

Formed as two creeks merge and simultaneously plunge 250 feet over the edge of Pitchstone Plateau, Union Falls is one of Yellowstone's most impressive waterfalls. There are five routes to Union Falls, and it is a relatively popular backcountry destination. The three easiest and shortest routes start from Grassy Lake Road (for driving directions to Grassy Lake Road, see introduction to the Bechler area, page 148).

GRASSY LAKE TO UNION FALLS (MOUNTAIN ASH CREEK TRAIL–EAST)   Map #26, 28

Grassy Lake Trailhead to:

Falls River Ford	1 miles	1.6 km
Proposition Creek	5	8
Mountain Ash Creek	5.5	9
Union Falls	7.5	12

To reach the Grassy Lake Trailhead, travel west from U.S. 89 on Grassy Lake Road for 11.3 miles, to Grassy Lake Reservoir. On the northeast end of the Grassy Lake Reservoir dam, there is a steep spur road leading downhill, that crosses an outlet stream before arriving at a parking area at the base of the dam. Rather than chance getting stuck down below, some people park at the top of this road and walk down the steep section (recommended if your car is not four-wheel drive). From the trailhead, the trail parallels, on the west side, the outlet stream and then Falls River, heading northwest. The trail soon meets a junction with a trail coming from Cascade Creek Trailhead. Stay right at this junction and you will immediately come to a crossing of Falls River. This wide ford can be thigh deep and swift before mid-July. After that, it subsides to an easy, but slippery, knee-deep crossing (wading shoes are mandatory).

After the ford, the trail climbs gradually up to the junction with the Pitchstone Plateau Trail, and then continues to climb 200 feet to the top of a lodgepole pine- and whortleberry-covered ridge. After staying along the top of this broad ridge for 2 miles, the trail descends steeply 600 feet to Proposition Creek, where you may see monkshood, paintbrush, sticky geranium, beargrass, and other flowers blooming (July to early August). Fallen logs make crossing the creek easy.

From Proposition Creek, the trail climbs up and over another 200-foot ridge to the trail junction at Mountain Ash Creek. The Mountain Ash Creek Trail continues west while the Union Falls Trail heads northeast (right). The Union Falls Trail follows Mountain Ash Creek upstream and then crosses it by bridge after ½ mile. Here, a small, unnamed creek joins Mountain Ash Creek from the west. Feel this stream's water and notice its warmth. About a mile farther up the Union Falls Trail, near the hitch rail, an unmarked spur trail turns left off the main trail and goes about ½ mile up to a small waterfall on that warm creek. The Union Falls Trail continues on to the right, and ends near the top of Union Falls. Stock are not allowed on the spur trail or at Union Falls. Getting to the base of Union Falls can be tricky because there is no trail and the steep slope is slippery due to the spray from the falls. ♣

FISH LAKE TO UNION FALLS   Map #26, 27, 28
(One-way distance: 6.5 miles 10.5 km)

This route is the shortest to Union Falls and has the least amount of elevation gain. The only drawback to the route is that you have to drive about 8 miles farther on Grassy Lake Road to reach the trailhead if you are coming from Yellowstone's South Entrance. And, if you don't have a high clearance vehicle, you will have to add 1.5 miles to the above hiking distance.

Take the Fish Lake/Loon Lake turnoff (Road #048, may not be signed) on Grassy Lake Road, about 8 miles west of Grassy Lake Reservoir. The Fish Lake/ Loon Lake Road forks after about ¼ mile. If you have a high clearance vehicle, drive up the road to the right (Road #047, may not be signed); otherwise, park at the fork in the road and walk to the Fish Lake Trailhead from here (about an extra 1.5 miles).

From the Fish Lake parking area, the trail heads north and soon crosses the park boundary, intersects the South Boundary Trail, and comes to the Falls

River within the first mile. The ford of the Falls River can have some tricky footing and should not be attempted before the water recedes in July. After that, it is knee to thigh deep. Wading shoes are a must.

The trail continues north from the Falls River through relatively level forest for a little less than 2 miles until it makes an easy crossing of Mountain Ash Creek and joins the Mountain Ash Creek Trail. Follow the Mountain Ash Creek Trail upstream (to the northeast) as it passes through willow meadows, makes another easy crossing of the creek, and climbs gently up toward the Union Falls Trail junction. From this junction, the Union Falls Trail follows Mountain Ash Creek upstream and then crosses it by bridge after ½ mile. Here, a small, unnamed creek joins Mountain Ash Creek from the west. Feel this stream's water and notice its warmth. About a mile farther up the Union Falls Trail, near the hitch rail, an unmarked spur trail turns left off the main trail and goes about ½ mile up to a small waterfall on that warm creek. The Union Falls Trail continues on to the right, and ends near the top of Union Falls. Stock are not allowed on the spur trail or at Union Falls. Getting to the base of Union Falls can be tricky because there is no trail and the steep slope is slippery due to the spray from the falls. ♣

BECHLER RANGER STATION TO UNION FALLS (MOUNTAIN ASH CREEK TRAIL–WEST)
(One-way distance: 11.9 miles 19 km)   Map #26, 27, 28

For those hikers wanting to reach Union Falls from the Bechler Ranger Station, this route uses parts of the Bechler River Trail and the Mountain Ash Creek Trail. Part of this route follows the old Marysville Road, a wagon road built by the Mormons in the 1880s that ran from Marysville, Idaho, to Jackson Hole, Wyoming. (For directions to the Bechler Ranger Station, see introduction to the Bechler area, page 148.)

From the Bechler Ranger Station, take the Bechler River Cutoff Trail to the Bechler River and then follow the river upstream to Rocky Ford. The hike along this section of the river is very pleasant. Rocky Ford is usually thigh deep after the water goes down in mid-July. The ford contains blocky rocks that can make for tricky footing—cross 30 feet downstream from the actual trail crossing. From the ford, the Bechler River Trail continues about another ¾ mile to the junction with the Mountain Ash Creek Trail. Turn right on to the Mountain Ash Creek Trail and follow it through areas of forest and meadows. After about 2.5 miles it meets the trail coming from Fish Lake. To reach Union Falls, stay on the Mountain Ash Creek Trail (see Fish Lake to Union Falls on the previous page for a description of this section of the trail). ♣

CAVE FALLS TO UNION FALLS   Map #26, 27, 28
(One-way distance: 9.5 miles 15 km)

This route starts by leaving the Cave Falls Road and heading east on the South Boundary Trail. (For directions to Cave Falls Road, see introduction to the Bechler area, page 148.) The trailhead is located about ¾ mile before (southwest of) Cave Falls proper, where the South Boundary Trail meets the road; however, there is no parking available at this location. Parking is available once the road comes to a dead-end, approximately one mile past the trailhead. Heading east from the trailhead, the trail immediately crosses the Falls River. This crossing is the biggest in the Bechler area, is very wide and swift, and shouldn't be attempted before the low water levels in August. Once across the river, continue on the South Boundary Trail for about 4 miles, past the meadows of Winegar Lake and Junco Lake, until you reach the junction with the Fish Lake Cutoff Trail (see Fish Lake Fish Lake Cutoff Trail (see Fish Lake to Union Falls on page 156 for a description of the remainder of the route to Union Falls). ❧

CASCADE CREEK TRAILHEAD TO TERRACED FALLS
AND UNION FALLS   Map #26, 28

Cascade Creek Trailhead to:

Mountain Ash Creek Trail Jct.	0.3 miles	0.5 km
Terraced Falls	1.6	2.6
Union Falls	7.5	12

This trail starts on Grassy Lake Road about 1.5 miles west of Grassy Lake Reservoir, approximately 13 miles from Flagg Ranch. Look for the sign for Cascade Creek Trailhead on the right (north); parking is available on the north side of the road. From the trailhead, the trail goes north along an old roadbed for about .3 mile and then comes to a trail junction. The right fork of this junction immediately crosses Cascade Creek and then travels about a mile to meet the Mountain Ash Creek Trail (see Grassy Lake to Union Falls on page 155 for a description of the remainder of the route to Union Falls). To go to Terraced Falls (no stock allowed), take the left fork of the trail. The trail continues for 1.3 miles through a forested area, paralleling first Cascade Creek and then Falls River, before reaching Terraced Falls—a multiple waterfall in a spectacular volcanic canyon. It's a great short day hike, especially in late summer or early fall. ❧

PITCHSTONE PLATEAU TRAIL   Map #26, 28, 29

Phantom/Pitchstone Trailhead on South Entrance Road to:

Phantom Fumarole... 4.5 miles......6 km
Phantom Campsite .... 5.5..............9
Benchmark 8715 .... 8.................13
Proposition Creek... 14.5............23
Mountain Ash Creek Trail... 16.5............26
Grassy Lake Reservoir .... 18..............29

The Pitchstone Plateau is an immense, solidified lava flow. The top of the plateau was, in the not too distant past, largely open meadows. Due to forest succession, the Pitchstone Plateau is now more heavily forested, but still has open grassy areas and volcanic rock outcrops to break up the scenery. This trail receives very little use, and finding the trail may be difficult. Surface water is scarce after the snow melts, so bring extra water with you. Cross-country navigating can be confusing for those considering off-trail travel. Also, due to the heavy snowfall during the winter, the Pitchstone Plateau Trail may not completely melt out before mid-July.

From the South Entrance Road, the trail starts at the Phantom/Pitchstone Trailhead about 2 miles south of Lewis Falls. The trail climbs steeply at first, and then more gradually as it nears the open grassland of the plateau. It reaches Phantom Fumarole after about 4.5 miles. This is a small thermal area containing steam vents and mudpots. A mile farther, the trail reaches a cold-water spring, shown on old maps as Phantom Campsite. Elk, mule deer, and coyotes all frequent this area for water. If you don't see them, you'll surely see their tracks.

From the spring, the trail continues to climb as it again enters the open grassland. The highest point of the trail (8,715 feet) is reached after about 2.5 miles from the spring. There are good views of the Falls River Basin to the southwest, the Grand Tetons to the south, and Mt. Sheridan to the northeast. Much of the trail above tree line, which is marked with rock cairns, receives very little use and may be hard to follow due to the little use it receives. The Pitchstone Plateau Trail then descends gradually about 1,200 feet in 6.5 miles to Proposition Creek. After a log crossing of the creek, the trail continues to descend through forest to the Mountain Ash Creek Trail. From this junction, it is 1.5 miles out to Grassy Lake Road. &

SOUTH BOUNDARY TRAIL–
GRASSY LAKE TO SOUTH ENTRANCE   Map #26, 28, 29

Beula Lake Trailhead to:

South Boundary Lake	2 miles	3.2 km
Polecat Creek	4	6.5
Tanager Lake	6	9.5
South Entrance	7	11.2

The best place to start this trail is at the east end of Grassy Lake Reservoir (on the Grassy Lake Road), at the Beula Lake Trailhead. Follow the Beula Lake Trail as it climbs up the forested ridge about ½ mile to the junction with the South Boundary Trail. The trail travels remarkably straight along the park's south boundary, through lodgepole pine, Engelmann Spruce, and sub-alpine fir forest. The trail descends to the pond-lily lined shores of South Boundary Lake. From the lake, the trail continues through forest to a good overlook of the Snake River Valley and Huckleberry Ridge to the east. The trail descends steeply from the overlook to Polecat Creek. There is no longer a bridge over the creek; the ford is only about 1-foot deep. The trail then climbs over a low ridge to Tanager Lake, where moose may be seen, especially in the meadows north of the lake. The South Boundary Trail then descends and exits at the South Entrance NPS horse corrals. ♠

BEULA LAKE TRAIL   Map #26, 28, 29
(One-way distance: 3 miles, 5 km)

The Beula Lake Trail starts from the east end of Grassy Lake Reservoir (on Grassy Lake Road) at the Beula Lake Trailhead. The trail immediately climbs 400 feet in elevation up a steep, forested ridge. Near the top, the South Boundary Trail crosses your path. The Beula Lake Trail remains on top of this ridge for about 1.5 miles and then descends gradually to the lodgepole-ringed shore of Beula Lake. In the past, trumpeter swans were seen on this lake. The Falls River flows out of the west end of Beula Lake. ♠

SNAKE RIVER AREA

Here starts the Snake River—a river that will flow through Wyoming, Idaho, and Washington before it joins with the Columbia River to be carried into the Pacific Ocean. In 2004, the Upper Snake River was designated a National Wild and Scenic River. Its headwaters in Yellowstone contain a potpourri of interesting, beautiful, and wild scenery. Here, elk feed in the high meadows of Big Game Ridge; twisted, wind-shaped whitebark pines sit atop Mt. Sheridan; Rustic Geyser erupts on the shore of Heart Lake; and the Snake River flows through pristine meadows and marshes. Yellowstone's Snake River Area was extensively burned during the 1988 fires, drastically changing the area from predominately mature, dark forest to a landscape with a much more open feel. When the trail passes through an unburned section of the former forest type, after miles and miles of the new post-fire regrowth, the contrast can be quite striking.

The area isn't for beginners. There are many streams and rivers to be crossed, long distances to be hiked, and steep ridges to be climbed. For those who do choose to hike here, the wilderness experience that can be gained is well worth the hardship. The best time to travel through the Snake River area is during August and September, when the streams, rivers, and mosquitoes are on their ebb. &

Yellowstone Lake and Mt. Sheridan

Heart Lake Trail

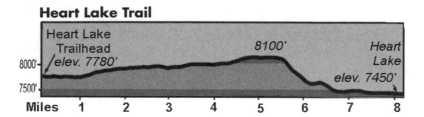

Miles   1   2   3   4   5   6   7   8

HEART LAKE TRAIL   Map #29, 30

Heart Lake Trailhead (5.4 miles south of Grant Village on the South Entrance Road) to:

Heart Lake .... 7.4 miles...... 11.9 km

Mt. Sheridan Trail Jct. .... 8 .... 12.9

Mt. Sheridan Lookout................................... 11.9............ 19

Sheridan Lake.. 12................ 19

Basin Creek Lake .... 14.5............ 23

Snake River .... 18................ 30

South Entrance.. 23.5............ 38

The Heart Lake Trail travels from the Heart Lake Trailhead to the South Boundary Trail. Heart Lake is the destination of many day hikers and backpackers, and receives relatively heavy use. The majority of people hiking the Heart Lake Trail start from the Heart Lake Trailhead, walk only as far as Heart Lake, and return by the same route. For those wishing to travel the entire length of this trail, it's best to travel north to south, as this avoids much of the altitude gain. Much of this area is good bear habitat and bear sightings are fairly common. After their reintroduction to Yellowstone in the mid-1990s, wolves have moved back into the area, and it's not unusual to hear their nighttime howling. On a more practical note, be aware that there is no drinking water to count on from the trailhead until you get to Heart Lake.

Starting at Heart Lake Trailhead, the first 5.5 miles of trail climbs very gradually through a forested area that was burned in the fires of 1988; now, 25 years later, the area is populated with thick lodgepole pine regrowth. The trail reaches an open thermal area with an impressive view, with Factory Hill and Heart Lake being the two most prominent features. From here, the trail drops down steeply into the Witch Creek drainage, which contains a number of hydrothermal features and provides dramatic clouds of water vapor on cold, clear mornings. The trail crosses Witch Creek on bridges and then arrives at a trail junction near the Heart Lake Ranger Station and the shore of Heart Lake. The trail to the left leads to campsites on the north shore of Heart Lake and to the Trail Creek Trail and Heart River Trail (take this route if you are following the CDT). The Heart Lake Trail continues southwest (right) at this junction and crosses another bridge over Witch Creek as it follows the shoreline of Heart Lake.

A few hundred yards down the trail, you'll cross the runoff channels of Rustic Geyser and other thermal features located on the hillside to the west. These thermal features can be reached by contouring over on a path that leaves the Heart Lake Trail near the Mt. Sheridan Trail junction. View these features from a safe distance; they are delicate and dangerous. By stepping in algae beds or on thin crust, you can wreck a fragile ecosystem and seriously burn yourself, as well. The animal bones spread around the bottom of these pools are testimony to the hazard of hot water.

After crossing the runoff channels, the Heart Lake Trail soon climbs up and away from the lakeshore. In about ½ mile, the trail meets the junction with the Mt. Sheridan Trail. The Heart Lake Trail continues on south of Heart Lake, passing Sheridan Lake and crossing Basin Creek. The section of trail between Sheridan Lake and campsite 8B1 has been significantly impacted by beaver activity. As of 2012, there was a 5-foot-high dam at the outlet of Sheridan Lake with water running over sections of the trail. Beavers are active throughout this area so don't be surprised by sections of submerged trail until the NPS is able to build trail reroutes. Along with the beavers, grizzly bears are active in this area during early summer, so stay alert. A short distance after crossing Basin Creek, you'll come to a trail junction. Here, the Basin Creek Cutoff Trail heads southeast (left) to hook up with the Snake River Trail.

The Heart Lake Trail continues south up to Basin Creek Lake. After a short climb above this lake, the trail crosses a notch in the ridge and descends into the meadows of the Red Creek drainage. Red Creek is crossed about 2 miles from the notch, and another 1.5 miles brings you to the Snake River. Crossing the Snake River in this area shouldn't be tried before mid-July, and after that it can still be thigh deep.

Once across the river, the Heart Lake Trail joins the South Boundary Trail. From this junction, it's 5.5 miles to the next crossing of the Snake River at the South Entrance. This ford is knee deep after mid-July with swiftly flowing water. After this ford, the trail climbs up the river embankment to the South Entrance Trailhead, located at the parking area behind the South Entrance Ranger Station. 🐾

MT. SHERIDAN LOOKOUT TRAIL   Map #29, 30
(One-way distance: 3 miles, 5 km)

The Mt. Sheridan Trail climbs about 2,700 feet in 3 miles from its starting point on the Heart Lake Trail. The trail ends at an ends at an unstaffed fire lookout station on top of the 10,308-foot peak. There is no easily accessible water along this trail, so bring enough for the roundtrip. Because snow lasts long into the summer, be careful selecting your route. Stay off steep, hard snow, and don't eat the watermelon-colored snow—it will make you sick. Once you finally arrive at the talus-covered summit of Mt. Sheridan, you'll have a marvelous view of Yellowstone Lake to the north, the Absaroka Range to the east, Pitchstone Plateau to the west, and the jagged peaks of the Teton Range to the south. The total distance from the Heart Lake Trailhead on the South Entrance Road to the summit of Mt. Sheridan is 11 miles, making this a popular two-day, one-night trip. If you plan to do it as a day hike, make sure you're in good enough shape to get up and down before dark. Due to the bear activity, this is no place to be wandering around at night. ❧

BASIN CREEK CUTOFF TRAIL   Map #29
(One-way distance: 2 miles, 3 km)

The Basin Creek Cutoff Trail follows Basin Creek, crossing the creek three times as it connects the Heart Lake Trail with the Snake River Trail. Due to recent (as of 2012) beaver activity, sections of this trail are flooded and the creek crossings can be 3- to 4-feet deep. Check at an NPS backcountry office for current conditions. Along with beavers, you may also spot moose feeding in or near Basin Creek. Grizzlies frequent this area throughout the summer. ❧

HEART RIVER TRAIL   Map #29
(One-way distance: 3 miles, 5 km)

The Heart River Trail starts 4.5 miles east of the Heart Lake Ranger Station and runs from the Trail Creek Trail to the Snake River Trail. It follows Heart River through boggy areas and burned forest. It makes two fords of the Heart River and one of Surprise Creek that are knee deep after mid-July. ❧

SOUTH BOUNDARY TRAIL

The eastern half of the South Boundary Trail travels from the South Entrance of Yellowstone to the Upper Yellowstone River Valley and Thorofare Ranger Station.   For most of this portion's 38 miles, it parallels the park's south boundary, traveling along the Snake River, climbing over Big Game Ridge and Two Ocean Plateau, and finally crossing the Yellowstone and Thorofare rivers. The variety of scenery is fascinating, including many miles of burned forest, but the hiking and stream crossings can be strenuous. The description of the South Boundary Trail is divided into three sections: (1) South Entrance to Harebell Patrol Cabin, (2) Harebell Patrol Cabin to Fox Creek Patrol Cabin, and (3) Fox Creek Patrol Cabin to Thorofare Ranger Station.

SOUTH ENTRANCE TRAILHEAD TO
HAREBELL PATROL CABIN   Map #29

South Entrance Trailhead to:

Heart Lake Trail Jct.	5.5 miles	9 km
Snake River Cutoff Trail Jct.	8	13
Harebell Patrol Cabin	12	19

The eastern half of the South Boundary Trail starts at the South Entrance Trailhead, which is located behind the South Entrance Ranger Station. To access the trailhead, park in the Snake River Picnic Area. Starting at this trailhead requires a deep crossing of the Snake River, usually not fordable until mid-July, or later, and knee deep and swift after that. Another possible starting point for this trail is on the south side of the highway bridge over the Snake River, about ½ mile south of Flagg Ranch (2.5 miles south of the South Entrance). This route (not an official trail) parallels the Snake River upstream on the hillside to the east, and then descends to the South Boundary Trail in the meadows across from the South Entrance Station. This route adds 3 miles to the distances listed above, and is unmarked and unmaintained (except for some occasional clearing done by hunting outfitters); by starting at this unofficial trailhead, no ford of the Snake River is necessary.

The South Boundary Trail follows the Snake River on an occasionally muddy trail, mainly through forest, to Snake Hot Springs, which are a small group of interesting thermal features located along the bank of the river. (During the winter, the runoff from these springs keeps the Snake from freezing immediately downstream of this area. Yet just upstream, at the Heart Lake

Trail ford, the river will usually be solid enough to ski across.) At 5.5 miles, the trail arrives at the junction with the Heart Lake Trail. From the junction, the South Boundary Trail turns southeast and passes through burned forest until it reaches a long meadow. At the north end of the meadow, you will arrive at the junction with the Snake River Cutoff Trail. The South Boundary Trail continues to the southern end of the meadow, and then leaves the Snake River and heads upstream on Wolverine Creek. The trail soon crosses Wolverine Creek, which requires a knee-deep ford (not fordable early in the season), and then comes to another trail junction. The trail heading south follows Wolverine Creek into the Bridger-Teton National Forest, though it is difficult to follow due to infrequent use. From this junction, the South Boundary Trail heads east (left), climbs 400 vertical feet in the next 1.5 miles and tops out on a ridge above Harebell Creek. Harebell Patrol Cabin is a mile farther. Near Harebell Patrol Cabin, there is a junction with the Harebell Cabin Cutoff Trail. This cutoff trail heads north, climbs over a burned ridge, and then descends about 500 vertical feet to a ford of the Snake River and then the junction with the Snake River Trail. ❧

HAREBELL PATROL CABIN TO
FOX CREEK PATROL CABIN   Map #29, 31
(One-way distance: 11.5 miles, 18.5 km)

From the Harebell Patrol Cabin, the trail follows Harebell Creek up the slopes of Big Game Ridge through heavily burned forest. Because of the lack of forest cover, this can be a hot and dusty climb on a sunny summer day. Be prepared, especially early in the hiking season, to find downed trees across this section of the trail. Harebell Creek is crossed twice in this section. Once out of the area of charred trees, you'll hike through open alpine meadows to the high point of the ridge (10,065 feet). You will have climbed about 2,400 feet in 7 miles from the cabin. On a clear day, the view from Big Game Ridge is well worth the climb. You can see Wyoming's two highest mountain ranges, the Teton Range to the southwest and the Wind River Range to the southeast. With a name like Big Game Ridge, it's only fitting that you'll probably also spot some elk. The elk feed on the grasses and forbs here from July through October. The descent from Big Game Ridge is steep, but enjoyable, as it passes through open stands of whitebark pine. Grizzlies feed on pine nuts in this area during the fall, so stay alert. Once down off the ridge, you'll come to the meadows of the Snake River Trail, reaching a trail junction before crossing the Snake River. The Snake River Trail heads north (left) at this junction, while the South Boundary Trail continues east across the river (an easy, knee-deep crossing after midsummer) to the Fox Creek Patrol Cabin. There is a trail heading south from the cabin area that goes into Bridger-Teton National Forest and leads to an extensive Forest Service trail system and the actual headwaters of the Snake River. ❧

FOX CREEK PATROL CABIN TO THOROFARE RANGER STATION (LYNX CREEK TRAIL)

Map #31, 33

Fox Creek Patrol Cabin to:

Two Ocean Plateau Trail Jct. .... 3 miles .... 5 km

Mariposa Lake .... 4 .... 6.5

Continental Divide 5.5 9

Yellowstone River Ford .... 11.5 .... 18.5

Thorofare Ranger Station 14 22

From Fox Creek Patrol Cabin, the South Boundary Trail travels up Plateau Creek, crossing it once, through intermittently burned forest. The trail crosses Mariposa Creek, then immediately comes to a junction with the Two Ocean Plateau Trail. The South Boundary Trail continues east up Mariposa Creek to Mariposa Lake. The trail gains about 900 feet in elevation from the cabin to Mariposa Lake—a shallow lake that contains cutthroat trout and is surrounded by meadows. East of the lake, the trail makes a shallow crossing of Mariposa Creek and continues up another 300 vertical feet through wet meadows and whitebark pine forest to the crest of Two Ocean Plateau (around 9,300 feet). Here, the path crosses the Continental Divide and descends into the drainage of the Atlantic Ocean.

The meadows of the Two Ocean Plateau are one of the highlights of this trail. Eagles, elk, moose, and bear all frequent this area throughout the summer and fall. Wildflowers abound. As you continue east down to the Lynx Creek side of the divide, there will be spectacular views of the Yellowstone River Valley and Trident Mountain to the east. Once the trail reaches the Yellowstone River Valley, you will have descended about 1,400 feet in the approximately 4.5 miles from the divide. Shortly after the last crossing of Lynx Creek, you will arrive at a trail junction on the South Boundary Trail near the confluence of the Yellowstone and Thorofare rivers. Fording the rivers at the confluence is actually easier than fording them separately later on. To take the spur trail to the confluence ford, turn left (northeast) at the trail junction and follow the path as it winds through an old burned section and then travels through a meadow area with tall willows—orange trail markers on snow stakes will lead the way. The ford, marked by orange squares on either side of the river, is slow moving and waist deep early in the season, subsiding to knee deep by late July or early August. After the ford, the spur trail continues past a side path to campsite 6Y4 and approximately 1.5 miles later ends at a "T" junction with another spur trail. Turn left (northeast) and you will soon come to the Thorofare Trail. Turn right (southwest) to return to the actual South Boundary Trail.

To continue on the South Boundary Trail instead of crossing at the confluence ford, turn right (south) at the trail junction mentioned in the preceding paragraph. The trail now parallels the Yellowstone River south through burned forest for about 1.5 miles until it reaches the Yellowstone River ford. This is a waist-deep ford, even late in the season. Luckily, the river flows fairly slowly through this section. There is a shallower place to cross if you diagonal upstream and look for the riffles. From the ford, the trail turns east and out into the meadows of the Yellowstone River Valley. From these meadows, you see mountains in all directions. It's a very special spot, and a long way from the nearest road. About a mile from the Yellowstone ford, the trail comes to a junction. The trail to Bridger Lake heads south (right) from here. A short distance farther on the South Boundary Trail, you will reach the ford of the Thorofare River. This is also a deep ford, but by scouting up or downstream a short way, you can usually find a shallower place to cross (thigh to waist deep after early August).

About ¼ mile east of the Thorofare Ford, the South Boundary Trail comes to a junction with a spur trail, which leads ¾ mile northeast to the Thorofare Trail. If your destination is somewhere north on the Thorofare Trail, Yellowstone Lake, East Entrance Road, etc., this spur is the trail you want to take. Continuing east on the South Boundary Trail, you will reach the Thorofare Ranger Station, which has a ranger living there most of the summer and fall. From a trail junction out in front of the pasture fence at the ranger station, you can either travel north on the Thorofare Trail or south to the Bridger–Teton National Forest and an extensive network of trails. ᚥ

SNAKE RIVER TRAIL   Map #29, 31

From Snake River Cutoff Trail Junction (8 miles east of South Entrance Trailhead) to:

Jct. with Trail from Harebell Patrol Cabin	3.3 miles	5.3 km
Basin Creek Cutoff Trail	5.9	9.5
Heart River Trail Jct. (CDT)	7.5	12.1
Fox Creek Patrol Cabin	18	30

This wild, seldom-hiked trail follows the Snake River through a variety of interesting terrain—including an 11-mile stretch through a scenic canyon. This is a good late summer or early fall hike. Moose, deer, and elk are all frequently seen here. The trail starts at the junction with the South Boundary Trail, 8 miles east of the South Entrance. From the junction, the Snake River Trail immediately crosses the river (around 2.5-feet deep in August). The Snake River Trail now climbs up and over a low pass, away from the river, for about 2.5 miles to the junction with the Harebell Cabin Cutoff Trail. The Snake River Trail crosses the river three more times in 15 miles as it makes its way through the canyon and joins up with the South Boundary Trail near the Fox Creek Patrol Cabin. The first ford is just east of the junction with the Basin Creek Cutoff Trail and is knee deep (but watch for a big hole). Next is a knee-deep crossing just before the junction with the Heart River Trail, and the final ford is calf deep and just a couple miles before the junction with the South Boundary Trail. These river crossings should not be attempted until after mid-July. &

RIDDLE LAKE TRAIL 🐻   Map #24, 29
(One-way distance: 2.5 miles, 4 km)

The Riddle Lake Trail starts at the Riddle Lake Trailhead approximately 2.5 miles south of Grant Village intersection. Even though it crosses the Continental Divide, the trail is very level. The Riddle Lake Trail travels mainly through small meadows where moose are often spotted. Intermittent streams through these meadows make the going very mushy until mid-July. Riddle Lake is a lovely little lake with a shoreline changing from marsh, to rock, to sandy beach. The Red Mountains and Mt. Sheridan provide a scenic backdrop as you hike along the lake's north shore. Sandpipers, Barrow's goldeneye, sandhill cranes, Canada geese, and even white pelicans are seen around Riddle Lake. The marshes are a haven for mosquitoes, which can be quite a nuisance throughout July. &

YELLOWSTONE LAKE OVERLOOK TRAIL   Map #24
(One-way distance: 1 mile, 1.6 km)

This scenic trail starts at the West Thumb Geyser Basin parking area, on the west side of the lot. The trail travels a few hundred yards through some meadows and then crosses the South Entrance Road. After the road, the trail travels through some wet areas and then gradually climbs (about 200 vertical feet) through meadows and burned forest until it reaches the overlook. From here, there is a good view of Yellowstone Lake and the Absaroka Range, which forms the park's east boundary. Elk, deer and grizzly bear travel through this area, although the bears are not often seen. The meadows can be filled with wildflowers in July. &

THOROFARE AREA

The Thorofare area has a lot of hiking potential. With hikes ranging in distance from 12 miles to over 50 miles, it contains a vast amount of honest-to-goodness breathtaking scenery. The remote arms of Yellowstone Lake, the wild marshes and meadows of the Upper Yellowstone River, and the snowy summits of Yellowstone's highest peaks are all contained in this area. To reach these spots, you've got to do some long hiking, wade some cold streams, and swat a few mosquitoes. To help you decide whether to brave the hardships, some of the area's interesting features are described below.

Most of the access routes to the Thorofare area involve a hike along the shore of Yellowstone Lake. This huge lake is over 20 miles long, 14 miles wide, 300 feet deep, and its clear water is always cold. For thousands of years, native cutthroat trout were the centerpiece of the lake's intricate food web. White pelicans, river otter, mink, mergansers, cormorants, gulls, osprey, eagles, and even grizzly bears had come to depend on the abundance of cutthroat in the lake and its tributaries. Then, in 1994, non-native lake trout were discovered in Yellowstone Lake, probably introduced years ago by anglers. Defenseless Yellowstone cutthroat trout are easy prey for lake trout—one adult lake trout may consume over 40 cutthroat trout per year. The cutthroat trout population is being displaced by lake trout, which is a devastating development not only for the cutthroat trout, but also for the lake ecosystem. Because lake trout dwell in the deeper parts of Yellowstone Lake, they are inaccessible as a food source for the mammal and bird species that depend on shallow-swimming cutthroat trout for a portion of their diets.

The decline in the cutthroat trout numbers is especially evident in Yellowstone Lake's tributaries. In 1978, 70,000 spawning cutthroat were counted in Clear Creek, located on the east shore of the lake. By 2008 that number had been reduced to less than 1,000. In tiny Bridge Creek, on the west shore, the numbers dropped from over 2,000 per year to only one solitary trout in 2004. These and other tributaries used to provide grizzly bears easy access to the cutthroat with each bear eating hundreds of trout per season, but by 2004 scientists concluded that the average grizzly bear was consuming fewer cutthroat trout than the average adult lake trout.

In an attempt to minimize the effect of the lake trout population, the NPS implemented an aggressive gill-netting program. In addition, Yellowstone's fishing regulations were amended to include a "catch-and-kill" policy for lake trout; anglers who catch a lake trout are required to remove it from the lake.

The good news is that, as of 2012, the combined efforts of NPS and contract fishery operations, and anglers, have removed 1.1 million lake trout from Yellowstone Lake.

Into the Southeast Arm of Yellowstone Lake flows the upper Yellowstone River. This remote river valley, with its marshes, meadows, and forest, is seen by few of the park's 3 million annual visitors. Its gravelly banks and lush marshes are home for spotted sandpipers, snipes, sandhill cranes, great blue herons, Canada geese, and a wide variety of ducks. Moose can be spotted occasionally. Elk may be seen feeding in the meadows early or late in the day. Bears are numerous, and their tracks are frequently visible on the trails. Since their reintroduction to the park in the mid-1990s, wolves have moved into the Upper Yellowstone River Valley and are hunting elk. The howls from the resident Delta pack are a bonus to the already perfect Thorofare nights.

The American Indians, trappers, and explorers of the region had long used this area as a route of travel. Artifacts left by the native people lead us to believe that the area has been traveled by humans for the last 10,000 years. There are still old tepee rings visible to the discerning eye in spots that would make beautiful campsites even today. Long before anyone had heard of Gore-Tex, *Giardia*, or GPS, people had used the area as a thoroughfare between Jackson's Hole and points north; they would travel over Two Ocean Pass, down into the Upper Yellowstone River Valley and then north along Yellowstone Lake, where they would then branch off in many directions. The names in this area remain as a reminder of these early travelers: Trapper's Creek, Colter Peak (named for John Colter, who was probably the first white guy to visit Yellowstone), Bridger Lake (named for Jim Bridger, famous mountain man and scout), and the Absaroka Range (named for the Absaroka Indians, also called the Crow Indians, who hunted this area during the summers). The scenery is just as they left it, even the burned areas.

Burned areas have been a part of the landscape here as long as there have been forests. Much of the Thorofare area was burned, to varying degrees, by both the fires of 1988 and by fires in subsequent years. If you hike through the burned sections, you'll find that the recent fires have added an extra dimension of interest to an already fascinating region. ❧

THOROFARE TRAIL   Map #31, 32, 33

Nine Mile Trailhead, also called Thorofare Trailhead, to:

Clear Creek.. 3 miles.........5 km
Park Point Campsites .... 6.5...............10.5
Columbine Creek .... 9..................14.5
Terrace Point... 15.5............25
Lower Ford Jct.. 19.5............31
Upper Ford Jct. .... 20.5............33
Mountain Ck. Trail Jct. .... 24.5............39
Mtn. Ck. Trail Jct. (south)... 26................41.5
South Boundary Trail Jct. .... 31................49.5
Thorofare Ranger Station .... 32................51
Bridger Lake.. 34................54.5

The Thorofare Trail provides the easiest access to the Upper Yellowstone River Valley, one of the jewels of Yellowstone's backcountry. It is possible to cut off about 9 miles of the first stretch of the Thorofare Trail by getting a boat drop-off near Columbine Creek on Yellowstone Lake. Contact Xanterra Services at (307) 242-3893 (June 1–early September) or (307) 344-5217.

The Nine Mile Trailhead is located about (you guessed it) 9 miles east of Fishing Bridge on the East Entrance Road. For the first 1.5 miles, the trail travels through a section of forest that was burned in 2003. This section, complete with plenty of fireweed, blackened trees, and new views of Yellowstone Lake and distant mountain formations, is a great example of the processes involved in fire ecology. Remember to use caution when hiking through this section in windy conditions—the standing dead snags can blow over with hardly any warning. The first major creek the trail reaches is Cub Creek, followed in another 1.5 miles by Clear Creek. Both creeks can have high, swift water early in the season. It may be possible to cross on fallen logs, but size up the consequences before you attempt to cross. Cub and Clear creeks are also both frequented by grizzly bears during the early season spawn. With the grizzlies intent on fishing for trout, and the roar of the creek, (and, in the case of Clear Creek, the dense forest), it is very easy to surprise a bear here. In recent years, there have been restrictions on travel in this area during spawning season, so check at a ranger station for current information before you plan on hiking this area. As you near Park Point, you will come to a more recently burned area—a result of the 2011 Point Fire. Just before reaching the Park Point campsites, the trail runs along the edge of a meadow where there is a good view of Mt. Doane and Mt. Stevenson. From Park Point beach, you can see Dot and Frank islands, the Promontory and the South and Southeast arms of the lake. As you might guess, watching the sunset across Yellowstone Lake from Park Point is a memorable experience. After crossing Meadow Creek, which is usually slow and shallow, the trail continues to travel through the woods, away from the shoreline. About ½ mile south of Meadow Creek, the trail travels for about a mile through an open grass and sage bench above the lake. Columbine Creek is about 2 miles farther, and can be crossed on logs or waded after water levels go down in mid-July.

From Columbine Creek to Terrace Point, the Thorofare Trail is in the trees with no views of the lake, mountains, or meadows. If you're one of the people who bemoaned the loss of trees during the fires of 1988 and have an affinity for thick lodgepole pine forest, then you'll love this section of trail.

At Terrace Point, the trail goes through a series of meadows where there is a fantastic panoramic view of the valley of the upper Yellowstone River, with Colter Peak to the east and Two Ocean Plateau on the west side of the valley. (To get an even better view, walk up the open slopes above the trail for about ¼ mile.) The crossing of Beaverdam Creek can be swift and knee deep throughout the summer and impassable early in the season. After crossing Beaverdam Creek, the trail winds through open meadows and a stretch of thick willows. It's difficult to see very far in front of you here, so make noise. No sense surprising a bear if you don't have to. These meadows are also home to elk, moose, sandhill cranes, and wolves. About a mile south of Beaverdam Creek, you'll encounter burned trees. From this point south, most of the forest along the way was burned to varying degrees by the fires of 1988 and more recent fires.

At 19.5 miles, the junction with the Trail Creek Trail (to Heart Lake) is reached. This junction is called the Lower Ford junction, because it leads to the Lower Ford of the Yellowstone River. One mile south of this junction is another junction with the Trail Creek Trail. This one is called the Upper Ford junction and, of course, leads to the Upper Ford of the Yellowstone River. Continuing south on the Thorofare Trail, you'll cross Trapper's Creek (knee deep after mid-July) and go through burned forest to Turret View meadows. Here is an impressive, full frontal view of Turret Mountain. About 1.5 miles south of Trapper's Creek, you'll travel through another big meadow that provides a good view of the Trident to the south.

At 24.5 miles, the Thorofare Trail meets the Mountain Creek Trail junction. (The Mountain Creek Trail leads to Eagle Pass.) About one mile south of the junction, the Thorofare Trail crosses Mountain Creek (knee deep after late July), and continues to the southern junction with the Mountain Creek Trail. The next 6 miles of the Thorofare Trail are quite scenic as it travels through meadows, forest, and in some places, along the Yellowstone River. You will go through areas burned by both the fires of 1988 and a fire from 2002. There are good views of the walls of the Trident directly above you to the east, and of Two Ocean Plateau across the valley to the west.

The Thorofare Trail crosses Cliff Creek about 4 miles past the southern Mountain Creek Trail junction. There are numerous fallen trees across the creek downstream from the ford. These can be a deadly hazard if you lose your footing and get swept into them during periods of high water. The good news is that the Cliff Creek crossing is usually easy and shallow for the majority of the summer and fall hiking season. About a mile north of Thorofare Ranger Station, the trail reaches the junction with a cutoff to the South Boundary Trail. Go right (southwest) at this junction to reach the South Boundary/Lynx Creek Trail and the South Entrance Trailhead. Go left (southeast) to stay on the Thorofare Trail and to reach Thorofare Ranger Station and the Thorofare Trail outside the park. You can reach Bridger Lake and Two Ocean Pass, in Bridger–Teton National Forest, by either route. Check with the U.S. Forest Service at Blackrock Ranger Station near Moran, WY or at Bridge Bay Ranger Station for status of Forest Service trails in this area.

After this last junction, the Thorofare Trail continues another 1.5 miles south, past Thorofare Ranger Station, to the park boundary. Just before the boundary, there is a turnoff for Bridger Lake. In 1998, a geographical research firm did an inventory and determined that the Thorofare Ranger Station area is the most remote spot in the lower 48 states, being 20 miles (as the crow flies, but a lot farther as the foot walks) from the nearest road of any kind. The Thorofare Trail continues outside Yellowstone National Park, and can be followed another 18 miles up to Deer Creek Pass, then down into the South Fork of the Shoshone River. That is only one of numerous possibilities for long trips in this remote area. ❧

Turret Mtn. *Table Mtn.* *Eagle Peak* *Eagle Pass*

Mountain Creek Area

MOUNTAIN CREEK TRAIL
(MONUMENT CREEK TRAIL)   Map #31

From Thorofare Trail Junction (24.5 miles south of Nine Mile Trailhead) to:

Dike Creek Trail Jct. .... 6.5 miles ..... 10.5 km

Eagle Pass .... 10 .... 16.5

Eagle Creek Campground on the North Fork Highway .. 27.5 44

The Mountain Creek Trail travels from the Thorofare Trail up through a beautiful mountain valley to Eagle Pass. The upper section of the trail is especially scenic, as it provides prolonged views of Yellowstone's highest peaks. Elk can be seen in these upper meadows, and bear and moose can be spotted along the lower stretch of trail. Most of the forest along this trail was burned in the fires of 1988. This is also the route of choice for those attempting to climb Eagle Peak. This peak is not a simple scramble, and has turned back and injured its share of would-be mountaineers. Check at Bridge Bay Ranger Station before attempting this climb.

The Mountain Creek Trail leaves the Thorofare Trail from two different junctions about a mile apart. Starting from the northern junction, the Mountain Creek Trail heads east through fairly level terrain. After about a mile, the trail passes the junction with the southern spur back to the Thorofare Trail. The Mountain Creek Trail now heads east along Mountain Creek, where there are good views of the Trident to the south. Soon, the trail leads uphill away from Mountain Creek and into the burned forest. For the next 3 miles, you'll travel through the burn, crossing many small creeks. Turret and Table mountains are right above you to the north. The trail then descends to the meadows of Howell Creek, crosses an unnamed side creek (that must be waded), and eventually passes the Dike Creek Trail junction. (The Dike Creek Trail climbs up into Bridger–Teton National Forest and over a short pass back to the upper reaches of Mountain Creek.)

From the Dike Creek Trail junction, the Mountain Creek Trail continues past the Howell Creek Patrol Cabin and through more burned forest. About a mile past the cabin, the trail starts climbing, and will gain about 1,000 feet in the next 2 miles up to Eagle Pass. The sheer walls of Eagle Peak fill the view to the northwest, and Pinnacle Mountain (100 feet higher than Eagle Peak) is above the trail to the northeast. Eagle Pass is a very special place. You can see a long way in every direction, and everything you see is wild country.

From the pass, the North Fork Highway to Cody is about 17.5 miles away via the Eagle Creek Trail. The first 3 miles are very steep. The trail makes 4 crossings of Eagle Creek (1.5–2 feet deep after late July). The trail ends at the Shoshone River, where there are some summer cabins. Veer left on the trail past these cabins and you'll arrive at a suspension bridge after 0.3 mile. This bridge will take you to Eagle Creek Campground. If you don't turn left past these cabins, you will remain on the Eagle Creek Trail. This will veer right (east), cross Eagle Creek another time, and end up a mile downstream at Eagle Creek Trailhead. This route requires a deep, fast ford of the Shoshone River, and is mainly used by horse parties. Check at the USFS Ranger Station at Wapiti for current conditions on the Eagle Creek Trail. ♦

TRAIL CREEK TRAIL
Heart Lake Ranger Station to:

Map #29, 30, 31

Heart River Trail/Trail Ck. Trail Jct.	4.4 miles	7 km
Outlet Lake	8	13
Two Ocean Plateau Cutoff Trail	13	21
East Jct. with Two Ocean Trail	15.5	25
Trail Creek Patrol Cabin	17	27
Yellowstone River Ford Jct.	21.5	34.5
Thorofare Trail	22	35

The Trail Creek Trail travels from the east end of Heart Lake to the Thorofare Trail. Along its 18-mile length, it provides access to Outlet Lake, the South and Southeast arms of Yellowstone Lake, Two Ocean Plateau Trail, and the upper Yellowstone River. The variety of scenery and wildlife along this trail makes it one of the more interesting hiking routes in the park. The trail is mainly level, with only one low pass to cross.

The shortest route (12 miles) to reach the western end of the Trail Creek Trail is to start at Heart Lake Trailhead and follow the Heart Lake Trail. Just past the Heart Lake Ranger Station, turn left off the Heart Lake Trail onto a trail that first travels east down the shoreline of Heart Lake for a few hundred yards and then turns up and away from the lake. There are frequent, impressive views of Mt. Sheridan (behind you) as the route roughly parallels the north shore of Heart Lake for 4 miles until it meets the Trail Creek Trail and Heart River Trail junction. From the junction, the Trail Creek Trail crosses Surprise Creek and begins climbing up the drainage of Outlet Creek. The trail crosses Outlet Creek in a long meadow. The trail then parallels the creek to the north end of the meadows (an abundance of wildflowers bloom here in mid-July to mid-August). From the meadows, the trail heads east into the burned forest and begins climbing up to the continental divide. The divide is at about 8,000 feet, which is only 500 feet higher than Heart Lake. Geologists believe that at one time Yellowstone Lake may have flowed into the Snake River/Pacific Ocean drainage instead of its present day Yellowstone River/Atlantic Ocean drainage. They think that the water may have flowed out via what is now the Outlet Creek valley.

From the divide, you will descend gradually through the meadows of Grouse Creek. Grouse Creek, along with most of the other creeks flowing into Yellowstone Lake, has spawning cutthroat trout from late June through mid-July. As you might guess, this easy source of fresh meat attracts grizzly bears, and this entire area south of Yellowstone Lake becomes a hotbed of bear activity early in the summer (hiking may be restricted in this area during spawning season). About 2 miles from the divide, the trail leaves Grouse Creek and heads into the forest, where it parallels the South Arm of Yellowstone Lake. The Trail Creek Trail meets the Two Ocean Plateau Cutoff Trail near a finger of the South Arm. This area is a haven for waterfowl and moose throughout the summer. The Trail Creek Trail continues another 2.5 miles through forest, meadow, and across Chipmunk Creek (calf deep after midsummer) to the junction with the actual Two Ocean Plateau Trail.

From the Two Ocean Plateau Trail junction, the trail travels through meadows and burned forest for another 1.5 miles until it arrives at the Trail Creek Cabin Bypass junction. At this junction, the trail to the left leads to the lakeshore and Trail Creek Patrol Cabin, a few hundred yards away. The Trail Creek cabin area contains a National Park Service cabin, barn, corral, and pasture to support the backcountry patrol operations. Walking past all this human development 25 miles from the nearest road can nudge you out of your wilderness state of mind. So unless you want to talk with the ranger, you should continue on the bypass trail, which turns to the right. After about ¼ mile on this trail, you'll come to a similar junction on the other side of the cabin area. Then, the Trail Creek Trail continues east, following the shoreline for the next ½ mile or so.

Leaving the lakeshore, the trail follows the meadows of Trail Creek, which are filled with migrating waterfowl and elk in the fall. The trail makes some log crossings of shallow spring creeks in this area. The bridge across Trail Creek itself is out, but the ford is slow and shallow.

After crossing Trail Creek, the trail continues east through forest burned in the 1988 fires. After about 0.2 mile, the trail then enters an area of forest that was burned in 1974 and burned again in 1988. The transition is subtle but noticeable. Thanks to the fires, there are now good views of Colter Peak to the east.

About one-half mile west of the Yellowstone River, the Trail Creek Trail splits. The trail to the left (north) goes to the Lower Ford of the Yellowstone River and the north portion of the Thorofare Trail. The trail to the right (south) goes to the Upper Ford and the southern portion of the Thorofare Trail. One ford is usually easier than the other, but it changes from year to year. Thus, the Lower Ford might be passable while the Upper Ford is not, or vice versa. The water levels at these crossings can fluctuate over the course of a couple of days, after heavy rainfalls. With the exception of periods of heavy rain, both crossings are usually passable (thigh to waist deep) by early August. After crossing at either ford, the Trail Creek Trail will meet the Thorofare Trail after a short climb through the forest. &

TWO OCEAN PLATEAU TRAIL   Map #31

From junction with Trail Creek Trail to:

South Boundary Trail	12.5 miles	20 km
Mariposa Lake	13.5	22
Fox Creek Patrol Cabin	15.5	25

The Two Ocean Plateau Trail connects the Trail Creek Trail with the South Boundary Trail as it travels up and over the plateau and the Continental Divide. The high meadows of Two Ocean Plateau are the summer home for herds of elk that migrate up from their wintering grounds in Jackson Hole. By migrating from lower to higher elevations, the elk follow the growing season for plants, as the season progresses, up the hillsides. This way, the elk arrive just in time for the new tender sprouts of plant growth. By moving to these higher, cooler, and windier places, the elk also escape the biting insects. The Two Ocean Plateau received its name because its streams flow into both the Atlantic and Pacific drainages.

The Two Ocean Plateau Trail receives little use, so expect the tread on the trail to be light in places. A topographic map is a must here. Starting from the

Trail Creek Trail (1.5 miles west of Trail Creek Patrol Cabin), the Two Ocean Plateau Trail follows Chipmunk Creek and its meadows, crossing the creek once, up to the confluence of Chipmunk Creek and Passage Creek. These meadows have nice wildflower displays in late July and early August, and are a good spot to see elk in late September. After a shallow crossing of Passage Creek, the trail climbs about 1,300 feet in 5 miles up to the continental divide, passing through a wide variety of vegetation types. Trail work in this area has eliminated five crossings of Passage Creek (the trail is shown incorrectly on pre-1978 topographic maps). Much of the Two Ocean Plateau was burned in the 1988 fires, as will be evident from the trail. After crossing the divide, the trail wanders in and out of beautiful meadows and then descends 700 vertical feet along a fork of Plateau Creek and joins the South Boundary Trail. From this point, Mariposa Lake is 1 mile to the east. ❧

AVALANCHE PEAK TRAIL   Map #32, 34
(One-way distance: 2 miles, 3 km)

This steep trail climbs 2,100 vertical feet in 2 miles to the summit of 10,566-foot Avalanche Peak. The view from the top is one of the most impressive in the park. The trail is minimally marked, but a Sierra Club work crew improved the tread work and drainage in 1988. Good traction soles on your shoes are a must. The trail starts at the picnic area at the west end of Eleanor Lake, 2 miles east of Sylvan Lake on the East Entrance Road. Across the highway (north) from the picnic area is a stream running down the hillside. The trail starts to the right of the stream and begins climbing steeply through the forest. About ½ mile up, the trail crosses the stream. From the stream, the trail traverses west a few hundred yards out into an old avalanche slide. Notice the trees in various stages of regrowth from the periodic avalanches. A few hundred yards farther, the trail traverses back east into the remnants of a mature whitebark pine forest that has experienced almost 100% mountain pine beetle kill in recent years.

About a mile from the trailhead, the trail finally comes out of the trees at the bottom of the southeast bowl of Avalanche Peak. You will be able to see the summit from this point. The trail now turns to the west and begins climbing up a steep scree slope. This will eventually take you up to the shoulder of the south ridge, and from this point there are a number of paths up the remaining scree slope to the summit ridge. Depending upon where you gain the summit ridge, the true summit will be a few hundred yards away, along the ridge top to the northeast. ❧

BACKCOUNTRY CAMPSITES

Northwest Corner (Maps #1, 2, 3)

NO.	PEOPLE	STOCK	CAMPSITE NAME / RESTRICTIONS
WD1	10	0	E Fork Specimen Creek
WD2	12	20	Sportsman Lake • No off-trail travel • No stock before 7/15
WD3	10	0	Sportsman Lake • No off-trail travel
WD4	10	0	High Lake • NWF
WD5	10	5	High Lake • NWF
WD6	12	25	High Lk/Sportsman Jct • Stock parties only • No stock before 7/15
WE1e	12	10	Specimen Creek Jct • 2 night limit • Pit toilet
WE4	12	0	Specimen Creek
WE5	8	0	Shelf Lake • NWF
WE6	8	0	Crescent Lake
WE7	8	0	Shelf Lake • NWF
WF1e	10	10	Black Butte Creek
WF2e	10	10	Upper Daily Creek

Gallatin Mountains and Mammoth Area (Maps #1, 3, 4)

NO.	PEOPLE	STOCK	CAMPSITE NAME / RESTRICTIONS
1B1e	10	0	Big Horn Pass Trail
1C1	10	0	Straight Creek South
1C2	10	6	Straight Creek North • Stock=llamas only
1C4	10	6	Winter Creek
1C5	10	6	Winter Creek SW
1F1	12	20	Fawn Creek-Gardners Hole • Stock parties only • Unavailable if 1G5 occupied
1F2	10	0	Fawn Lake • No off-trail travel
1G2	10	0	Gardners Hole
1G3	10	0	Gardner River • No off-trail travel
1G4	10	0	Upper Gardner River • No off-trail travel
1G5	12	25	Soldiers Corral • Stock parties only • Unavailable if 1F1 occupied
WB1	10	0	Gallatin River
WB3	12	25	Gallatin River • Stock parties only • Unavailable if WB4 occupied • No off-trail travel
WB4	12	25	Gallatin River • Stock parties only • Unavailable if WB3 occupied • No off-trail travel
WB6	10	0	Gallatin River • No off-trail travel
WC2	10	0	Fan Creek
WC3	12	25	Fan Creek • Stock parties only
WC4	12	25	Fan Creek/NE Fork • Stock parties only

NWF = No Wood Fires, **BMA** = Bear Management Area,
e = Easy Access Site (site is within 2 miles of the trailhead)

Lower Yellowstone River Area (Maps #4, 5, 6)

NO.	PEOPLE	STOCK	CAMPSITE NAME / RESTRICTIONS
1A1e	10	6	Lower Blacktail Creek
1A2e	10	0	Rescue Creek
1A3e	6	0	Lava Creek • NWF
1R1	12	6	W Cottonwood Creek • NWF •Stock limit 2 nights
1R2	6	0	E Cottonwood Creek • NWF
1R3	10	10	Little Cottonwood Creek • NWF • Stock limit 2 nights
1Y1	10	0	Yellowstone River Trail • NWF • Bearproof box
1Y2	10	0	Yellowstone River Trail • NWF • Bearproof box
1Y4	6	0	Crevice Lake • NWF
1Y5	6	0	Yellowstone River Bridge • NWF
1Y6	6	0	E of Blacktail Cabin • NWF • Bearproof box
1Y7	10	6	Yellowstone River Trail • NWF • Stock limit 2 nights
1Y8	6	0	Oxbow Creek • NWF • Bearproof box
1Y9	8	0	Yellowstone River Trail • NWF
2B1	10	16	Buffalo Plateau • Closed after 9/13
2C1	8	0	Coyote Creek
2C2	8	0	Coyote Creek
2C3	10	16	Coyote Creek • Stock parties only
2H1	8	0	N Yell/Hell Confluence • NWF
2H2	6	0	S Yell/Hell Confluence • NWF
2H3	10	0	Hellroaring Creek • NWF
2H4	6	0	Hellroaring Creek • NWF
2H5	8	0	Hellroaring Creek • NWF
2H6	8	0	Hellroaring Creek • NWF
2H7	10	0	Hellroaring Creek • NWF
2H8	8	0	Hellroaring Creek • NWF
2H9	8	0	Hellroaring Creek

Tower Area (Map #14)

NO.	PEOPLE	STOCK	CAMPSITE NAME / RESTRICTIONS
2Y1	8	0	Agate Creek • Closed Fri. of Memorial Weekend to 7/15

NWF = No Wood Fires, **BMA** = Bear Management Area,
e = Easy Access Site (site is within 2 miles of the trailhead)

Northeast Corner (Maps #7, 8, 9)

NO.	PEOPLE	STOCK	CAMPSITE NAME / RESTRICTIONS
2S1*	8	12	Lower Slough Creek
2S2*	6	0	Lower Slough Creek • Bearproof box
2S3*	8	0	Slough Creek • Bearproof box
2S4*	8	0	Slough Creek
2S6*	8	0	Upper Slough Creek
2S7*	12	20	Upper Slough Cr. • Stock parties only • 1 party per night in either 2S7 or 2S8
2S8*	12	20	Upper Slough Creek • Same as 2S7
3P1	12	0	Pebble Creek
3P2	12	0	Bliss Pass Jct
3P3	6	0	Bliss Pass Jct
3P4	12	20	Upper Pebble Creek
3P5e	12	0	Upper Pebble Creek

*Only three nights allowed per permit for all 2S sites 6/15 – 9/15

Lamar River Area (Maps #7, 9, 10, 11, 12)

NO.	PEOPLE	STOCK	CAMPSITE NAME / RESTRICTIONS
3C2	12	20	Lower Cache Creek • 2 night limit for stock
3C3	12	25	Upper Cache Creek
3C4	12	0	Upper Cache Creek
3F1	6	0	Cold Creek
3F2	12	25	Lemon City
3L1	12	8	N Lower Cache Creek • Stock = llamas only
3L2	12	0	S Lower Cache Creek
3L3	12	0	Lower Lamar
3L4	12	0	Lower Lamar
3L6	12	20	Middle Lamar • Stock parties only • 2 night limit
3L7	12	0	Middle Lamar
3L8	12	0	Timothy Creek
3L9	12	20	Warm Spring Meadow
3M1	12	25	Appaloosa Meadows • 2 night limit for stock
3M2	12	0	Lower Miller Creek
3M3	12	20	Lower Miller Creek
3M4	6	0	Upper Miller Creek
3M5	12	0	Upper Miller Creek
3M6	12	0	Hoodoo Basin
3M7	12	20	Boundary • No stock before 8/1 • 1 night stock limit
3T2	12	12	Mist Creek Meadows • 2 night limit
3T3	12	25	Mist Creek Pass • 2 night limit
3U1	12	25	Lower Willow Creek
3U2	12	0	Lower Willow Creek
3U3	12	0	Little Saddle Creek
3U4	12	25	Cold Creek Jct • Stock parties only

NWF = No Wood Fires, **BMA** = Bear Management Area,
e = Easy Access Site (site is within 2 miles of the trailhead)

Canyon Area (Maps #10, 11, 12, 14, 16, 17, 18)

NO.	PEOPLE	STOCK	CAMPSITE NAME / RESTRICTIONS
4B1	6	0	Joseph's Coat Spring • Off-trail travel required • 2 night limit
4B2	6	0	Broad Creek • Off-trail travel required
4B3	12	6	Broad Creek • Off-trail travel required
4B4	12	10	Broad Creek
4C1	8	0	Old Seven Mile Hole • No stock allowed on trail •NWF
4C2	8	0	Seven Mile Hole • No stock allowed on trail • NWF
4C3	8	0	Seven Mile Hole • No stock allowed on trail • NWF
4E1	8	0	Washburn Meadow • No stock allowed on trail
4M2	12	6	Moss Creek
4R1e	8	0	Ribbon Lake
4R2e	8	0	Ribbon Lake
4W1	12	6	Wrangler Lake
4W2	8	0	Wapiti Lake
4W3	8	0	Wapiti Lake
5B1	20	25	Broad Creek
5B2	12	15	Broad View
4D1e	6	0	Ice Lake North • NWF
4D2e	8	0	Ice Lake East
4D3e*	4	0	Ice Lake South
4E2	4	0	Cascade Lake
4E3	8	0	Cascade Lake
4E4e	8	12	Cascade Lake
4F1e	8	0	Norris Meadows
4G2	8	0	Grebe Lake
4G3	8	6	Grebe Lake • NWF
4G4	8	6	Grebe Lake
4G5	8	6	Grebe Lake
4G6	8	12	Wolf Lake
4G7	8	0	Wolf Lake
4P1	8	0	Observation Peak • NWF

Reservable only by parties with special needs. Wheelchair accessible with assistance.

Madison Valley Area (Map #21)

NO.	PEOPLE	STOCK	CAMPSITE NAME / RESTRICTIONS
WA1	10	20	Gneiss Creek • Closed 3/10 through 6/30 • No off-trail travel

NWF = No Wood Fires, **BMA** = Bear Management Area,
e = Easy Access Site (site is within 2 miles of the trailhead)

Firehole Valley Area (Maps #22, 23)

NO.	PEOPLE	STOCK	CAMPSITE NAME / RESTRICTIONS
OB2	6	0	Mallard Lake SE
OB3	6	0	Mallard Lake E
OB4	6	0	Mallard Lake Outlet • NWF
OD1e	6	0	Fairy Meadows • NWF
OD2	10	0	Firehole Meadows
OD3	6	0	Firehole Falls
OD4	12	0	Imperial Meadows
OD5e	6	0	Goose Lake • Handicapped accessible • 1 night limit
OE1	6	6	Summit Lake
OG1e	8	0	Sentinel Meadows East • NWF

All OD and OG sites are closed from 3/10 until Friday before Memorial Day (BMA)

Shoshone Lake Area (Maps #24, 25, 26, 29)

NO.	PEOPLE	STOCK	CAMPSITE NAME / RESTRICTIONS
OA1e	12	10	Lone Star
OA2	6	0	Upper Firehole
OA3	6	0	Firehole Springs
8G1	12	0	Shoshone Meadows • Site located on Shoshone Lk Trail & isn't visible from the Bechler–Old Faithful Trail • 1 night limit
8M1	8	15	Moose Creek
8M2	8	15	Moose Creek Meadow • 2 night limit
8Q1*	8	0	S Narrow Point • Boat access only
8Q3	8	0	S Narrow Beach • Boat access only
8Q4	8	0	Moose Creek Point • Boat access only
8Q6**	8	0	Moose Creek Outlet • Boat access only
8Q7**	8	0	Moose Creek Beach • Boat access only
8Q9	8	0	Channel • Boat access only
8R1	8	0	Windy Point • Boat access only
8R2*	8	0	Bluff Top • Trail or boat access
8R3	8	0	Cove • Trail access only
8R4	8	0	Flat Top • Boat access only
8R5	8	0	Basin Bay Point • Trail access only
8S1	8	0	Outlet • 2 Party site (1 trail access only and 1 boat access only)
8S2	8	0	DeLacy Creek • Trail or boat access
8S3	8	0	Coyote • Trail access only
8S4*	8	0	N Grizzly Beach • Boat access only
8S5*	8	0	S Grizzly Beach • Boat access only
8S7*	8	0	North Narrows • Boat access only
8T1*	4	0	Basin Beach • Trail access only • Limit of 1 tent
8T3**	8	0	Hillside • Boat access only
8T5**	8	0	Tranquility • Boat access only

Wood fires are prohibited at all these sites except OA1, OA2, OA3, & 8M2

*Not reservable before 7/1 **Not reservable before 7/15

NWF = No Wood Fires, **BMA** = Bear Management Area,
e = Easy Access Site (site is within 2 miles of the trailhead)

Bechler River and Falls River Area (Maps #26, 27, 28, 29)

NO.	PEOPLE	STOCK	CAMPSITE NAME / RESTRICTIONS
8P1	8	6	Phantom Campsite • Stock use not recommended
8P2	8	0	Phantom Campsite
8A1	8	0	Beula Lake
8A2	6	0	Beula Lake
9A0	12	25	Upper Boundary Creek • Stock Parties Only
9A1	12	20	Boundary Creek Meadows
9A2	12	0	Upper Boundary Creek
9A3	12	0	Dunanda Fall
9A4	12	25	Talus Terrace
9A5	12	25	Buffalo Lake
9A6	12	25	Robinson Creek
9A7	12	0	Little Robinson Creek
9B1	12	0	Lower Boundary Creek • 2 night limit • NWF
9B2	12	0	Bechler Ford • 2 night limit • NWF
9B3	20	25	Trail Spring • Stock Parties Only • 2 night limit
9B4	12	0	Ouzel Falls • 1 night limit
9B5	12	0	Colonnade Fall • 1 night limit
9B6	12	0	Lower Ford • 1 night limit
9B7	12	0	Talus Spring • 1 night limit
9B8	12	0	Upper Ford • 1 night limit
9B9	12	0	Albright Falls • 2 night limit • NWF
9B0	12	25	Three Rivers Meadow • 2 night limit • NWF
9C1	12	0	Rocky Ford • 2 night limit
9D1	12	0	Ferris Fork • 1 night limit • NWF
9D2	12	0	Gregg Fork • 1 night limit
9D3	12	25	Douglas Knob Meadow • 1 night limit • NWF
9D4	12	0	Continental Divide • 1 night limit • NWF
9F1	12	0	Lower Falls River
9F2	12	0	Upper Falls River • 1 night limit
9M1	12	25	Lower Boundary Creek • Stock Parties Only • 2 night limit • NWF
9M2	12	25	Bechler Ford • Stock Parties Only • 2 night limit • NWF
9U1	12	25	Falls River Cutoff
9U2	12	0	Mountain Ash Creek
9U3	12	0	Mountain Ash Creek • NWF
9U4	12	0	Union Falls • 2 night limit
9U5	12	12	Union Falls • 2 night limit • NWF

NWF = No Wood Fires, **BMA** = Bear Management Area,
e = Easy Access Site (site is within 2 miles of the trailhead)

Snake River Area (Maps #29, 30, 31)

NO.	PEOPLE	STOCK	CAMPSITE NAME / RESTRICTIONS
6M3*	8	0	Mariposa Lake • NWF
6M4*	12	25	Two Ocean Trail Jct • No stock before 7/20
6M5*	12	25	Upper Passage Creek • No stock before 7/20
6M7	12	0	Fox Creek
8C1	8	0	Snake River • May not be fordable until mid-July
8C2	12	25	Snake River
8C4	12	6	Snake River
8C6	8	0	Snake River Ford
8C7	12	25	Snake River • Stock parties only
8C9	12	20	Crooked Creek

All sites listed below are closed 4/1–6/30 (BMA)

NO.	PEOPLE	STOCK	CAMPSITE NAME / RESTRICTIONS
8B1	4	0	Basin Creek
8B2	12	6	Basin Creek Lake
8B3	12	20	Basin Creek • Stock parties only • Unavailable if 8B4 occupied
8B4	12	20	Basin Creek • Stock parties only • Unavailable if 8B3 occupied
8B5	8	0	Basin Creek
8C5	12	10	Snake River
8H1**	8	0	South Bay • NWF
8H2**	6	0	Sheridan Creek
8H3**	4	0	Hideaway
8H4**	8	0	West Shore • NWF
8H5**	6	0	Sheridan Trail • NWF
8H6**	6	0	Rustic • NWF
8J1**	8	0	Beaver Creek
8J2	12	25	Beaver Creek Meadow • Stock parties only • 2 night limit
8J3	8	0	Surprise Creek
8J4	8	0	Heart River
8J6	4	0	East Shore
8O2	6	0	Outlet Lake • No travel east of Outlet Lake before 7/15

*All 6M sites except 6M7, no off-trail travel except 7/15 – 8/21 (BMA)• Must obtain a permit for off-trail travel at the South Entrance

**All 8H sites and 8J1 have a limit of 2 nights per trip 7/1 – 9/1

NWF = No Wood Fires, **BMA** = Bear Management Area,
e = Easy Access Site (site is within 2 miles of the trailhead)

The Thorofare Area (Maps #29, 30, 31, 32, 33)

NO.	PEOPLE	STOCK	CAMPSITE NAME / RESTRICTIONS
5E1	12	0	Beaverdam Trail • Trail access only • Closed 4/1– 7/14
5E3	12	0	Brimstone Point • No off-trail travel 4/1–7/14 • Trail or boat access • Boats must be entirely removed from water
5E4	12	0	Brimstone Bay • No off-trail travel 4/1–7/14 • Trail or boat access • Boats must be entirely removed from water
5E6	12	25	Columbine Meadow N • No off-trail travel 4/1–7/14 • Trail or boat access • Boats must be entirely removed from water • One night limit
5E7	12	25	Meadow Creek • Closed 4/1–7/14 • Trail access only
5E8	12	0	Park Point S • Closed 4/1–7/14 • Trail or boat access • Boats must be entirely removed from water
5E9	12	0	Park Point N • No off-trail travel 4/1–7/14 • Trail or boat access • Boats must be entirely removed from water
6A3	12	0	Trail Point • No travel from campsite 5/15 – 7/14 • Trail or non-motorized boat access only • Trail access may be restricted during early season due to inability to ford the Yellowstone River • Can anchor sailboat
6A4	12	0	Trail Bay • No travel from campsite 5/15 – 7/14 • Trail or non-motorized boat access only • Trail access may be restricted during early season due to inability to ford Yellowstone River • Can anchor sailboat • Bearproof box
6B1	20	20	Lower Ford • No off-trail travel 5/15 – 7/14 • 1 night limit for stock • River may not be fordable until late July/early August
6B2	8	0	Upper Ford • Closed 5/15 – 7/14 • River may not be fordable until late July/early August
6B4	20	20	Beaverdam Meadow • Closed 4/1–7/14
6C1	20	15	Colter Meadows • Keep stock from spring source
6C2	20	25	Rivers Edge • 1.5 miles west of main trail
6C3	10	0	Turret View
6D1	20	10	Mountain Creek
6D2	20	0	Mountain Creek Ford
6D3	20	25	Mountain Creek • Stock parties only
6D5	20	20	Upper Mountain Creek
6D6	20	25	Howell Creek
6D7	20	0	Howell Creek
6D8	20	10	Howell Creek • Often has snow until July • No stock after 9/1
6T1	20	20	South Thorofare • Creek may be unfordable until mid/late-July
6T2	20	0	North Thorofare • On north side of Thorofare Creek
6Y2	12	0	South Yell River • River may be unfordable until mid/late-July
6Y4	20	25	East Confluence • Limited picketing for stock
6Y5	20	0	Cliff Creek
6Y6	20	25	Three Mile Bend
6Y7	20	25	Yellowstone Meadows • Stock parties only
5L2	8	10	Monument Camp • Closed 5/15 – 7/14 • Trail or boat access
7G1	12	20	Grouse Creek • Closed 5/15 – 7/14 • Unavailable if 7G2 occupied
7G2	12	20	Grouse Creek • Closed 5/15 – 7/14 • Unavailable if 7G1 occupied

NWF = No Wood Fires, **BMA** = Bear Management Area,
e = Easy Access Site (site is within 2 miles of the trailhead)

APPENDIX

References

Gibson, Ken. "Mountain Pine Beetle Conditions in Whitebark Pine Stands in the GYE, 2006." *Forest Health Protection*. February 2006. 9 February 2008 <www.fs.fed.us/r1-r4/spt.fhp/publications/bystate/R1Pub06-03_MPB_Yellowstone_gibson/pdf>.

Gookin, John. "NOLS Backcountry Lightning Safety Guidelines." The National Outdoor Leadership School, 2000.

Greater Yellowstone Coordinating Committee Whitebark Pine Subcommittee. "Whitebark Pine Strategy for the Greater Yellowstone Area." May 2011. 27 November 2012 <fedgycc.org/documents/WBPStrategyFINAL5.31.11.pdf>

Gunther, Kerry. "Yellowstone National Park Bear-Related Injuries/Fatalities." *Bear Management Office Information Paper No. BMO-1*, U.S. Department of Interior, National Park Service, Yellowstone National Park. March 2012. 27 November 2012 <www.nps.gov/yell/naturescience/injuries.htm>.

Hatch, Cory. "Hope for the Westslope Cutthroat." *Jackson Hole News & Guide* 23 August 2006. 14 November 2007 <http://www.jacksonholenews.com/print/php?art_id=822&pid=news>.

Herrero, Stephen. *Bear Attacks: Their Causes and Avoidance.* The Lyons Press, 2002.

Herrero, Stephen, and Andrew Higgins. "Field Use of Capsicum Spray as a Bear Deterrent." *Ursus* 10 (1998): 533-537.

National Safety Council, Wilderness Medical Society. *Wilderness First Aid: Emergency Care for Remote Locations.* Jones and Bartlett Publishers, Inc., 1997.

Robbins C.T., C.C. Schwartz, K.A. Gunther, and C. Servheen. "Grizzly Bear Nutrition and Ecology Studies in Yellowstone National Park." *Yellowstone Science* 14 (2006):19-26.

Robison, Hillary. 2002. "Ecological Relationship Between Grizzly Bears and Army Cutworm Moths." Pages 37-40 in C.C. Schwartz and M.A. Haroldson. *Yellowstone Grizzly Bear Investigations: Annual Report of the Interagency Grizzly Bear Study Team.* Bozeman, Montana: USGS, 2001.

Rockwell, Robert L. "Giardia Lamblia and Giardiasis, With Particular Attention to the Sierra Nevada." *Yosemite Association* Newsletter 4 (2002).

Schullery, Paul. *The Bears of Yellowstone.* High Plains Publishing Co., Inc., 1992.

Smith, D.W., et al. *Yellowstone Wolf Project: Annual Report, 2011.* National Park Service, Yellowstone Center for Resources, Yellowstone National Park, Wyoming, YCR-2012-01. 3 December 2012 <www.nps.gov/yell/naturescience/upload/Wolf_AR_2011.pdf>.

Smith, T. S., S. Herrero, T. D. DeBruyn, and J. M. Wilder. "Efficacy of Bear Deterrent Spray in Alaska." *J. Wildl. Manage.* 72(3): 640-645.

Wilkerson, James A. *Medicine for Mountaineering and Other Wilderness Activities.* 4th ed. The Mountaineers Books, 1992.

Yellowstone Resources and Issues. Yellowstone National Park, Wyoming: Division of Interpretation, 2012. 28 November 2012 <www.nps.gov/yell/planyourvisit/Yellowstone-resources-and-issues-handbook.htm>.

"Yellowstone to Begin Westslope Cutthroat Trout Restoration Project." NPS.gov. 10 July 2006. 14 November 2007 <www.nps.gov/yell/parknews/0643.htm>.

Water Treatment and Dehydration

For general information, go to:

The Center for Disease Control (CDC): www.cdc.gov
The Rehydration Project: www.rehydrate.org
For information on dehydration while on a backcountry trip, go to:
www.gorp.com

Maps

U.S. Geological Survey (for 7.5-minute maps)
P.O. Box 25286, Denver, CO 80225
1-888-ASK-USGS Website: www.usgs.gov

National Geographic Trails Illustrated Maps

Maps are available through National Geographic by calling (800) 962-1643
or through their website: maps.nationalgeographic.com/maps

Printed maps also available through the Yellowstone Association. To order,
call (877) 967-0090 or go online to: www.YellowstoneAssociation.org

Know Before You Go

The more you know about what you're seeing in Yellowstone's backcountry,
the greater your enjoyment will be. Here are some sources of information:

Backcountry Office of Yellowstone National Park

This office offers copies of the *Backcountry Trip Planner*, advance backcountry
campsite reservations, and general park information.
Backcountry Office • P.O. Box 168 • Yellowstone NP, WY 82190 • (307) 344-2160
• www.nps.gov/yell/planyourvisit/backcountrytripplanner.html

Yellowstone National Park's website: www.nps.gov/yell/

This is a great resource for everything from park opening dates and the online version
of the park newspaper to updates on resource issues and scientific papers. Check out
the Nature & Science section—it has information on wolves, bears, moose, bison, birds,
geothermal resources, archaeology, and more.

National Park Service Ranger-Naturalist Programs

The National Park Service provides evening slide programs, guided walks, and short
informational talks that are free of charge, are presented by park rangers, and cover all
aspects of Yellowstone's natural and human history. The guided walks are particularly
beneficial for hikers. Look in the park newspaper or check at any NPS visitor center for
program schedules.

The Yellowstone Association Institute

The Yellowstone Association Institute is a field school that offers in-depth educational
programs throughout the year in Yellowstone National Park. Course topics include:
plant identification, animal tracking, geology, history, birds, photography, grizzly bears,
wolves, and backpacking skills. For a complete listing of courses or to order books on
Yellowstone, contact the association by phone, (877) 967-0090, or through their website,
www.YellowstoneAssociation.org.

If there are errors or confusing sections in this book, or if you have suggestions, please
contact us c/o Yellowstone Association, P.O. Box 117, Yellowstone NP, WY 82190, or
e-mail us at: mcmarschall@hotmail.com.

THE MAPS IN THIS BOOK

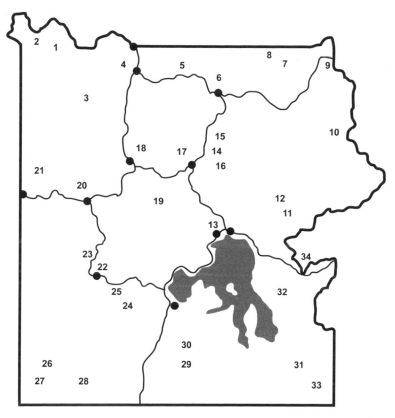

Map#	Area	Page #
1	Northwest Corner	191
2	Northwest Corner (enlarged)	192, 193
3	Gallatin Mountains	194, 195
4	Mammoth	196, 197
5	Lower Yellowstone	198
6	Tower	199
7	Slough/Pebble Creeks	200
8	Slough Creek	201
9	Northeast Corner	202, 203
10	Lamar	204, 205
11	Pelican Valley	206
12	Pelican Valley (enlarged)	207
13	Lake/Fishing Bridge	208
14	Canyon	209
15	Mt. Washburn	210
16	Canyon (enlarged)	211
17	Grebe/Cascade Lakes	212
18	Norris	213
19	Central Plateau	214
20	Madison	215
21	Gneiss Creek	216
22	Firehole Valley	217
23	Old Faithful	218
24	Shoshone Lake	219
25	Shoshone Lake (enlarged)	220, 221
26	Bechler	222, 223
27	Bechler (enlarged)	224, 225
28	Grassy Lake	227
29	Snake River	228, 229
30	Heart Lake	231
31	Thorofare	232, 233
32	Yellowstone Lake (east)	234
33	Thorofare (enlarged)	235
34	Avalanche Peak	236

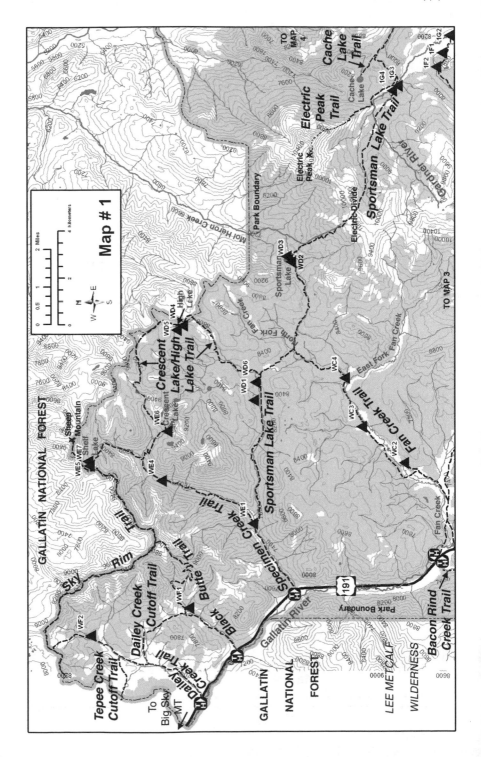

192

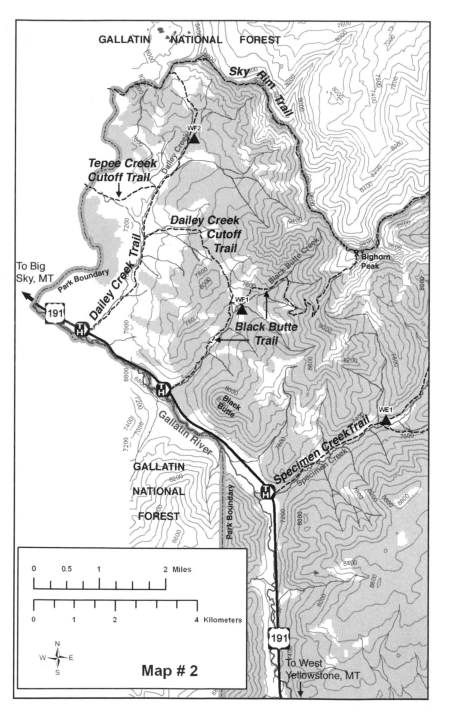

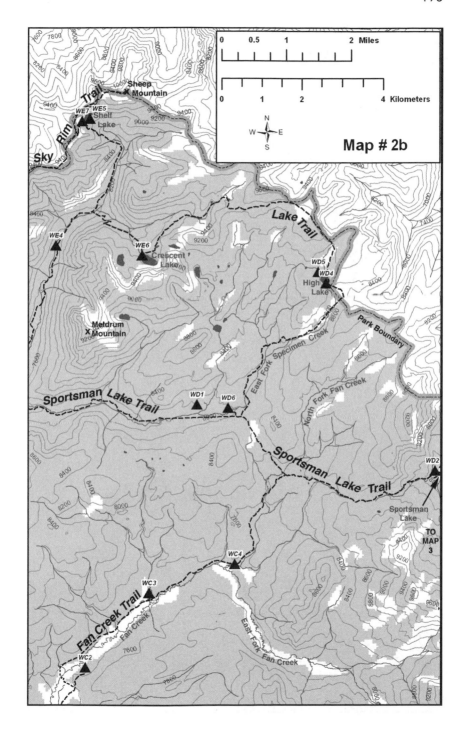

194

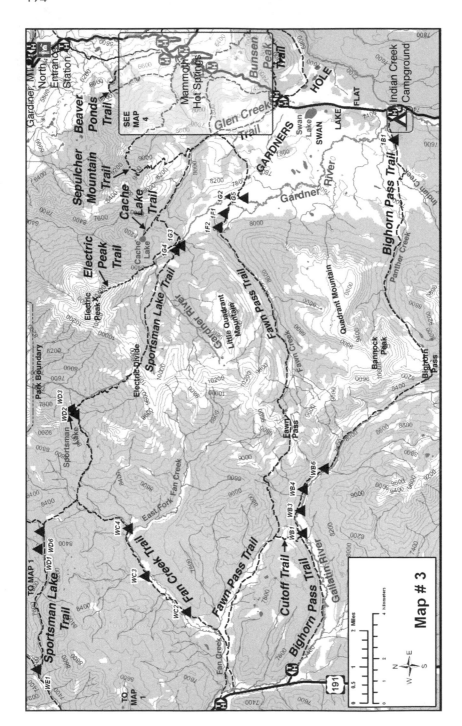

Map # 3

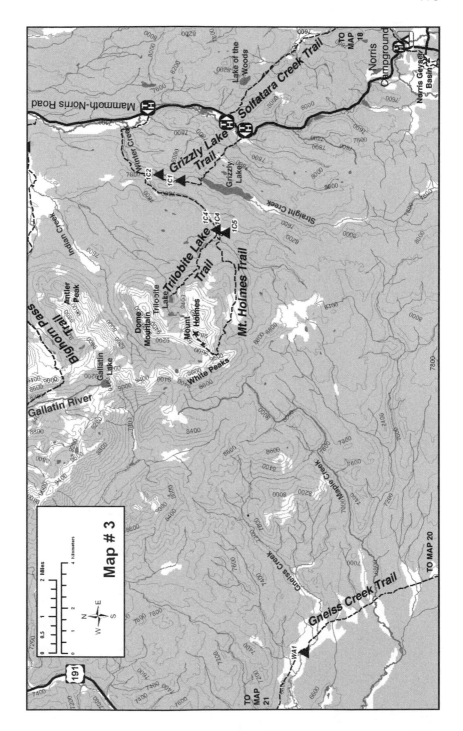

Map # 3

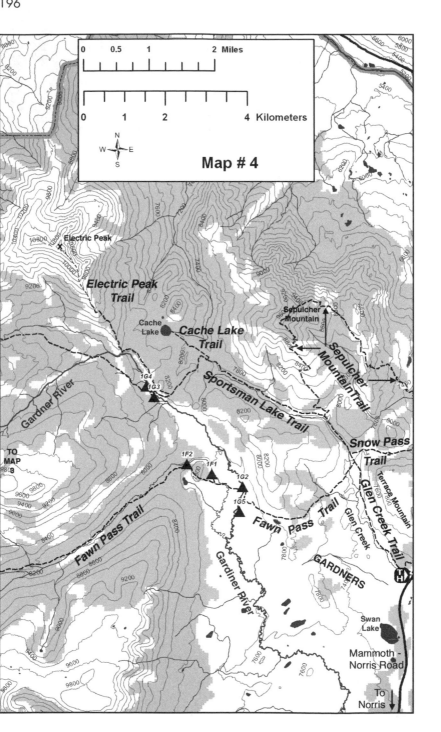

Map # 4

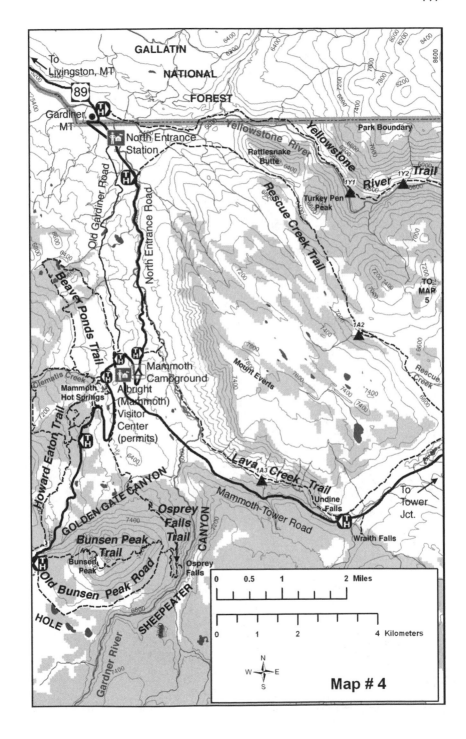

Map # 4

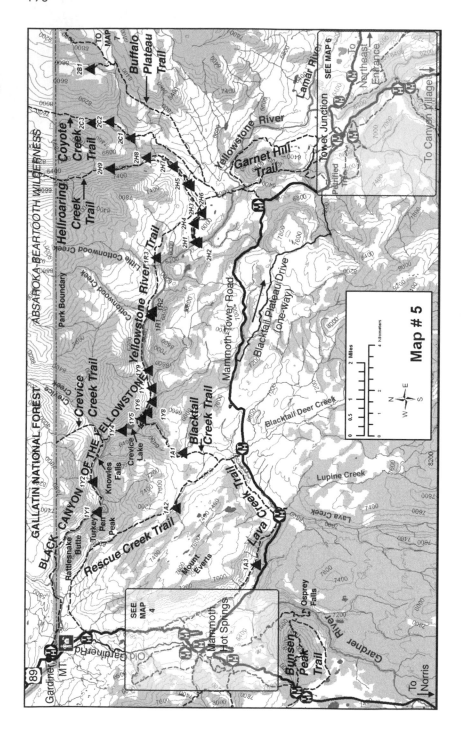

Map # 5

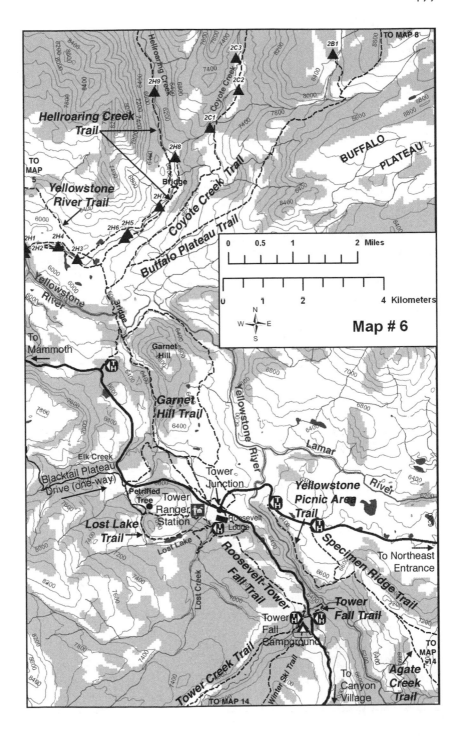

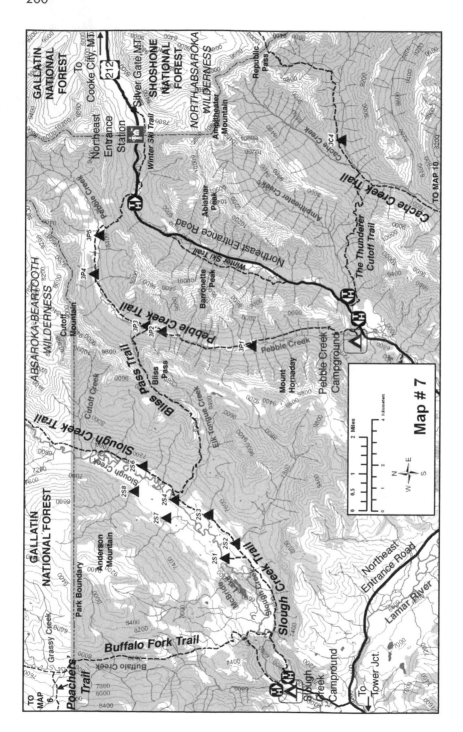

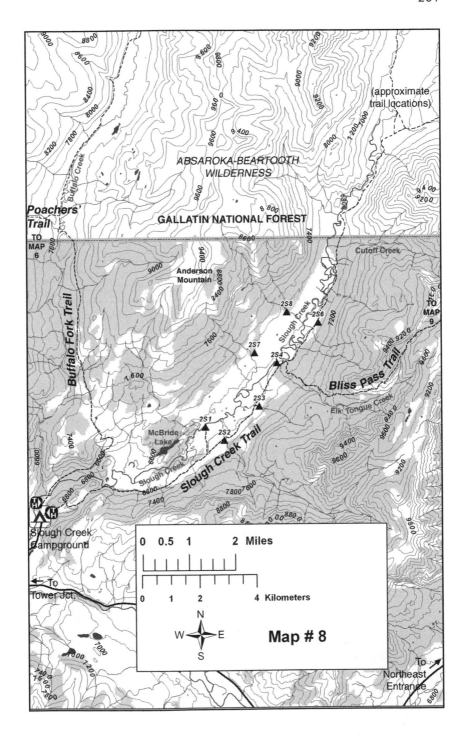

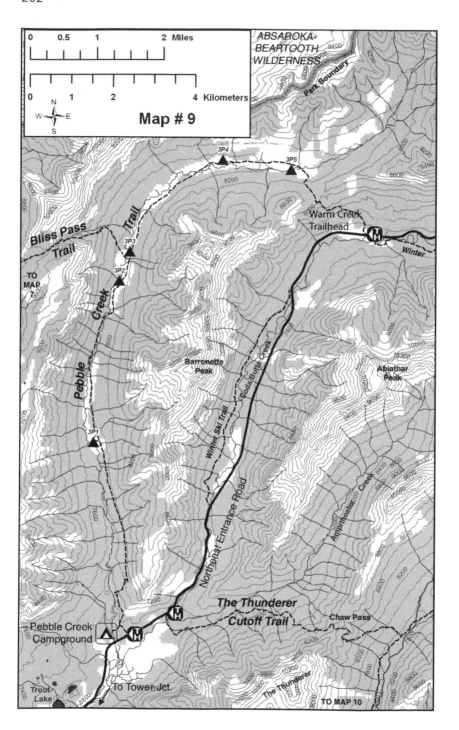

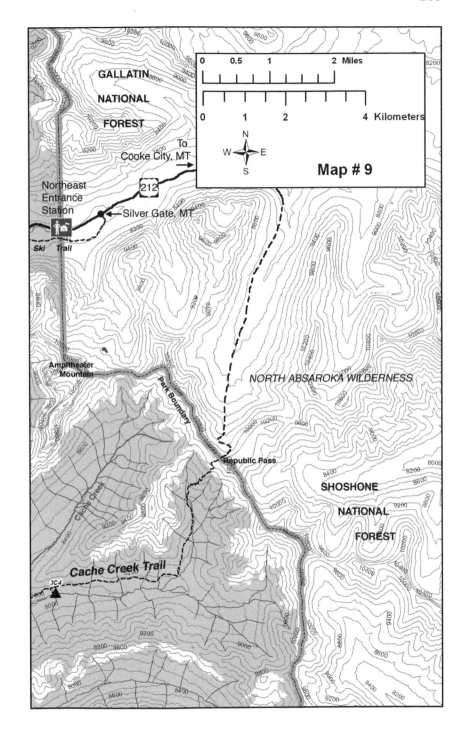

GALLATIN
NATIONAL
FOREST

To
Cooke City, MT

Northeast
Entrance
Station

212

Silver Gate, MT

Ski   Trail

Amphitheater
Mountain

Park Boundary

NORTH ABSAROKA WILDERNESS

Republic Pass

SHOSHONE

NATIONAL

FOREST

Cache Creek

Cache Creek Trail

3C4

0   0.5   1   2 Miles

0   1   2   4 Kilometers

N
W   E
S

Map # 9

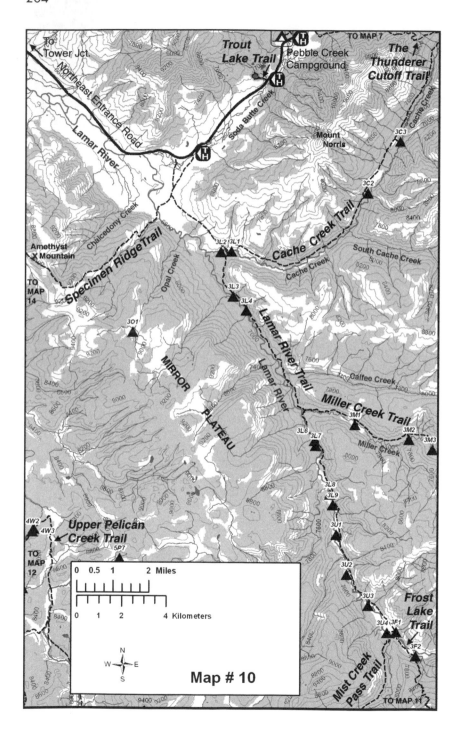

Map # 10

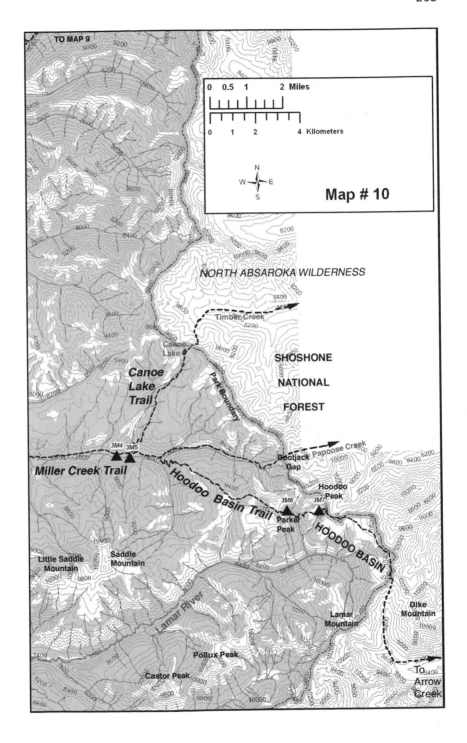

TO MAP 9

0   0.5   1   2 Miles

0   1   2   4 Kilometers

N
W · E
S

Map # 10

NORTH ABSAROKA WILDERNESS

Timber Creek

Canoe Lake

SHOSHONE

NATIONAL

FOREST

Canoe Lake Trail

Park Boundary

3M4 3M5

Miller Creek Trail

Hoodoo Basin Trail

Bootjack Gap

Papoose Creek

Hoodoo Peak

3M6 3M7

Parker Peak

HOODOO BASIN

Little Saddle Mountain

Saddle Mountain

Lamar River

Lamar Mountain

Dike Mountain

Pollux Peak

Castor Peak

To Arrow Creek

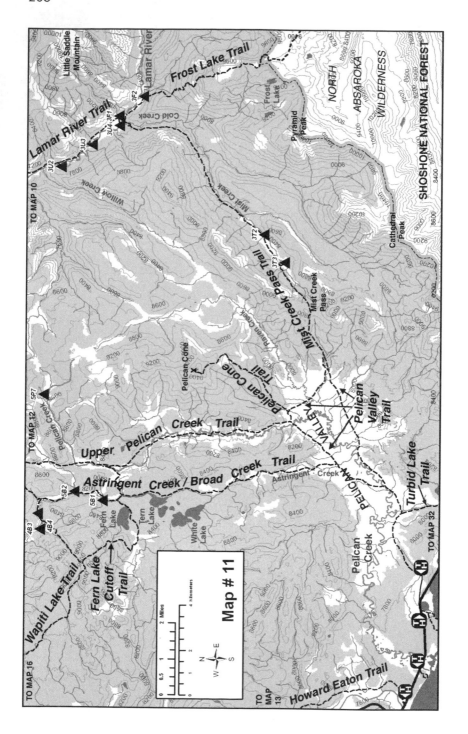

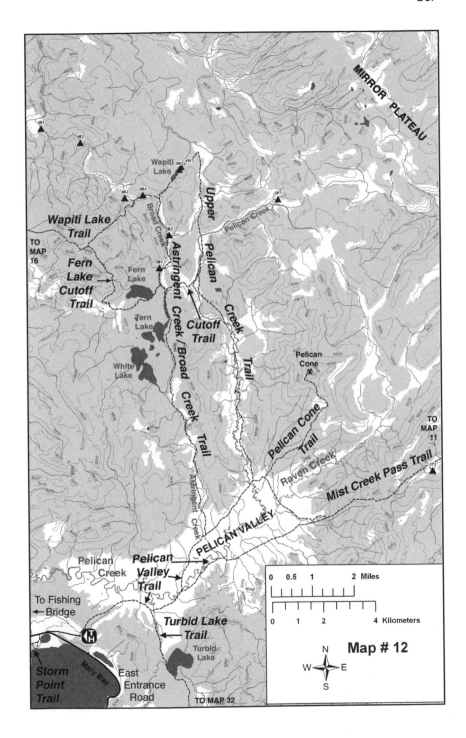

MIRROR PLATEAU

4B1

4B2

Wapiti
Lake

4W2 4W3

6P1

Upper

Pelican Creek

4B3 4B4

Wapiti Lake Trail

5B2

TO
MAP
16

Fern Lake Cutoff Trail

5B1

Fern
Lake

Broad Creek

Astringent Creek / Broad Creek Trail

Pelican

Creek

Trail

Cutoff Trail

Tern
Lake

White
Lake

Pelican
Cone

TO
MAP
11

Pelican Cone Trail

Raven Creek

Mist Creek Pass Trail

Astringent

Creek

PELICAN VALLEY

Pelican
Creek

Pelican Valley Trail

Turbid Lake Trail

Turbid
Lake

To Fishing
Bridge

Storm Point Trail

Mary Bay

East
Entrance
Road

TO MAP 32

| 0 | 0.5 | 1 | | 2 Miles |

| 0 | 1 | 2 | 4 Kilometers |

Map # 12

N
W E
S

208

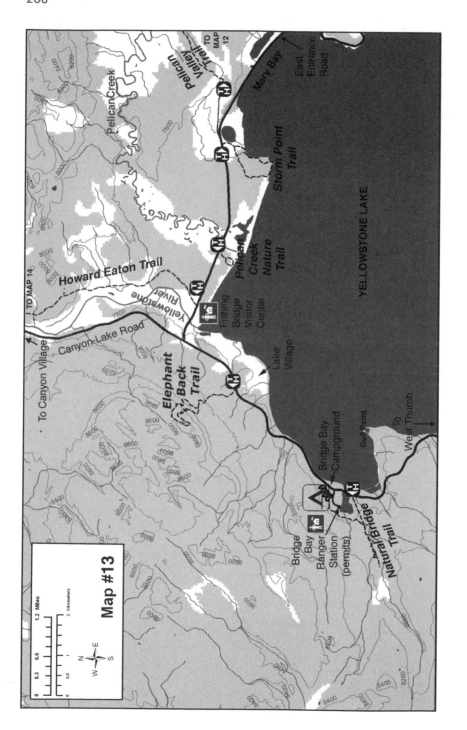

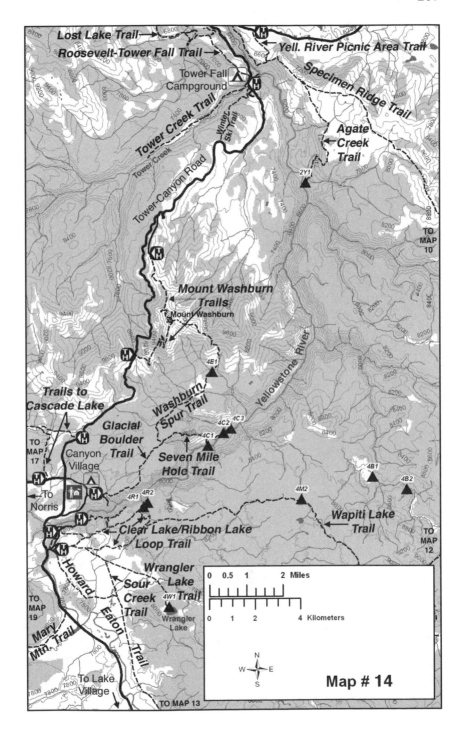

Lost Lake Trail
Roosevelt-Tower Fall Trail
Yell. River Picnic Area Trail
Specimen Ridge Trail
Tower Fall Campground
Agate Creek Trail
Tower Creek Trail
Winter Ski Trail
Tower Creek
Tower-Canyon Road
2Y1
TO MAP 10
Mount Washburn Trails
Mount Washburn
4E1
Trails to Cascade Lake
Washburn Spur Trail
Yellowstone River
Glacial Boulder Trail
4C2 4C3
TO MAP 17
Canyon Village
4C1
Seven Mile Hole Trail
4B1
4B2
To Norris
4R1 4R2
4M2
Wapiti Lake Trail
TO MAP 12
Clear Lake/Ribbon Lake Loop Trail
Howard
Wrangler Lake Trail
Sour Creek Trail
4W1
Mary Mtn Trail
Eaton Trail
Wrangler Lake
TO MAP 19

0	0.5	1		2 Miles

0   1   2   4 Kilometers

N
W   E
S

Map # 14

To Lake Village

TO MAP 13

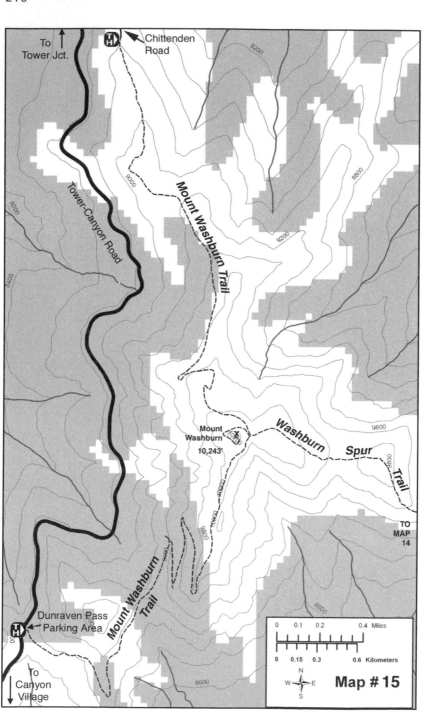

To
Tower Jct.

Chittenden
Road

Tower-Canyon Road

Mount Washburn Trail

8200

9000

8800

8000

9200

8400

Washburn

Spur

Trail

9600

9600

Mount
Washburn
10,243'

TO
MAP
14

Mount Washburn

Trail

9800

Dunraven Pass
Parking Area

To
Canyon
Village

8600

8600

| 0 | 0.1 | 0.2 | | 0.4 Miles |

| 0 | 0.15 | 0.3 | | 0.6 Kilometers |

N
W E
S

Map # 15

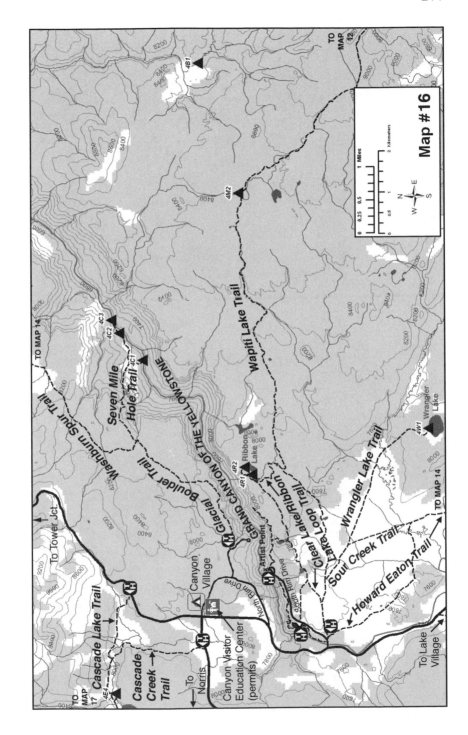

Map #16

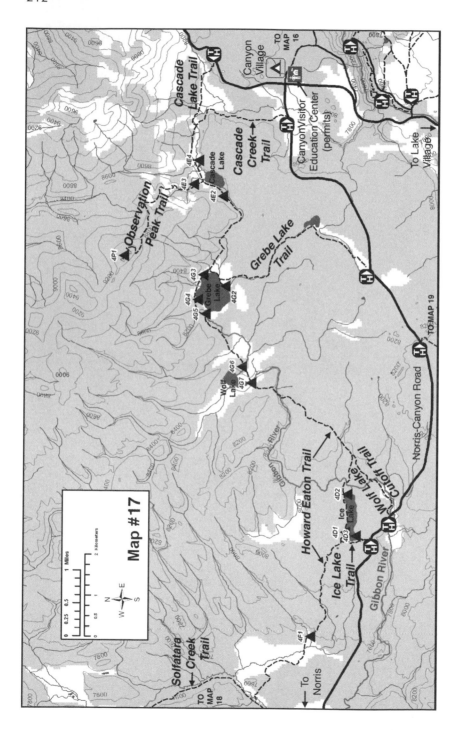

Map #17

213

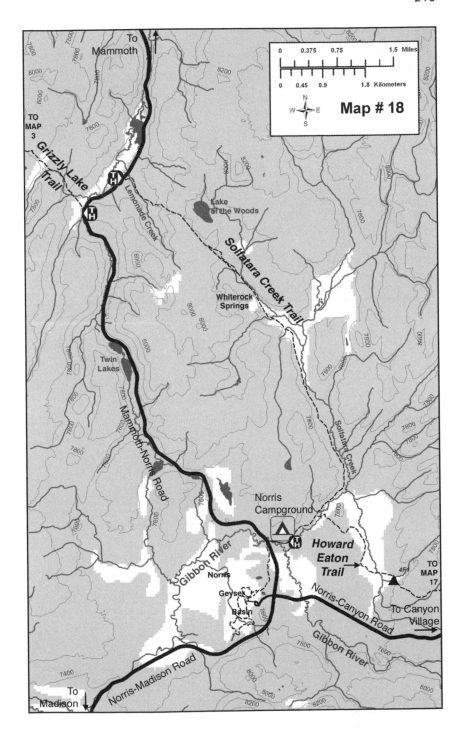

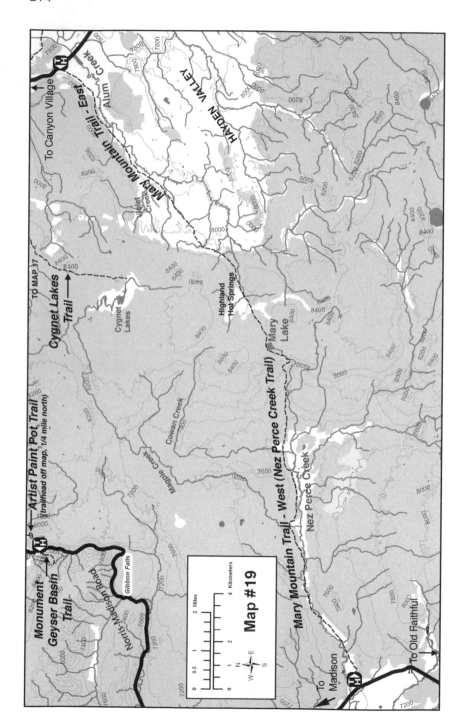

Map #19

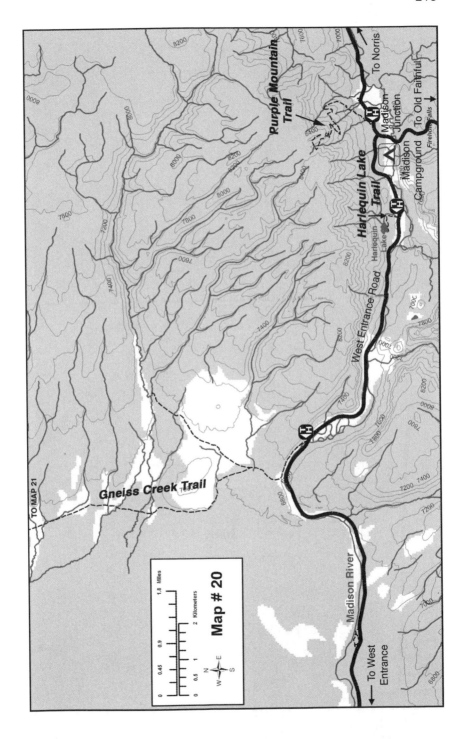

Map # 20

Purple Mountain Trail

Harlequin Lake Trail

West Entrance Road

Gneiss Creek Trail

Madison River

TO MAP 21

To Norris

To Old Faithful

Madison Junction

Firehole Falls

Madison Campground

Harlequin Lake

To West Entrance

0 0.45 0.9 1.8 Miles

0 0.5 1 2 Kilometers

N
W   E
S

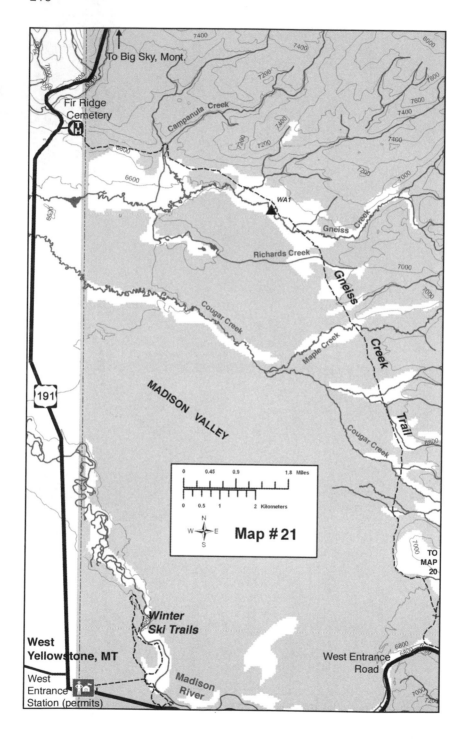

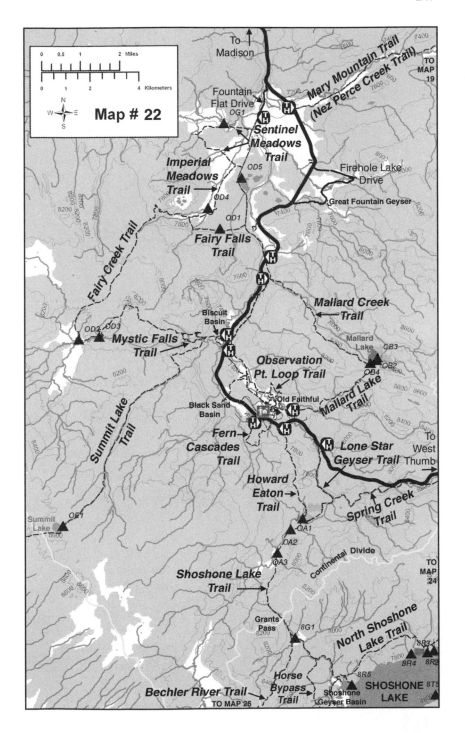

218

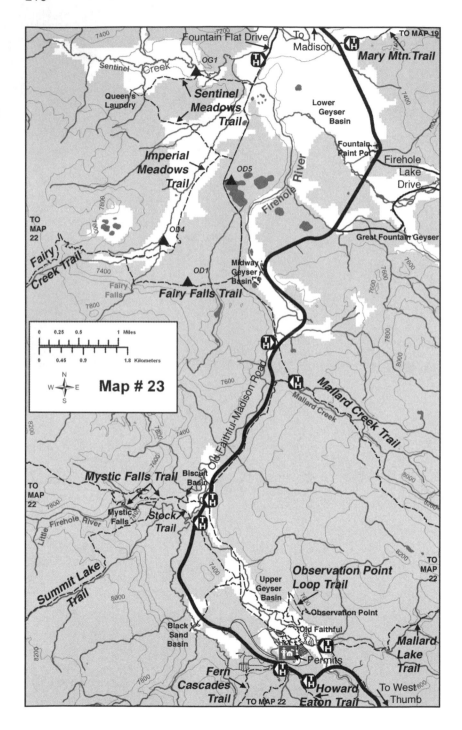

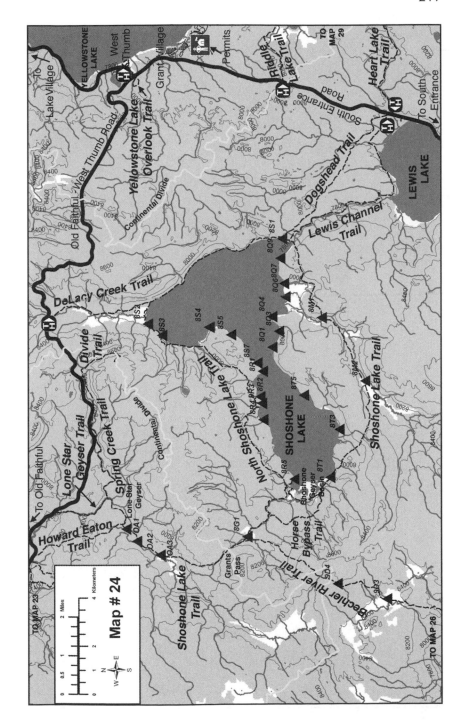

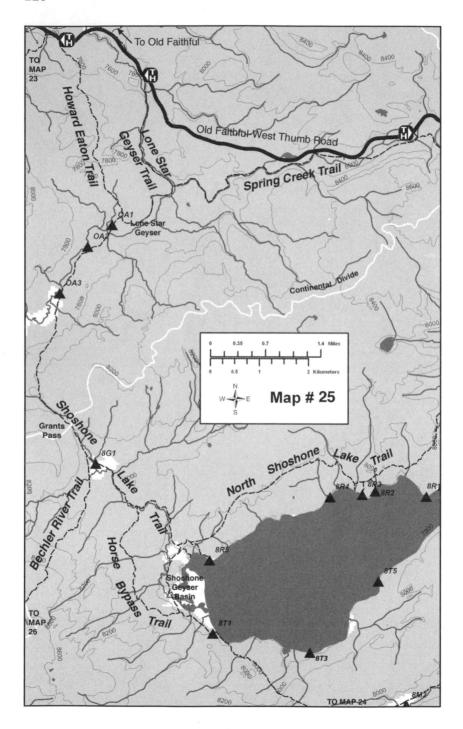

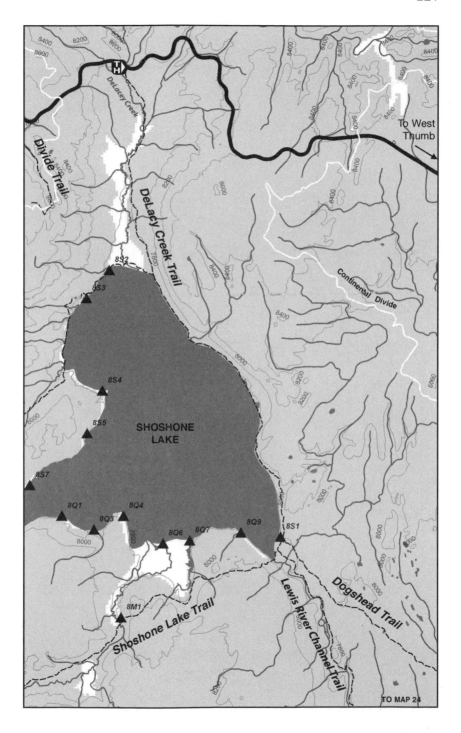

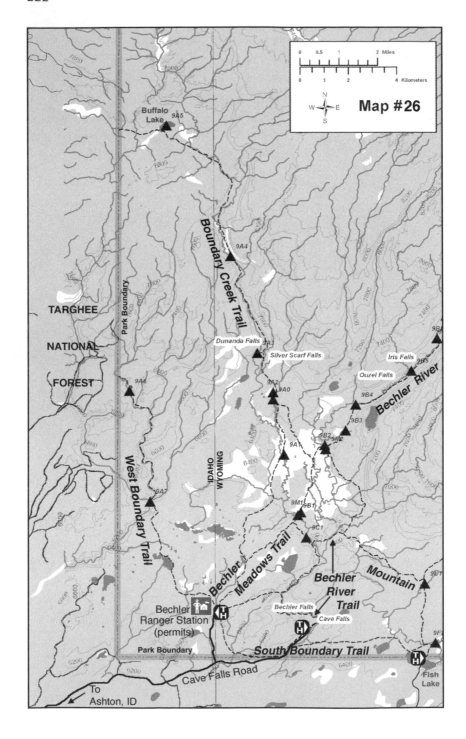

Buffalo Lake 9A5

9A4

Boundary Creek Trail

Map #26

0   0.5   1   2 Miles
0   1   2   4 Kilometers

N
W   E
S

TARGHEE

NATIONAL

FOREST

Park Boundary

9A6

Dunanda Falls 9A3
Silver Scarf Falls

9A2 9A0

Iris Falls 9B5
Ouzel Falls
9B4

9B6

Bechler River

9B3

9B2 9M2

9A1

West Boundary Trail

OHIO

WYOMING

9A7

9M1 9B1

9C1

Bechler Meadows Trail

Bechler River Trail

Mountain

9D1

Bechler Ranger Station (permits)

Bechler Falls
Cave Falls

Park Boundary

South Boundary Trail

9F1

Fish Lake

Cave Falls Road

To Ashton, ID

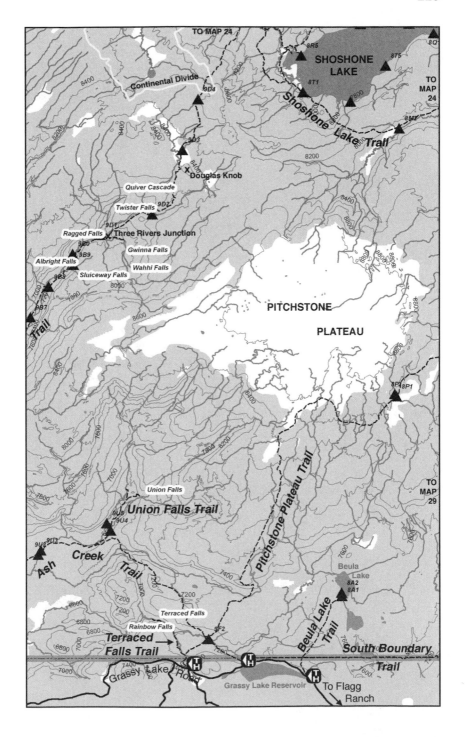

TO MAP 24

8R5

SHOSHONE
LAKE

8Q
8T5

8T1

Shoshone Lake Trail

TO
MAP
24

8A2

8400

Continental Divide

9D4

8600

8800

9D3

X Douglas Knob

8200

Quiver Cascade

Twister Falls   9D2

8400

8000

Ragged Falls   Three Rivers Junction

9B0

Gwinna Falls

9B9

Albright Falls

Wahhi Falls

9B8

Sluiceway Falls

8090

9B7

7000

7800

PITCHSTONE

PLATEAU

8800

8000

8600

8400

8P2 8P1

Trail

8000

7600

7000

7600

7000

7800 8200

8600

8400

Union Falls

TO
MAP
29

Union Falls Trail

9U5

9U4

9U2 9U3

7600

Ash   Creek   Trail

Beula
Lake

8A2
8A1

Pitchstone Plateau Trail

Terraced Falls

7200

7200

7400

7000

Beula Lake Trail

Rainbow Falls

9F2

Terraced
Falls Trail

6800

6800

7000

6800

South Boundary
Trail

Grassy Lake Road

7400

7000

Grassy Lake Reservoir

To Flagg
Ranch

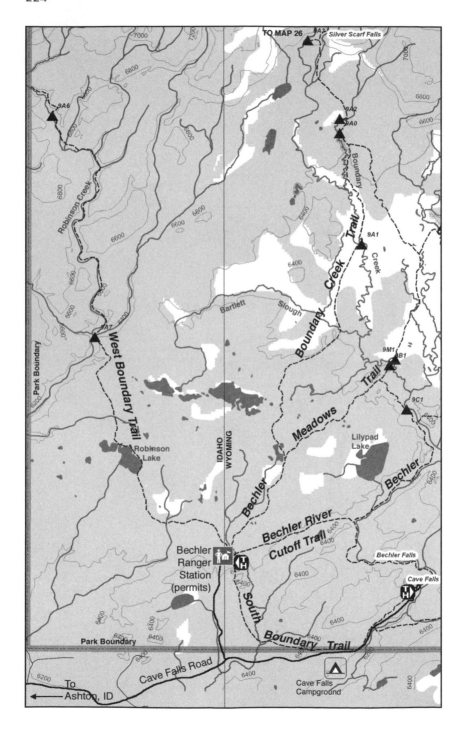

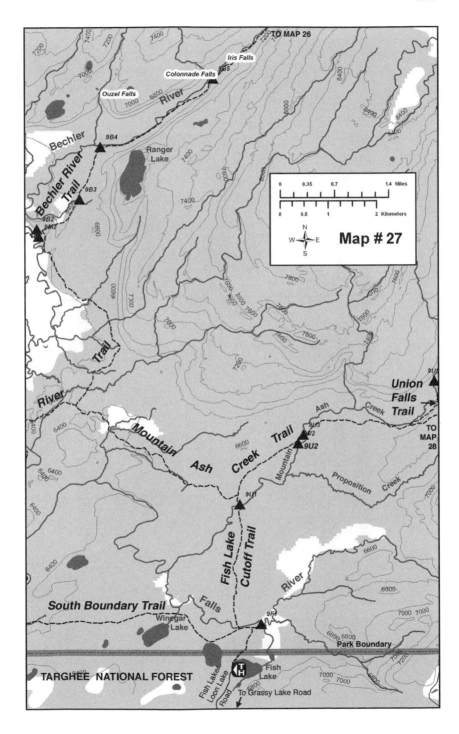

Iris Falls
9B5

Colonnade Falls

Ouzel Falls

River

Bechler

9B4

Ranger
Lake

Bechler River Trail

9B3

9B2
9M2

Trail

Union
Falls
Trail

9U5

River

Mountain

Ash

Creek

Trail

Ash

Creek

9U3
9U2

Mountain

TO
MAP
28

Proposition

Creek

9U1

Fish Lake Cutoff Trail

River

South Boundary Trail

Falls

Winegar
Lake

9F1

Park Boundary

TARGHEE NATIONAL FOREST

Fish Lake
Loon Lake
Road

Fish
Lake

To Grassy Lake Road

Map # 27

0   0.35   0.7   1.4 Miles

0   0.5   1   2 Kilometers

N
W   E
S

Union Falls

227

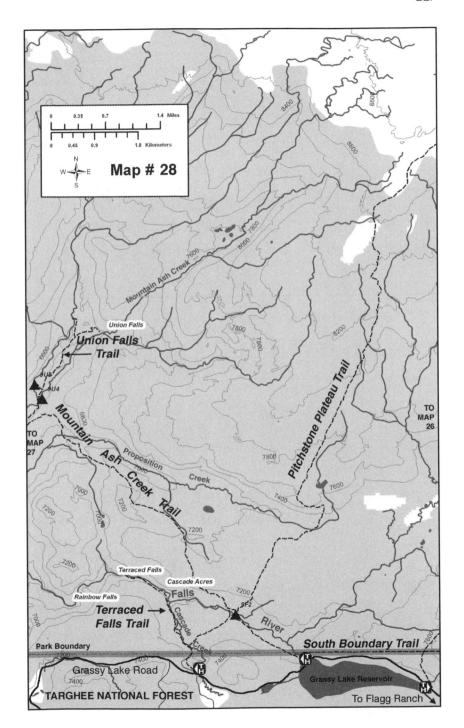

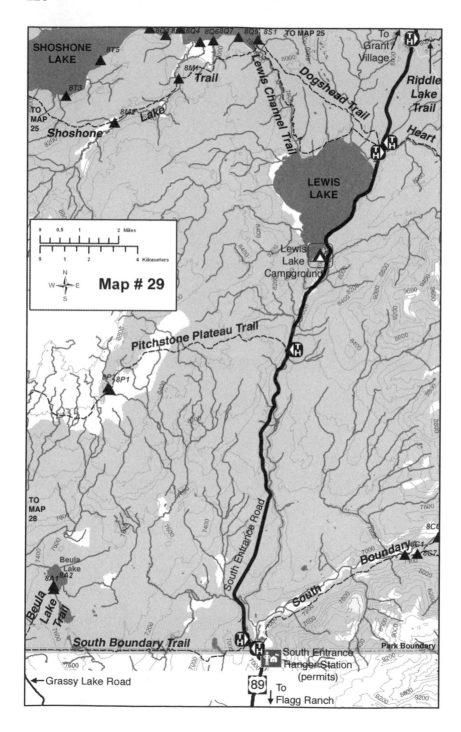

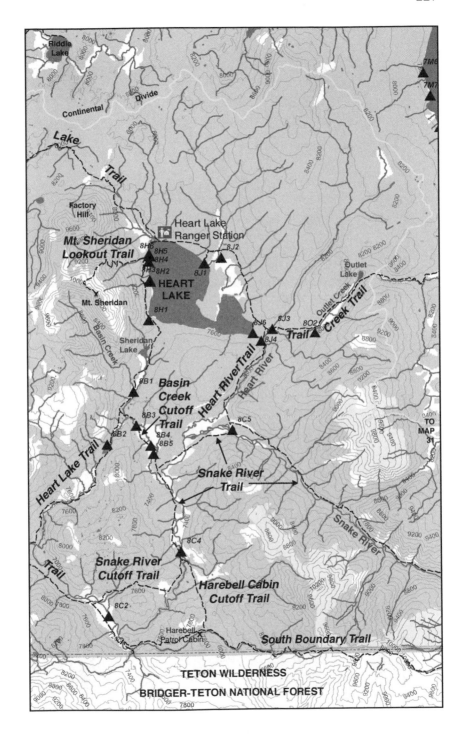

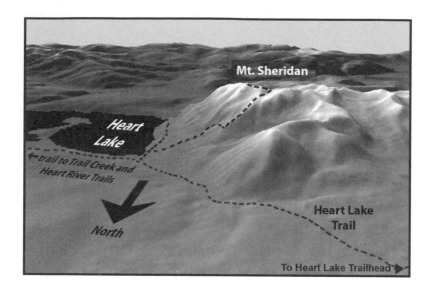

Heart Lake and Mt. Sheridan

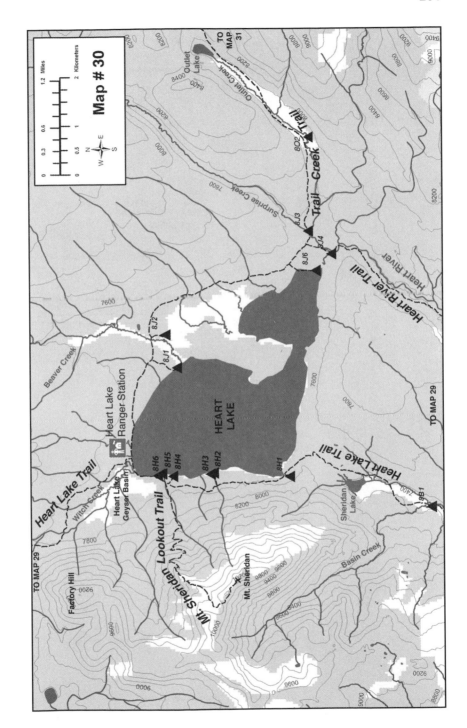

232

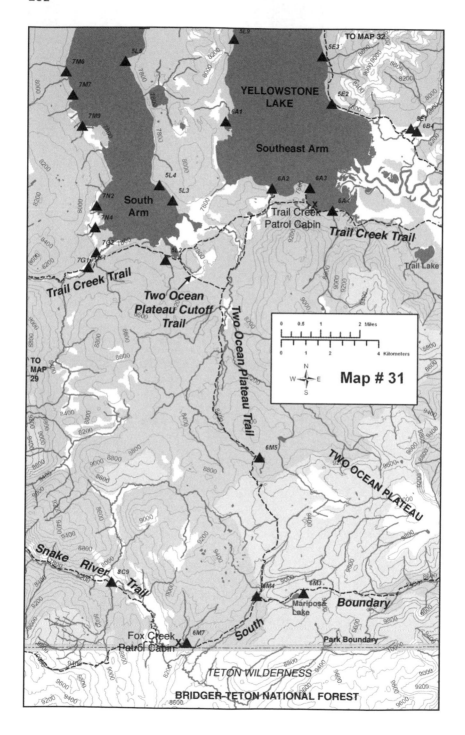

TO MAP 32

5L9

5E3

5L5

7M6

7M7

7M9

6A1

YELLOWSTONE
LAKE

5E2

5E1
6B4

Southeast Arm

5L4

5L3

7N2

South
Arm

6A2   6A3

6A4

7N4

Trail Creek
Patrol Cabin

Trail Creek Trail

7G2

7G1

5L2

Trail Lake

Trail Creek Trail

Two Ocean
Plateau Cutoff
Trail

TO
MAP
29

Two Ocean Plateau Trail

Map # 31

6M5

TWO OCEAN PLATEAU

Snake
River
Trail

8C9

6M4   6M3

Mariposa
Lake

Boundary

Fox Creek
Patrol Cabin

6M7

South

Park Boundary

TETON WILDERNESS

BRIDGER-TETON NATIONAL FOREST

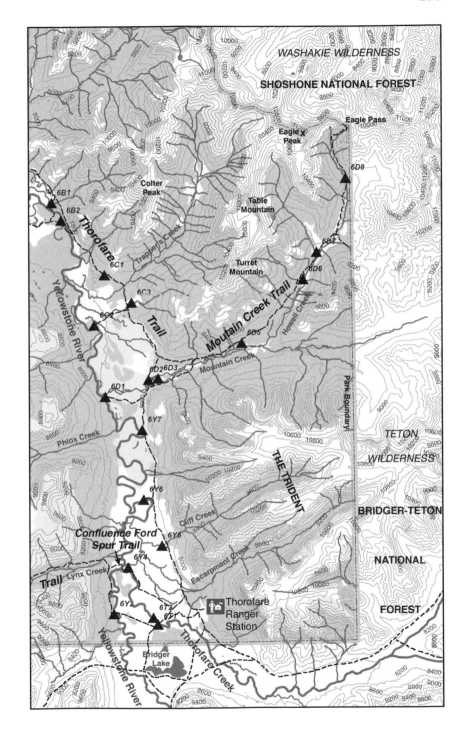

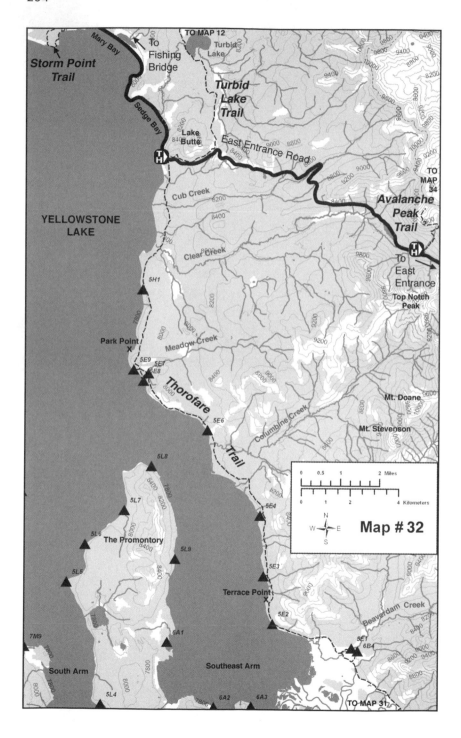

Map # 32

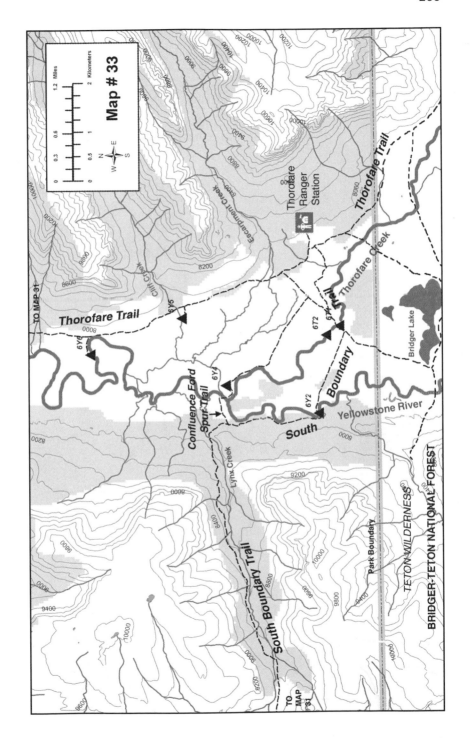

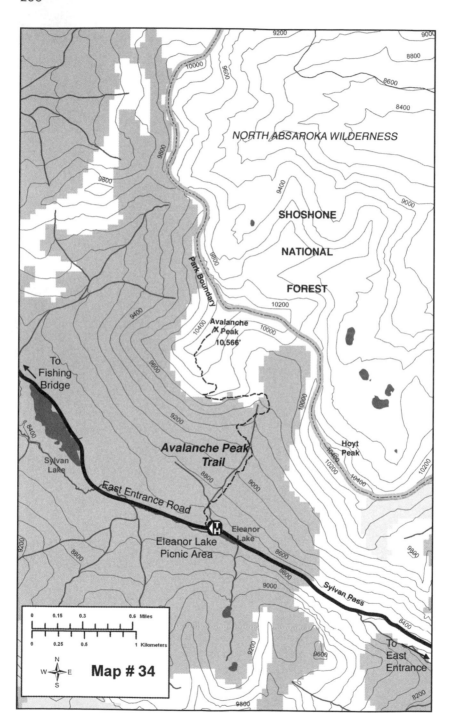

INDEX

A

Agate Creek Trail 86
Alum Creek 130
Amethyst Mountain 89
Amphitheater Springs 124
Anderson Mountain 82-83
Appendix 188
Artemisia Trail 137, 140
Artist Paint Pot Trail 126
Artist Point 117
Astringent Creek/Broad Creek Trail (Tern Lake Trail) 108
Avalanche Peak Trail 179

B

Backcountry camping 21
Backcountry campsites 180
Backcountry permits 16
Backcountry regulations 4
Backpacking equipment 19
Bacon Rind Creek Trail 75
Bannock Peak 65
Barronette Peak 93
Barrow's Goldeneye 63
Basin Creek Cutoff Trail 164
Bears
    black 23, 45
    grizzly 23, 42-43, 128
Bears, coexisting with 24
Bear encounters 25
Beaver Ponds Trail 73
Beaverdam Creek 173
Bechler/Falls River Area 148
Bechler Falls Trail 154
Bechler Ranger Station to Union Falls 157
Bechler Meadows Trail 150
Bechler River Trail 150
Beula Lake Trail 160
Big Game Ridge 166
Bighorn Pass Trail 64
Bighorn Peak 54, 55
Bighorn sheep 47, 113-114, 115, 119
Birds 47
Biscuit Basin Parking Area 137, 138
Bison 44, *127*, 128
Black Butte Trail 54
Black Canyon of the Yellowstone 77, 79, 83
Blacktail Creek Trail 81
Blacktail Ponds 73
Bliss Pass Trail 94
Bootjack Gap 99
Boundary Creek Trail 153
Bridger Lake 168, 171, 174
Broad Creek 106, 108, 109, 119, 120
Buffalo Ford 112
Buffalo Fork Trail 82
Buffalo Lake 153, 154
Buffalo Plateau Trail 82
Bunsen Peak Trail 72

C

Cache Creek Trail 96
Cache Lake Trail 69
Calfee Creek 96
Campanula Creek 132
Campsite setup 22
Campylobactor 32, 33
Canoe Lake Trail 100
Canyon Area 113
Capsicum bear repellents 29-30, 31
Cascade Corner 148
Cascade Creek Trailhead to Terraced Falls and Union Falls 158
Cascade Lake Trails 121
Castle Geyser 136
Cave Falls 148, 149, 150, 151, 154, 158
Cave Falls/Bechler Falls Loop Trail 154
Cave Falls to Union Falls 158
Central Plateau Area 127
Chaw Pass 98
Chemical repellents 29-30
Chipmunk, least 142
Chipmunk Creek 177, 179
Chittenden Bridge Picnic Area 112, 117
Clark's Nutcracker 55
Clear Creek 172, 173
Clear Lake/Ribbon Lake Loop Trail 117
Cliff Creek 174
Colonnade Falls 150, 151
Columbine Creek 172, 173
Continental Divide Trail 17-18
Cottonwood Creek 79
Cougar Creek 132
Cowan Creek 128, 129
Coyote Creek Trail 84
Coyotes 45, *46*
Crandall Ranger Station 99, 101
Crescent Lake/High Lake Trail 57
Crevice Creek Trail 79
Crevice Lake 79, 81
Crystal Creek 90
Cub Creek 172
Cutoff Mountain 91, 92, 93
Cygnet Lakes Trail 129

D

Dailey Creek Trail 51
Day hiking 19-20
Death Gulch 96
Dehydration 34, 189
DeLacy Creek Trail 146
Dike Creek Trail 176
Divide Trail 141
Dogshead Trail to Shoshone Lake 147
Dome Mountain 63
Douglas Knob 152
Dunanda Falls 148, 153

INDEX

E

Eagle Creek Trail 176
Eagle Pass (Mountain Creek Trail) 175, 176
Eagle Peak 175, 176
Eagles 126
East Fire 110, 172
Eleanor Lake 179
Electric Divide 68, 69
Electric Peak 71
Electric Peak Trail 69
Elephant Back Trail 130
Elk 44, *104*

F

Fairy Creek Trail 138
Fairy Falls Trails 139
Falls River Area 148
Fan Creek Trail 74
Fawn Pass Trail 66
Fern Cascades Semi-Loop Trail 134
Fern Lake 108, 120
Ferris Fork Trail 152
Fir Ridge Cemetery 132
Firehole Valley Area 133
Fish 48
Fish Lake to Union Falls 156
Fishing Bridge Trailhead 111
Floating Island Lake 83
Food storage 21-23
Forest fires 39
Fossil forests 41
Fox Creek Patrol Cabin to Thorofare Ranger
    Station (Lynx Creek Trail) 167
Frost Lake Trail 101

G

Gallatin/Mammoth Area 60
Gallatin Petrified Forest 55
Gardners Hole 58, 67, 68
Garnet Hill Trail 88
Giardia 32-33
Glacial Boulder Trail 116
Glen Creek Trail 67, 68, 71
Gneiss Creek Trail 132
Grants Pass 144, 152
Grassy Lake to South Entrance (South
    Boundary Trail) 160
Grassy Lake to Union Falls 155
Gray Jay 55
Grebe Lake Trail 120
Grizzly Lake Trail 61
Grouse Creek 177

H

Harebell 59
Harebell Patrol Cabin to Fox Creek
    Patrol Cabin 166

Harlequin Lake Trail 131
Hayden Valley 127-128
Heart Lake Trail 162
Heart River Trail 164
Hellroaring Creek Trail 83
Hellroaring Mountain 76, 84
High Lake 57, 58
Highland Hot Springs 130
Hoodoo Basin Trail 100
Hoodoos 71
Howard Eaton Trail to Lone Star Geyser 134
Howard Eaton Trail–Fishing Bridge
    to Canyon 111
Howard Eaton Trail–to Ice Lake, Wolf Lake
    and Grebe Lake 122
Howard Eaton Trail–Mammoth
    to Glen Creek 71
Howard Eaton Trail–Norris Campground
    to Ice Lake 125
Hydrothermal areas 38
Hypothermia 36

I

Ice Lake Trail 122
Imperial Geyser 138, 139
Imperial Meadows Trail 139, 140
Indian Creek 65
Indian Pond 103, 105, 111
Iris Falls 150, 151
Irma Mine Road 97

K

Kepler Cascades 133
Knowles Falls 77, 78, 79, 81

L

Lake Butte 110
Lake of the Woods 124
Lake Trout 48, 170
Lamar River Area 95
Lamar River Trail 95
Lava Creek Trail 73
Lee Metcalf Wilderness Area 75
LeHardy's Rapids 112
Lemonade Creek 124
Lewis River Channel Trail 147
Lightning 36
Little Cottonwood Creek 78, 79
Little Firehole Meadows Trail 138
Little Gibbon Falls 123
Lone Star Geyser Trail 133
Lost Lake Trail 87
Lower Yellowstone River Area 76
Lynx 47
Lynx Creek Trail (Fox Creek Patrol Cabin
    to Thorofare Ranger Station) 167

INDEX

M

Madison Valley Area 131
Magpie Creek 129
Mallard Creek Trail 135
Mallard Lake Trail 135
Mammoth Area 60
Maps 14-15, 189, 190-236
Mariposa Creek 167
Mariposa Lake 167, 179
Mary Mountain Trail–East 130
Mary Mountain Trail–West (Nez Perce
  Creek Trail) 129
Mary Lake 129, 130
Meldrum Mountain 56
Miller Creek Trail 99
Mist Creek Pass Trail 109
Monument Creek Trail (Mountain Creek
  Trail) 175
Monument Geyser Basin Trail 125
Moose 47
Moose Creek 145
Mountain Ash Creek Trail–East 155
Mountain Ash Creek Trail–West 157
Mountain Creek Area 175
Mountain Creek Trail 175
Mountain Lions 47
Mountain Pine Beetle 55, 179
Mt. Everts 73, 74
Mt. Holmes Trail (Winter Creek Trail) 62
Mt. Sheridan Trail 164
Mt. Washburn Trails 113
Mushpots 105-106
Mystic Falls Trail 137

N

Nez Perce Creek Trail (Mary Mountain–
  West) 129
Nez Perce Ford 112
Nez Perce Indians 128
Nine Mile Trailhead 172
Norris Area 124
Norris Campground to Ice Lake (Howard
  Eaton Trail) 125
Northeast Corner 91
North Shoshone Lake Trail 146
Northwest Corner 51

O

Observation Peak Trail 122
Observation Point Loop Trail 135
Osprey 105
Osprey Falls Trail 72
Outlet Creek 177
Ouzel Falls 148
Owl Fire 56, 59
Owl, great gray 18

P

Pahaska Tepee 101
Panther Creek 65
Papoose Creek Trail 99
Park Point 173
Parker Peak 100
Passage Creek 179
Pebble Creek Trail 92
Pelican Cone Trail 106
Pelican Springs Creek 104
Pelican Valley 39
Pelican Valley Area 102
Pelican Valley Bear Management 107
Pelican Valley Trail 102
Pepper Spray 30-31
Petrified Trees 41, 87, 90
Phantom Campsite 159
Pipeline Hot Springs 135
Pitchstone Plateau Trail 159
Plateau Creek 167, 179
Playing Dead 28
Polecat Creek 160
Ponuntpa Hot Springs 108, 120
Proposition Creek 156, 159
Purple Mountain Trail 131

Q

Quadrant Mountain 60, 65
Queen's Laundry 140

R

Rattlesnake Butte 80
Raven Creek 104
Red Creek 163
Republic Pass 97, 98
Rescue Creek Trail 80
Ribbon Lake 117-118
Riddle Lake Trail 169
River & Stream Crossings 35
Robinson Lake 154
Roosevelt Lodge to Tower Fall Campground 87
Russell Creek 104
Rustic Geyser 161, 163

S

Sandhill Crane 120
Sentinel Meadows Trail 140
Sepulcher Mountain Trail 70
Seven Mile Bridge Trailhead 132
Seven Mile Hole Trail 116
Shelf Lake 52, 54, 55, 56
Sheep Mountain 54, 56, 74
Sheepeater Canyon 72
Shooting Star 101
Shoshone Geyser Basin Trail 145
Shoshone Lake Area 143

INDEX

Shoshone Lake East Shore Trail 144
Shoshone Lake, North Trail 146
Shoshone Lake Trail 144
Silver Cord Cascade 118
Silver Scarf Falls 153
Silver Tip Ranch 91, 92
Sky Rim Trail 52
Slough Creek Trail 91
Snake Hot Springs 165
Snake River Area 161
Snake River Trail 168
Solfatara Creek Trail 124
Sour Creek 112, 118, 120
South Boundary Trail–
    Grassy Lake to South Entrance 160
South Boundary Trail–
    South Entrance to Thorofare R.S. 165
South Entrance to Harebell Patrol Cabin 165
South Shoshone Trail 144
Specimen Creek Trail 56
Specimen Ridge Trail 89
Sportsman Lake Trail–East 68
Sportsman Lake Trail–West 58
Spotted Sandpiper 37
Spring Beauty 20
Spring Creek Trail 141
Squirrel, golden-mantled ground 142
Storm Point Trail 110
Straight Creek 61
Summit Lake Trail 138
Sunlight Basin Road 99, 100, 101
Sylvan Lake 179

T
Tepee Creek Trail 52
Tern Lake 108
Tern Lake Trail (Astringent Creek/
    Broad Creek Trail) 108
Terrace Mountain 67, 68, 71
Terrace Point 173
Terraced Falls 158
Thorofare Area 170
Thorofare Trail 172
Three Rivers Junction 152
Thunderer 98
Thunderer Cutoff Trail 98
Tower Area 85
Tower Creek Trail 85
Tower Fall Trail 86
Trail Creek Trail 176
Trail Descriptions 49
Trapper's Creek 171, 173
Trilobite Lake Trail 63
Trout *48*, 57, 170
Trout Lake Trail 94

Turbid Lake Trail 110
Turkey Pen Peak 80
Twister Falls 152
Two Ocean Plateau Trail 178

U
Undine Falls 73, *226*
Union Falls Trails 155
Upper Pelican Creek Trail 105

V
Violet Creek 130

W
Wahb Springs 96
Wapiti Lake Trail 119
Warm Creek Trailhead 93, 94
Washburn Hot Springs 115
Washburn Spur Trail 115
Water filter 32
Water treatment 32
Waterfalls 40
Weather 36
West Boundary Trail 154
Western Fringed Gentian 75
Westslope Cutthroat Trout 57
White Lake 108
White Peaks 62
Whiterock Springs 124
Wildlife 42-48
Winter Creek Trail (Mt. Holmes Trail) 62
Witch Creek 162-163
Wolf Lake Cutoff Trail 123
Wolverine Creek 166
Wolves 45, *46*, 107, 128
Wrangler Lake Trail 118

X
Xanterra Services 172

Y
Yancey's Hole 88
Yellowstone Caldera 127
Yellowstone Cutthroat Trout *48*, 170
Yellowstone Lake 161
Yellowstone Lake Overlook Trail 169
Yellowstone River Picnic Area Trail 86
Yellowstone River Trail 77